THINK, PLAY, DO

Think, Play, Do

Technology, Innovation, and Organization

Mark Dodgson
David Gann
Ammon Salter

OXFORD
UNIVERSITY PRESS

T
173,8
.D64
2005

OXFORD
UNIVERSITY PRESS

Great Clarendon Street, Oxford ox2 6DP

Oxford University Press is a department of the University of Oxford.
It furthers the University's objective of excellence in research, scholarship,
and education by publishing worldwide in

Oxford New York

Auckland Cape Town Dar es Salaam Hong Kong Karachi
Kuala Lumpur Madrid Melbourne Mexico City Nairobi
New Delhi Shanghai Taipei Toronto

With offices in

Argentina Austria Brazil Chile Czech Republic France Greece
Guatemala Hungary Italy Japan Poland Portugal Singapore
South Korea Switzerland Thailand Turkey Ukraine Vietnam

Oxford is a registered trade mark of Oxford University Press
in the UK and in certain other countries

Published in the United States
by Oxford University Press Inc., New York

© M. Dodgson, D. Gann, and A. Salter 2005

British Library Cataloguing in Publication Data
Data available

Library of Congress Cataloging in Publication Data
Data available

Typeset by SPI Publisher Services, Pondicherry, India
Printed in Great Britain
on acid-free paper by
Biddles Ltd., King's Lynn, Norfolk

ISBN 0-19-926808-8
ISBN 0-19-926809-6 (Pbk.)

'I found this book very refreshing and original, because of the way it intersperses numerous fascinating examples from the 'real world' of firms and industry, science, engineering and design, with more theoretical reflection and analysis of the whole process of innovation. It is a wonderful book which could be a key book for courses all over the world, as well as for many individual readers.'

Chris Freeman, Professor Emeritus, Science Policy Research Unit, Sussex University

'*Think, Play, Do* goes to the core of how our industry needs to approach innovation. It provides excellent examples of the benefits of Innovation Technology with wide applicability across industry, particularly in engineering.'

Keith Clarke, Chief Executive, Atkins plc.

'Innovation has become a core business process at CSC. We recognize the need to work at the leading-edge of innovation practice, providing new services to our customers. *Think, Play, Do* provides deep insights that will help us stay at the top in providing IT services to our clients.'

Keith Wilman, President Northern and EMEA Region, Computer Sciences Corporation

'As a leading international project-based firm, Laing O'Rourke needs to use new tools for innovation to deliver value to our clients. Processes of Thinking, Playing and Doing supported by Innovation Technology provide the platform for our approach to radical innovation.'

Ray O'Rourke, Chairman, Laing O'Rourke

'The prosperity of advanced nations will hinge on listening closely to leading edge customers and bringing innovative solutions to market as fast as possible. This important book is bristling with new ideas and insights to enhance our innovative capabilities.'

Daniel T Jones, Chairman, Lean Enterprise Academy, Co-author of The Machine that Changed the World, Lean Thinking and Lean Solutions.

'This book explains how Innovation Technology supports the new innovation process, providing major improvements in efficiency and effectiveness in industrial innovation. It describes and analyses leading-edge management of research, development and design. It demonstrates the importance of combining expertise in business strategy, engineering and the sciences.'

Sir Richard Sykes, Rector, Imperial College London, former Chairman and CEO, GlaxoSmithKline

'The Think, Play, Do framework and the concept of Innovation Technology provide new and valuable insights about the ways innovation is changing, and how to manage the crucially important relationships between science and business.'

Catherine Livingstone, Chairman, CSIRO

'Willmott Dixon has been a long-term collaborator with the authors and is enjoying the benefits of successful implementation of innovation strategies based on ideas in this book. In particular, the development of Matrix 1 – our proprietary approach to engaging our clients in our innovation process, demonstrates the benefits of investing in Innovation Technology.'

Rick Willmott, CEO, Willmott Dixon Group Ltd

'This is a superb and compelling book which takes the study of innovation in business onto a new plane. It should be compulsory reading for all those trying to understand the innovation process – whether in industry, government or academia'

Professor Mike Hobday, Director, CoPS Innovation Centre, SPRU, University of Sussex

'The nature of science is changing because of the use of a range of new technologies. The concept of Innovation Technology clearly describes the use of simulation, modelling and Grid technologies and how they are affecting experimentation in science.'

Professor Dame Julia Higgins FRS FREng

'Through rich and contemporary case studies, the authors demonstrate how technologies such as computer-based simulation and modeling, visualization and virtual reality, rapid prototyping, and data mining, are transforming the innovation process increasing the speed and efficiency of innovation in a wide range of industries and public sector organizations.'

Robert J. DeFillippi, Chair of Management and Director, Center for Innovation and Change Leadership, Sawyer School of Management, Suffolk University, Boston, MA

'The book gives a new perspective on how innovation processes are organized around and supported by a new family of 'innovation technologies' with the potential to speed up and intensify innovation. It is an original contribution with far-reaching theoretical and practical implications.'

Bengt-Åke Lundvall, Professor of Economics, University of Aalborg

'TPD provides a readable and rigorous approach to innovation management for firms that appreciate how innovative design can generate both tactical and strategic advantage.'

Michael Schrage, MIT Media Lab and author, Serious Play

'This book provides a powerful intellectual stimulus for debates on the modern innovation process'

Richard Lester, Director, MIT Industrial Performance Centre, co-author, Innovation – the missing dimension

'Economists need to understand the major changes occuring in innovation processes. Firms engage in innovation processes for the creation of value and efficiencies, and yet innovating is difficult, due to factors such as the uncertainties of search and the combination of high costs and skewed returns. This book provides a fascinating and useful analytical lens through which to explore the major changes occuring, as businesses apply innovation technology 'IvT'. This intensification of innovation, the authors argue, affects not only the firms themselves but also future options for society.'

Professor Maureen McKelvey, Department of Technology Management and Economics, Chalmers University of Technology, Sweden

'This book helps define the future of innovation studies, articulating a forward looking alternative to well understood, but increasingly dated concepts, the authors explain how emerging technologies shape innovation in services as well as manufacturing. Universities seeking collaboration with industry need to understand this new world.'

Professor Diana Hicks, Chair of the School of Public Policy, Georgia Institute of Technology

'Innovation Technology is what IBM does. This book provides a rigorous analysis of the evolution and application of innovation processes that create on demand solutions adding value to customers in every industry. Through the use of compelling examples, the book presents a strong case for recognising and applying Innovation Technology to increase innovation success by reducing the impact of uncertainty.'

Robert Berry, IBM Distinguished Engineer, CTO, Messaging Technology, IBM

'The relationship between science and industry is crucial for economic and social development. This book proposes some exciting new ideas on how this relationship is changing and how a new innovation process that merges the worlds of ideas and their applications can be managed.'

Professor John Hay, AC, Vice-Chancellor, The University of Queensland

'*Think, Play, Do* draws on ideas we have exchanged with the authors over a long period of collaboration with them. Its welcome insight and rigour brings some order to the apparently haphazard processes of innovation. The power of Innovation Technology and its role in gaining market advantage comes through very clearly'.

Dr John Miles, Director, Arup Group

In memory of Roy Rothwell (1941–2003)

Preface

Something profound is happening to the innovation process. It is changing in ways that have important implications for organizations and individuals who are, or want to be, innovative, for governments that want to increase innovative activity, and those like us who study it.

In *Think, Play, Do* we bring together new material and insights into the innovation process. As academics we are steeped in the study of innovation, with sixty years between us spent in its examination. We are also inculcated with the usual academic concern for caution and method. But there is a time to be cautious, and there is a time to be bold. This book, we believe, makes a number of very bold and novel assertions. For example, we make the following claims:

- A new category of technology, what we call 'innovation technology' has emerged over recent years and is increasingly being applied to, and changing, the innovation process. It complements and builds upon existing technologies.
- The use of this technology, when combined with appropriately supportive organization and skills, can lead to the intensification of innovation. That is, these technologies can make the innovation process more economical and less uncertain.
- The contemporary innovation process can be characterized by a new schema of 'thinking', 'playing', and 'doing'. This breaks away from traditional notions of research, development, and engineering, and emphasizes the importance of design and prototyping in innovation.
- Successful implementation of innovation technology depends upon the development and use of a range of new 'craft' skills and new forms of, usually project-based, organization.

We provide a diverse range of evidence in support of these assertions. We examine the innovation activities of two large multinational companies, Procter & Gamble (P&G) and GlaxoSmithKline (GSK); two engineering services companies, Arup and Ricardo; and Frank Gehry's architectural practice. We discuss case studies of new product development in cameras and brassieres, the fashion industry, Formula 1 racing, house building, automotives, and consumer products. We consider the use of innovation technology in public programmes, like the London Congestion Charge and the project that prevented the Leaning Tower of Pisa collapsing. We describe the way innovation technology has been used to confirm the safety of a chemical reactor following an accident, to plan advanced manufacturing processes, and in the mining industry. We describe examples of new Internet-based innovation intermediaries, such as InnoCentive, Yet2.com, and NineSigma. We analyse the way technology has been used to improve the acoustics in the Sydney Opera House in Australia, to stop the Millennium Bridge wobbling in London, and to plan for greater safety in the Twin Towers replacement building in New York. This diversity of evidence supports our contention that innovation technology and its use in thinking, playing, and doing in the innovation process is ubiquitous.

We have benefited enormously from access to many brilliant thinkers, players, and doers in our respective institutions of Imperial College London and the University of Queensland. These colleagues have not only been kind enough to provide case study material on their cutting-edge research but have also generously given of their time to comment on drafts of our work.

Our ideas have been critically examined in numerous seminars and conferences around the world and they have been tested on a large number of knowledgeable people and corporate groups. Nonetheless, we believe that there is still much work to develop and question these ideas and we welcome attempts to do so. In part, the boldness of our assertions reflects a concern that there seems to be a paucity of new and exciting ideas in the study of innovation. We study innovation. Let's be innovative in our thinking about it.

This is a book for all those engaged with, or interested in, the innovation process. It is for managers who have a strategic concern with improving the innovation performance of their companies, for industry analysts, and for researchers in business, public policy, and innovation studies who want to understand the evolving nature of one of the most powerful sources of competitiveness. It is for students, particularly in business and engineering, who wish to appreciate the way the world in which they are going to work is changing and where their future contributions may most valuably lie.

Ideas never emerge in a void, and there are many excellent pieces of work upon which we build. Amongst the more contemporary literature we would particularly like to acknowledge is the work of Henry Chesbrough, Stefan Thomke, and Michael Schrage. We owe these authors an immense intellectual debt.

Our concern has been to place our ideas in a theoretical and conceptual context and wherever possible support them with empirical evidence, which is in contrast to many management books on innovation. We refer to theories of evolutionary economics and techno-economic paradigms and, from the business strategy literature, to resource-based and dynamic capabilities theory.

We have also taken a historical approach, again in contrast to many other books in the field. This may make it seem overly 'academic' for some readers used to the 'gee-whiz', simple-solution-to-complex-problem type of management book. We do not believe it is but in any case we are unapologetic as we wish to present substance to our arguments.

The ideas in the book have been tested at seminars at the following business schools and universities: Imperial College London, Said Business School (Oxford University), University of Brighton, Cranfield University Business School, Manchester School of Management, Copenhagen Business School, Hanken Helsinki Business School, London School of Economics, Salford University, National University of Singapore, Australian National University, Macquarie Graduate School of Management, University of Queensland, Melbourne Business School. Academic papers have been presented at the R&D Management Conference in Wellington, New Zealand; the DRUID Conference in Elsinore, Denmark; the EGOS Conference in Copenhagen, Denmark; and the ASEAT Conference in Manchester, UK.

The following people have been particularly helpful in the development of ideas for our study: Mike Addison, Peter Bressington, John Burland, Keith Clarke, John Darlington, Andy Foster, Stephen Glaister, Richard Haryott, Tony Hey, Dame Julia Higgins, Nicole Hoffman, Ian Hughes, Richard Jones, Steve Jones, Neil McGlip, Maureen McKelvey, John Miles, Mehmet Kizil, Tim Napier-Munn, Toke Reichstein, Roger Ridsill-Smith, Brendan Ritchie, Michael Schrage, Tony Sheehan, David Siddle, Anne Trefethen, and Glenn Wallington.

The following people have been kind enough to comment on particular chapters and papers: Andrew Amis, Erik Baark, Catelijne Coopmans, Andrew Davies, Mike Hobday, Alice Lam, Keld Laursen, Maureen McKelvey, John Steen, Bruce Tether, Anne Trefethen.

John Bessant, Jane Marceau, Denis Towill, and Jennifer Whyte were kind enough to comment on early drafts.

We wish to acknowledge the excellent research assistance provided to us during the course of this study by Sheridan Ash. She assisted with a number of the case studies and her persistence in pursuing interviews was instrumental to their completion. We are also grateful to Virginia Harris for her assistance in preparing the text and bibliography.

The research on which this book is based was conducted over a four-year period. It entailed enormous amounts of travel back and forth between the UK and Australia and places in between, and we wish to acknowledge the significant support we have received from our respective employers: University of Queensland Business School and Tanaka Business School, Imperial College London.

We particularly acknowledge the financial support received from the Engineering and Physical Sciences Research Council's Innovative Manufacturing

Preface

Programme in the UK, the University of Queensland Business School in Australia, and the Innovator-in-Residence Program University of Queensland.

The book is structured into eight chapters. Chapter 1 introduces the idea of innovation technology. Chapter 2 discusses the nature of innovation. In Chapter 3 detailed case studies of two companies, P&G and Arup, are provided to illustrate our argument. Chapters 4, 5, and 6 consider 'think', 'play', and 'do', and each incorporates a range of empirical and case study material. Chapter 7 considers the strategic management of innovation. In Chapter 8 we speculate on the future development and challenges of innovation technology. Throughout the book, we include short sections, or 'boxes', which are designed to add to the argument by reporting case and technical material and short reviews of relevant literature, but can be read separately without affecting the flow of the argument.

Finally, we wish to acknowledge the enduring legacy of Professor Roy Rothwell. Roy was one of the pioneers of innovation studies, and he saw many of the changes we analyse long before anyone else. Roy understood the innovation process, and all his substantial contributions to the management and public policy literature derived from that knowledge. He was a physicist who knew that there is no point at all talking about technological innovation without understanding the market. He was a disciplined scholar who knew that you should not write about innovation without understanding the ill-disciplined and messy activities that often go on in firms. He was contemptuous of academic pomposity and bureaucracy, and subverted both whenever possible. In these, and many other ways, he remains a wonderful role model.

Mark Dodgson
David Gann
Ammon Salter

Contents

Contents

List of Figures

List of Tables

List of Boxes

1 Innovation Technology

1.1 Introduction

The Latin proverb *Nihil simul inventum est et perfectum* means 'nothing is invented and perfected at the same time'. Like many proverbs, this one has stood the test of time, and is still apposite. But everything changes; nothing stays the same, and the search for 'inventions' that are 'perfect' at birth is a continuing quest for innovators. Present changes occurring in the innovation process that result from the application of a range of new technologies and management practices are part of that quest. We describe the new technology—including simulation and modelling tools, virtual reality, data mining and rapid prototyping—as *innovation technology* (IvT). We contend that the changes associated with their introduction leads to the *intensification of innovation*. We argue that it is being applied to an innovation process that can be characterized by *thinking*, *playing*, and *doing*.

Understanding these changes is important because innovation is the means by which economic, social, and environmental resources are reconfigured and used to advantage. Industries and businesses thrive and decline as a result of the way they deal with the many, and increasing, challenges of innovation. An innovation process that successfully matches market demand with technological opportunity is a key source of sustainable competitive advantage. In essence, innovation is what enables firms and nations to pave their way in the world, and a deep comprehension of the process of innovation enables better use of the resources we have to support it. At a time when markets and customers are becoming more sophisticated and demanding, and technological developments are producing ever-expanding opportunities and threats, any approach that enables the innovation process to be better understood and managed is welcome.

IvT is increasingly being applied to, and changing, the innovation process, and influences the creative tasks and the ways knowledge is constructed, shared, and used. It affects the ways in which we think about and conceive innovations. IvT changes the way we experiment with, test, and prototype new products, processes, and services (Thomke 2003). It contributes to the process of what Schrage (2000) calls 'serious play', placing prototyping and design centrally in the innovation process. It can be integrated with advanced manufacturing and operations technologies, such as computer-aided machine tools, and marketing and customer management systems, thereby linking product, service, and process innovations. IvT provides the technological means to unite the diverse range of inputs into the innovation process.

IvT is built upon the massive power and speed of information and communication technologies and the infrastructure and tools they create, notably broadband and open systems of software and hardware production. In the language expressed throughout this book, IvT has the ability to affect *thinking*, *playing*, and *doing* in the innovation process. Thinking is facilitated by technologies, such as those supporting e-science (or cyberscience as it is known in the USA), that build virtual research communities and permit new ways of finding and combining information through data searching. It is assisted by recent developments in Grid computing and artificial intelligence. Playing is facilitated by simulation, modelling, and visualization technologies, which build upon existing technology platforms, such as computer-aided design (CAD), and the developing capacities of virtual reality. Doing is facilitated by rapid prototyping technologies, which build upon existing design and manufacturing systems.

There are a number of reasons why the schema of innovation—Think, Play, Do—was developed.[1] First, the concern is with the innovation *process*: the managerial and organizational practices that combine to successfully exploit new ideas. Much research into innovation is focused on innovation *inputs*, such as R&D expenditure, and *outputs*, including patents and new products, and tells us little about the flow of connected and iterative activities that turns inputs into outputs.

Second, traditional descriptions of 'research', 'development' and 'engineering' are unhelpful for a number of reasons. Traditional categories imply organizational boundaries: between institutions (university/industry); within institutions (research function/engineering function); and between professions (scientists/engineers; mechanical/chemical/civil/electronic engineers). This is counter to the contemporary innovation process, which is characterized by highly fluid boundaries and networked and distributed contributors. There is no implied linearity in our schema; thinking, playing, and doing occur at all stages of the innovation process and, whilst the IvT we describe is primarily linked with particular activities, it is used by them all.

Third, in contrast to the traditional categories, the schema better captures the importance of *design* and *prototyping* in innovation. Design (the process of making choices about function, cost, quality, and impact, including aesthetics) and prototyping (the creation of new types or forms that serve as a basis or standard for later stages of development) play a central role in our analysis and will be examined in depth in Chapter 5.

Fourth, the Think, Play, Do schema provides a more useful and contemporary idiom of an innovation process in the kind of evolving, creative companies, industries, and practices described in this book. Notions of R&D apply more readily in large integrated manufacturing firms, which comprise an increasingly small element of overall innovation activity. Indeed, most firms do no formal R&D, and the usual R&D measures have failed to fully recognize the innovative activities of small firms and innovation in services.[2] Think, Play, Do does not apply only to new and emerging sectors. The schema is applicable in very traditional industrial sectors, including mining and welding, and in services and public projects.

As a result of the application of the technologies mentioned above, the innovation process—and the thinking, playing, and doing activities that support it—has intensified. The intensity is a result of strenuous efforts directed towards improved productivity, and the more efficient and effective utilization of resources applied to more perfectly identified aims in innovation. The key characteristics of this intensification are the search for greater economies of effort, and precision and clarity in aim, in innovation investments. Figure 1.1 illustrates how thinking, playing, and doing can be supported by the use of IvT set within a new innovation process, to intensify innovation and ameliorate risk and uncertainty, giving rise to more successful outcomes than traditional approaches.

Used effectively, IvT has the potential to radically alter the ways in which innovation occurs and to ameliorate many of the uncertainties associated with it, bringing greater predictability and direction to the process. Technology alone, however, will never completely remove the inherent uncertainties and risks associated with innovation, never producing the completely efficient process that captures in one go both available technological possibilities and the requirements of markets and customers. The technologies that we describe allow people to think, play, and do, and iterate between these activities in new ways, but their use, and their effect on innovation, is determined by the social and organizational choices and behaviours that surround them. Innovation is, and will remain, a socially determined and hence unpredictable process.

Indeed, one of the benefits of IvT is its capacity to encourage thinking and creativity by expanding the variety of potential scientific and technological ideas, experiments, and options and thereby increasing one kind of uncertainty in innovation. In periods of dramatic and disruptive technological change, when there is a high degree of fluidity and uncertainty about the form of emerging technologies, the value of IvT lies in the ways it increases opportunities for innovation by adding to the set of possible technological outcomes. It expands the range of possibilities available and creates new ones that could not have been imagined without it.

Think, Play, Do

The technologies used to assist thinking, playing, and doing are valuable in helping firms to do things differently (the so-called disruptive innovation) and also to do existing things better (incremental or 'normal' innovation). IvT helps firms understand when and how they can do new things, and enables better processes of product and service development.

Whilst IvT can help managers better exploit existing incremental activities, and explore disruptive ones, it does not 'control' the innovation process. A controlled, routine innovation process may be attractive in the rare circumstances when technologies and markets are stable and predictable ('we just need to do more of the same'). But thoughts of increased control over innovation are misplaced where there is a high degree of environmental uncertainty ('what do we need to do, and how do we do it?'). With both incremental and disruptive innovations, IvT can valuably produce greater *intensity* in the innovation process. It liberates creative people from mundane tasks, enabling them to experiment more freely and widely, producing a variety of options (think). It enables them to design, prototype, and test more cheaply and effectively and to delay choices about investments until market and

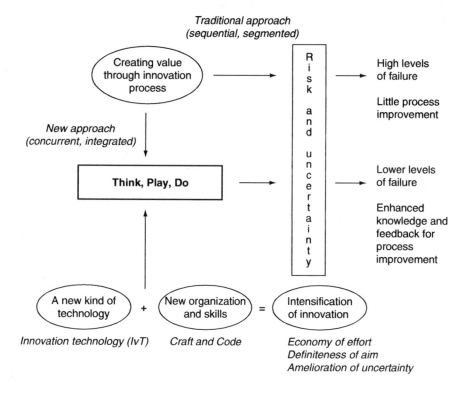

Fig. 1.1 The intensification of innovation

4

technology patterns become clearer (play). The extent of digital integration with other kinds of technology provides greater confidence for innovators in the ability of new ideas and designs to be successfully transformed into products and services (do). IvT is a technology that helps create a collaborative environment where ideas and knowledge can be effectively and economically represented and shared. The value of IvT does not lie with greater automation of innovation, where humans are replaced with machines, but derives from the way it can assist people to obtain clear and valuable objectives in innovation.

The technology we discuss is not disembodied; it is developed and used by people with particular objectives. Box 1.1 describes the way IvT is used by one engineering design team.

Given the importance of innovation in contemporary economies and societies, IvT and the intensification of innovation have major implications for businesses, governments, research institutes, and all those organizations and individuals that seek to benefit from technological change. Without a thorough understanding of the innovation process and the way it is changing, it is impossible for firms and research organizations to develop strategies and for governments to develop policies for innovation.

The changes associated with IvT are ubiquitous. IvT is found in large multinational manufacturing firms and small service providers, in for-profit firms, and in public-good organizations. 'High-tech' sectors, such as pharmaceuticals and biotechnology, and 'low-tech' sectors, such as mining, use IvT. Knowledge-intensive services, such as those provided by engineering design firms, use IvT extensively. The technologies are used in thinking, playing, and doing activities, and IvT increasingly both unites and blurs the distinctions between them. IvT is used to attract and please customers in markets and to improve the performance of public infrastructure. It helps improve the functionality and quality of products, processes, and services, from pharmaceuticals to home products to financial services, and delights us through its ability to aid researchers and engineers to design new products, such as buildings and clothes, creating desirable and affordable artefacts that once we only dreamed about.

Whilst the technologies are ubiquitous in the range of activities to which they are applied, they vary in the way they are used. As with previous vintages of technology, there is no simple pattern of use determined by the technology itself. As shown in the case studies described in Chapters 3–6, organizations and firms have choices about their application, choices which can have a profound impact on these firms' ability to develop new products and services, shaping their position in the market. As seen in the case of the engineer described below, the use of IvT involves the combination of the new digital code in IvT with existing and developing craft skills and flexible, often project- and network-based organization.

Box 1.1   A new kind of player

In early 2003, fire engineers at Arup Fire offices in London were helping to design Freedom Tower, the replacement for the Twin Towers destroyed in the terrorist attacks on New York on 11 September 2001. The engineers collaborated with a number of architectural firms as well as other Arup colleagues in New York and London. Arup has developed a reputation as a world leader in engineering for extreme events, and in this project it is seeking a design solution that will ensure that if there is a fire, the evacuation of the new building will be achieved quickly and safely. Arup engineers are fully exploiting the new technologies and materials of fire protection. Fire engineering has been revolutionized by the development of new models, simulations, and methods, and Arup Fire engineers have been at the forefront of utililizing the powerful computational capabilities of IvT to predict and explore different design options.

The Arup Fire work is the embodiment of how IvT affects the ways engineers design and the significant changes occurring in the broad nature of business and innovation. Arup Fire engineers use IvT to considerably enhance their capacity to think about design options and to play with and find solutions to problems in a quick, economical, and definitive way. The software that they use, often developed in-house, assists the team to accomplish their tasks by complementing their professional knowledge and judgement. Sitting alongside and supporting their engineering craft skills, it enables them to draw on repositories of useful information and to experiment and test ideas and concepts in a manner that is relatively unconstrained by cost or by delays resulting from the need to produce physical prototypes.

The Arup Fire team is also participating in a new form of virtual organization structure. From their London desks, they are designing with architects, engineers, and their customers around the world. The search for a design solution requires the Arup Fire team to undertake a range of activities, including:

- Face-to-face meetings and videoconferencing with architects to discuss their designs to
  o learn about patterns of use: the number of people in the building, on each floor, type of people (children, those with disabilities, etc.)
  o learn about the materials and mechanical and electrical systems to be used in the building
  o understand the impact of architectural features, such as stairs, windows, and elevator positions
- Preliminary calculations: testing initial ideas and determining broad outlines of fire control in the new design
- Initial conversations with Arup Fire colleagues, including quick design critiques, brainstorming, and sketches of fire management strategies
- Placing the initial fire strategy into Arup Fire models and simulations, including:
  o evacuation models
  o structural stability models
  o 3-dimension (3D) virtual reality models of the building and people moving through it
  o computational fluid dynamics (CFD) models of fire and smoke movements[3]
- Outlining potential extreme events that might cause disaster, including fire, terrorist attacks, earthquakes, and hurricanes
- Playing with different scenarios and seeing the response of the design to extreme events
- Viewing in 3D models the behaviour of people and the building under these various conditions
- Working with architects and the rest of the project to refine and develop the initial design to account for extreme events, the goal being to embed the latest practices and ideas on safety into the design

1.2. Three generic technologies

We distinguish between information and communications technology (ICT), operations and manufacturing technology (OMT), and innovation technology (IvT)[4] (see Figure 1.2).

ICT is an *enabling* technology for innovation through the provision of a ubiquitous digital infrastructure for the inexpensive, rapid, and secure storage and transfer of information and data. It facilitates the exchange of ideas and information moving from one place to another. ICT infrastructure supports a whole range of value-adding services, notably Web services, enterprise resource planning, and customer relations management. Its development trajectory is directed towards improved speed, processing power, connectivity, and physical interfaces. The benefits of ICT are based on large improvements in these areas coupled with cost reductions in equipment, and open computer systems architectures that enable the cumulative development of technological advances.

OMT is the technology for *implementing* innovation or making it operational. OMT essentially provides the technological mechanisms in production and coordination for transforming inputs into outputs. Its development trajectory is directed towards increasing reliability, flexibility, and accuracy, and reducing prices and costs. This technology has generic uses beyond conventional manufacturing industry and can be applied in science-based areas such as biotechnology and services such as entertainment. As well as the digital elements of this trajectory, extremely important developments are also taking place in the material used by OMT, such as nanotechnology. The benefits of OMT are based on combinations of various machines, such as computerized machine tools and robots, which process, make, and assemble varieties of products predictably, quickly, and cheaply alongside technologies that improve

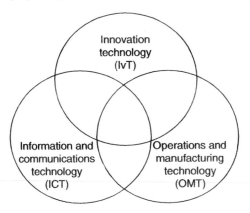

Fig. 1.2 Three generic types of technology (1)

networking and coordination through the management of information. In essence, OMT is concerned with the flow of information, components, and products, and the automation and standardization that assist in its control.

IvT is the technology for *creating* innovation. It provides the means by which people are technologically assisted in their innovation tasks, and the multiple inputs into the innovation process are united. The development trajectory of IvT is towards achieving economies of effort and definiteness of aim in innovation. These technologies help create new environments for people to think about new options, to engage other parties, including users, in design, playing or experimenting with different solutions to problems, and to ensure that ICT and OMT are used to maximum effect in the delivery of product, process, and service innovation. Figure 1.3 illustrates some examples of the various types of technology in each category.[5] We shall now describe some innovation technologies.

1.3 Innovation technology (IvT)

Computer-based simulation and modelling is replacing the traditional, laborious drafting, physical testing, and model building approach to many design tasks. Models provide simplified representations of a system and are used in a wide range of design and engineering tasks, including diagnostics, analysis, verification, and design optimization. Standard modelling tools include CFD, which can be used to model many different characteristics of movement and flow. There is a trend towards the use of non-linear models, and CFD reveals patterns in such areas as airflow, where characteristics that defy simplistic predictions can be explored.

Computers can reliably and realistically imitate the aggregate behaviour of materials. A classic example of the use of simulation techniques is in computer-generated crash tests for automobile designers (see Chapter 3). This technology, based on CAD programs, simulates crash behaviour and through repeated redesign stages assists in the optimization of designs. The advantages for the automaker are significant. First, the market demands regular production of new models and, by avoiding the need for slow production of prototypes for safety testing at early stages in the design process, development times are shortened. Second, the expense of crashing physical prototypes is avoided.[6] Third, the quality of data from the simulation is better than that derived from physical prototypes, with resulting improvements for safety.[7] Physical tests are still conducted at later stages but by then prototypes are much better developed and significant time and costs have been saved. Advanced 3D and 4D CAD systems, such as CATIA,[8] on which models are created and simulations conducted are used to improve the design quality of products as diverse as helicop-

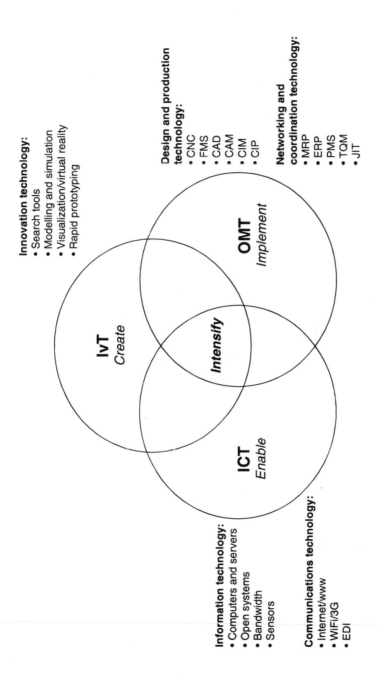

Innovation technology:
- Search tools
- Modelling and simulation
- Visualization/virtual reality
- Rapid prototyping

Design and production technology:
- CNC
- FMS
- CAD
- CAM
- CIM
- CIP

Networking and coordination technology:
- MRP
- ERP
- PMS
- TQM
- JIT

Information technology:
- Computers and servers
- Open systems
- Bandwidth
- Sensors

Communications technology:
- Internet/www
- WiFi/3G
- EDI

IvT
Create

OMT
Implement

ICT
Enable

Intensify

Fig. 1.3 Three generic types of technology (2)

9

ters (Sikorsky), automobiles (Rolls-Royce, BMW, Volkswagen), aircraft (Boeing), buildings (Bilbao Guggenheim Museum), shoes (Nike), and home appliances (Braun) (see, for example, Debackere 1999; Debackere and von Looy 2003).

Simulation is the no-risk way of gaining experience before making any investments and the elegant alternative to costly and time-consuming series of tests. The aim is always to analyse, predict, gain experience from the future, and improve. Simulation makes it possible to gain an overview of complex processes.... It is even possible to conduct experiments by computer which are not feasible in reality, or are too expensive, too dangerous or ethically unacceptable. (Miller 2001: 6)

Visualization technologies enable people to overcome natural limits of their capacity to extract knowledge from enormous data-sets. *Virtual reality*, for instance, combines at the top end supercomputers, high-speed networks, image-generating software, graphical interfaces, and advanced curved screen projection systems, and at the bottom end uses personal computers, to allow researchers and designers to visualize complex data-sets and enable high-performance modelling and prototyping (Whyte 2002). Such technologies allow design ideas to be shared from early concept to detailed articulation (Dahl et al. 2001; Oxman 2002; Whyte 2002). Graphical images enable more effective and faster assimilation of complex information (Johnson and Hansen 2004). Uses range from pharmaceutical development to mining or planning theatrical productions. In drug development, complicated molecular structures can be represented, displaying distances and angles of chemical bonds and the ways these can be modified by the introduction or substitution of molecules or atoms, enabling more creative and efficient drug design. High-throughput chemistry and simulations can increase the speed of the drug discovery process. In the mining industry the visualization of the properties of ore bodies enables economically efficient and environmentally less-damaging mining. In the theatre, virtual reality can be used for efficient set design and can also represent views of the stage from particular seats.

An example of the ways in which visual representation technologies make complex data, information, perspectives, and preferences from diverse groups visible and comprehensible is provided by the design of a new building. Virtual representation can assist architects in their visualization of the eventual design and help clarify clients' expectations, as they get a good understanding of what a building will look like before work begins, and inform contractors and builders of specifications and requirements (Anumba et al. 2000; Whyte 2002, 2003).

Rapid prototyping is the production of a physical 3D solid object from CAD data. It enables the examination of a variety of design concepts before the final design is fixed. As well as making models from traditional material, such as plastic and wood, models can be constructed from the layering of thermoplastics;

through stereolithography, which uses an ultraviolet (UV) photosensitive epoxy resin; and selective laser sintering. It is used for purposes as diverse as Boeing's design of parts for NASA's Space Station to the work of Therics, a US pharmaceutical company, which uses the technology to enable it to print 'designer pills' with unique time-release capabilities. It can be used both to manufacture consumer products, such as sunglasses, in quantities of hundreds of thousands, and to produce for 'markets of one'. Research is being undertaken towards using rapid prototyping in the development of relatively large-scale products, such as 25-m yachts. These technologies have the potential to become very widely diffused indeed, with Hewlett-Packard, for example, planning to introduce home rapid prototyping kits in the form of 3D printers.

Data mining, searching, and browsing. The enormous amount of information collected in various databases enables 'data mining', which assists the discovery of commercially and scientifically valuable knowledge. Data mining is helped by easy-to-use, intuitive navigation and search tools that can valuably assist in making sense, and deriving patterns, from the previously unobservable or incomprehensible. DNA micro-array techniques, for example, can test hundreds of thousands of compounds against a target field in a matter of weeks. It previously took months to analyse a few hundred (see Watson 2004). The ability to visualize and navigate within data-sets, recognizing patterns and finding new relationships has emerged as a new 'craft' skill (Hutchins 1996; McCullough 1996). We distinguish here between searching and browsing. Searching implies intent: the search for specific data or information. Browsing, in contrast, implies casual scanning: the quest for serendipitous information and connections. Internet businesses, such as Google, assist both searching and browsing. Both may be critical for innovation.

Artificial intelligence is used to help manage this data and information and guide good practice and support decision-making processes in product development and engineering projects. It is used across a variety of sectors, from component selection in Japanese house-building to semiconductors to medical practice. Steinmueller (2000), in his study of the semiconductor industry, refers to the necessity of automated tools for managing the user's cognitive processes in the use of 'working models', simulations, and large-scale computer-supported collaboration. He argues that the extent to which progress is being made in simulation techniques and the construction of virtual models of physical systems is controversial but, nonetheless, there exist widely used symbolic systems for representations of designs and specifications in electronics. He uses the example of simulation program integrated circuit emphasis (SPICE) and other circuit simulation models and symbolic languages for the description of integrated circuit fabrication that allow the reproduction of highly sophisticated working electronic systems and devices (Steinmueller 2000: 372).

These technologies provide the next generation of tools that will increase added value and improve efficiencies and competitiveness across a wide range of industries and sectors. Their use will be discussed in the following chapters. Although there are very porous boundaries we concentrate our discussion of particular technologies within the specific framework of thinking, playing, and doing. We therefore use the model illustrated in Fig. 1.4.

1.4 The importance of innovation

The prime medium for innovation is the firm, and the prime motive for innovation is enhanced competitiveness through the creation of value and efficiencies. It is the way that firms are motivated and rewarded for innovations through the mechanism of competition that underpins economic performance—their own, and in aggregate. Simply put, firms innovate in order to generate products and services which customers want to buy at price levels that maintain or improve competitive positions.

The creation of efficiencies and value is of concern for organizations beyond individual businesses including universities, research organizations, and a range of public institutions—any organization, in fact, interested in achieving economies of effort and definiteness of aim in innovation. Later chapters will show the advantages of IvT in a range of public sector settings, from the design of the congestion charge in London to the conduct of large-scale research experiments in universities. It is also of relevance for housing and health providers.

Innovation is not an end in itself. It is a means to an end. This book is concerned with the use of technology for broadly defined business purposes. It is less concerned with technical wizardry and the astonishing developments in research seen currently in the physical, life, and information sciences and more with the impact that technology can and does have on the business processes that create efficiencies and value. The focus is on the use of IvT to transform and unite the innovation process, the ways in which organizations use it, the choices they make and how they make them. The emphasis is on choice: there is no predetermined path that technology fixes for organizations to follow.

The intimate relationship between capitalism and innovation has long been recognized. Over sixty years ago, Schumpeter (1942) argued that it is not price competition which counts but 'the competition from the new commodity, the new technology, the new source of supply, the new type of organisation... competition which commands a decisive cost or quality advantage and which strikes not at the margins of the profits and the outputs of the existing firms but at their foundations and their very lives'.

Contemporary economists concur. Baumol (2002: 13), for example, argues that 'virtually all of the economic growth that has occurred since the eighteenth

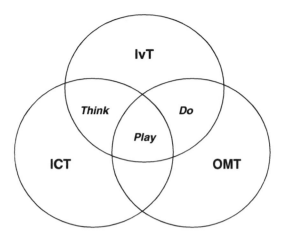

Fig. 1.4 Three generic types of technology (3)

century is ultimately attributable to innovation'. He also argues that 'under capitalism, innovative activity... becomes mandatory, a life-and-death matter for the firm' (2002: 1), and that '*innovation has replaced price* as the name of the game in a number of important industries' (2002: 4).

Essentially, innovation is what allows firms and nations to continue to pave their way in the world in a sustainable way. It enables firms to survive and grow, pay salaries and dividends, and it provides governments with resources to pay for services such as health and education.

Empirical evidence

The importance of innovation is seen in the level of resources devoted to it. The Organization for Economic Cooperation and Development (OECD) nations annually spend in excess of $600 billion on R&D, which is but one input to innovation. Several major corporations spend over $5 billion on R&D each year, and in some high-tech sectors, like pharmaceuticals and electronics, an allocation of 5–10 per cent of annual sales to R&D expenditure is not uncommon. The fact that such large investments are made reflects the very high returns that are possible when the right decisions about innovation are taken. IBM's investment of $1 billion in complementary metal oxide semiconductor (CMOS) technology in the early 1990s is estimated to have returned the company $19 billion between 1997 and 2001 (Gerstner 2002). It is not only the absolute level of investment in innovation that denotes its importance but also the relative levels. Many entrepreneurial individuals and firms invest substantial proportions of their wealth or sales in innovative activities.

It remains difficult to estimate the level of investment made by firms in innovative activities. The oft-used measure of R&D expenditures is a partial one, under-reporting the R&D activities of small firms and service providers (Patel and Pravitt 2000). Industrial sectors differ in their propensity to develop innovations through investments in formal R&D. In some sectors, such as pharmaceuticals, formal R&D activities are common. In others, informal design and engineering activities account for vast majority of innovative effort and under the current definition of R&D they remain unmeasured. R&D figures also significantly underestimate the levels of investment required by the firm to bring an innovation to the market. Indeed, R&D statistics only account for the costs of creating the first successful commercial prototype, and not its costs of designing, manufacturing, and marketing. Using data from the UK Innovation Survey, it is possible to roughly estimate these additional costs. In the survey, firms were asked to estimate their expenditures on the range of innovation-related activities not included in R&D statistics, including marketing, manufacturing, and training. Although these figures are difficult for firms to calculate, they do show that R&D represents less than 30 per cent of total innovative expenditures, indicating that R&D statistics may underestimate total innovative investment by up to three times (Stockdale 2002). If these figures hold at the national level, then the total investment in innovation is well above the 2–3 per cent share of R&D of gross national product (GNP) that is typical amongst OECD countries. Indeed, the actual levels of investment in innovative activities may be closer to 6–9 per cent of GNP. The gap between the measured levels of R&D and these rough estimates is simply the level of our ignorance about the costs of innovating.

Measuring the innovation activities of services firms is complex, but we do know that formal R&D activities are becoming an increasingly important part of service industries. Services R&D accounts for an ever-greater share of total industrial R&D expenditures across the OECD. Until the early 1980s, services R&D accounted for less than 5 per cent of total R&D in the USA, but by 2001, this increased to 39 per cent. Within services, the growth of R&D in the USA has been concentrated in software ($13 billion in 2002), professional and technical services ($22 billion in 2002), and trade, normally associated with distribution and retail ($24 billion in 2002) (NSB 2004). In Norway, Australia, Spain, and Denmark along with the USA, services now account for more than 30 per cent of total industrial R&D expenditures. In other countries, where services R&D only accounts for 10 per cent of total industrial R&D, this may reflect measurement shortcomings. In many OECD countries, services R&D accounts for the fastest growing portion of the R&D system (OECD 2004: 7).

If R&D is a partial measure of inputs into innovation, then patents are a partial output measure. There was a vast increase in the number of patents granted in the USA in the 1990s. In 1991, 96,512 patents were granted by the US Patent and Trademark Office (USPTO). In 2001, this figure had increased to 166,037 (NSB 2004). The fastest growing areas of technology patented were pharmaceuticals, biotechnology, mechanical equipment, and computer peripherals (Hicks et al. 2001). There are a variety of competing explanations for these increases, including the rise in the number of university patents and patent examiners at the USPTO, the growth of the ICT sector, and a greater emphasis on formal intellectual property rights protection on the part of industrial firms. For a review of this debate, see Kortum and Lerner (1999). Regardless of the reasons for the increase, it is clear that mounting expenditures in R&D in the USA have, in part, been reflected in a rise in the number of patents. Although it would be unwise to simply suggest that the rate of innovation in the USA dramatically changed in the 1990s, the growth in US patents does suggest that an increasing share of innovative efforts is leading to formal property rights. This does not, however, indicate that other informal forms of appropriating innovation, such as trade secrets and fast lead times, are becoming less important. The Carnegie Mellon survey of industrial R&D laboratories suggests that informal means of appropriating innovation have continued to be important and that firms patent for a number of strategic reasons that have little to do with a measure of innovative outputs, such as to engage in the trading of intellectual property rights (Cohen et al. 2002). In the UK, the 2001 Innovation Survey indicated that informal means of appropriability remain more widely used than formal methods (Laursen and Salter 2004).

Although almost all firms do attempt to innovate at some time, many fail. Recent innovation surveys in Europe and Canada reveal that the majority of manufacturing and services firms are actively trying to innovate. Yet only a small number are able to succeed. For example, in the UK, 8 per cent of firms indicated that they were able to develop a product that was new for their market between 1998 and 2001 (Stockdale 2002). Indeed, major radical or disruptive innovations are rare and in some industries they may appear only once every thirty years (Tushman and Anderson 1986). Most firms live off their past innovations, making small modifications in their product offerings. For these firms, significant innovations are highly unusual. Among UK innovators, incremental product innovations account for close to 35 per cent of total turnover. Only 8 per cent of their turnover comes from products that are new for the market (Stockdale 2002).

Innovation can, however, pay great rewards. Research into investments in new product development consistently shows the benefits that accrue (Cooper 1998).[9] According to one estimate, new products, that is those introduced in the past five years, account for 50 per cent of annual sales in many industries

(Schilling and Hill 1998). Innovation also increases a firm's export potential (Bleaney and Wakelin 2002), profits over long periods and during recessions (Geroski et al. 1993), credit ratings (Czarnitzki and Kraft 2004), chances of surviving in the market (Cefis and Marsili 2004), and market value (Hall 2000; Toivanen and Stoneman 2002).

1.5 Why study innovation

The high levels of investment in innovation, and the substantial contribution it makes, provide compelling reasons for studying it. Perhaps what is even more compelling is that, whereas at a macro level it is relatively straightforward to claim the association between more investment and more innovation (see Fagerberg 1987; Freeman 1994), at the micro level of the individual innovation and organization it is far more difficult. Choices about how to manage the innovation process itself matter.

Essentially, whilst innovation is an important activity, it is also one that is characterized by a high degree of uncertainty and failure. Empirical studies show that firms frequently fail in their R&D and new product development projects. Of the thousands of potential new drugs currently in development, for example, only one or two will eventually succeed in the marketplace. Schilling and Hill (1998) estimate that roughly one-third to two-thirds of new products that actually reach the market fail to produce a financial return. Governments often fail in the policies they develop to encourage innovation (Cohen and Noll 1991).

The work of Scherer (1999) shows that returns from innovation are highly skewed. Only a few innovations in a portfolio produce significantly above-average returns. Similarly, only a small number of academic publications get very highly cited, a small number of patents produce most income, and a small number of products yield the majority of sales. Although the performance of incremental innovations tend to be less skewed than radical innovations, the implications of these skewed returns are clear: as Scherer argues, the chances of success in innovation are such that an appropriate metaphor is that of a lottery. Spending more on innovation, or buying more tickets, provides more chances of success but large expenditure does not ensure that you win.

Theoretically, innovation can be conceived as a process whereby organizations invest in developing innovations in a variety of forms, some of which are selected for use by markets, governments, or partner organizations, and a few of which are thereafter successfully propagated and diffused. Variety, as argued by economists such as Nelson and Winter (1982), Cohen and Malerba (2001), and Metcalfe (1997) is the engine of growth in capitalism. In the view of evolutionary economists there is considerable attrition between the production of variety and the propagation of innovations resulting from a whole range of uncertainties around selection processes (this theoretical approach will be expanded upon in Chapter 2).

In these circumstances where innovation is so important, but only a limited number of innovations succeed, it is clearly important to study how organizations might achieve greater efficiencies and predictability in their innovative activities. It is useful to know how more variety can be produced with more predictable and less uncertain selection processes, thereby improving the likelihood of successful diffusion and propagation. The benefits of greater understanding would clearly accrue to firms, but also to research organizations and nations, since any resources saved could be reinvested more effectively and any reduction in failure rates could stimulate greater investments. In circumstances where uncertainty provides opportunity, and where firms are confronted by disruptive changes and need to do things differently, IvT can cost-effectively help create a wider range of innovative options from which to select.

Understanding changes in the ways the innovation process is managed and organized and can be improved is critical to

- better allocating resources to meet organizational aims, enhancing the skills and performance of creative and productive individuals and teams;
- benefiting consumers and users through better utility, functionality, and quality of products and services, through reduced costs and the creation of things that delight us;
- increasing the range of future options available to businesses and society that are so important in uncertain and unpredictable environments, helping us better select between them and ensure their development and diffusion.

Organizations differ in their capacities to innovate and very few can continually innovate over extended periods of time. One of the major reasons why organizations find innovation so troublesome is the wide range of different kinds of uncertainty that surrounds it.

1.6 Risk and uncertainty in innovation

As Bernstein (1996: 207) puts it in his history of risk: 'We are never certain: we are always ignorant to some degree.' In addition to the usual risks of investments associated with changing markets, volatile finance, and the continuing challenges of organizing resources and people, there are many types of uncertainty around technological innovation that explain in large part why it is so inherently risky.

One of the major determinants of risk is, of course, the substantial resources that are often invested in innovation and stand to be lost if the innovation fails.

Risk is also a function of the uncertainties that surround innovation. Here we must distinguish—as Frank Knight did in his 1921 book, *Risk, Uncertainty and Profit*—risk (which is measureable) from uncertainty (which is unmeasurable). Our concern is with efforts to help assess and limit uncertainty. Various broad forms of uncertainty can be described: technical, market, social, political, cultural, and those derived from time, speed, and complexity.

Technical and market uncertainty

The first two forms of uncertainty include the broad issues about what new technologies might develop in the future and their impact on markets. It is virtually impossible to predict with any degree of certainty what innovations will emerge and therefore assess what potential threats exist for current technologies, products, and services. As Metcalfe (1998: 6) puts it:

While we know a great deal about innovation processes and their general dependence on opportunities, incentives, resources and management capabilities we will never, I claim, develop this knowledge to such a fine level that we can predict the kind of product and process innovation that will emerge.

In these circumstances it is perhaps apposite to claim—as the founder of Intel, Grove (1996), put it—that 'only the paranoid survive'.

There is frequent uncertainty about specific technology choices. When Edison embarked on the long search for a suitable filament for the incandescent electric light bulb, it took his team fourteen months. According to one of his assistants, the fibres used for carbonization of the filament included cotton, flax, silk, hemp, horsehair, fish line, teak, spruce, boxwood, vulcanized rubber, cork, celluloid, grass fibres from everywhere, linen twine, tar paper, wrapping paper, cardboard, tissue paper, parchment, holly wood, absorbent cotton, rattan, California redwood, raw jute, corn silk, New Zealand flax, and the hair from the beards of several laboratory workers (quoted in Carey 1995: 169).

There are many ways potential innovations fail. Some innovations fail simply because the technology does not deliver what was expected of it: think of the *Titanic*. Some innovations succeed technologically but fail to win the market that was expected of them: Concorde, Sony's Betamax, and IBM's OS/2 are examples. Indeed, Christensen (1997) in his study of disruptive technologies, such as PCs, discount retailing, and off-road motorcycles, goes so far as to argue that not only are the market applications for such technologies *unknown* at the time of their development, they are *unknowable*. Some innovations fail on both counts. Ford's Edsel automobile was overdesigned, difficult to make, and unloved by motorists. The Apple Newton was overpriced, oversized, and poorly engineered. Its handwriting recognition software was initially fairly inaccurate and required considerable time to learn the user's writing style before becoming effective. Nintendo's Virtual Boy, released in 1995, which used a twin eyeglass style projector to display the games in 3D, was heavy, non-portable, and had little software. In order to prevent legal proceedings, Nintendo added an automatic stop feature that reminded users to take frequent breaks. This reminder scared off many customers. The UK Government's Millennium Dome, although constructed on time and on budget, was a complete commercial flop, attracting only six million of the thirteen million expected visitors. After closing in December 2000, it has been a continuing drain on public funds.

The ambiguous and messy notions of success and failure need to be fully incorporated into discussions of innovation. Even if the contribution of a particular innovation can be quantified exactly, producing a substantial return on investment, there may be an issue of what consequence that innovation has for other areas of existing business: has it diverted resources and compromised existing markets? Or the innovation may have taken the firm down a particular technological path that may not be the most advantageous for it in the long run. Similarly, an innovation that has been a spectacular failure in accounting terms may have enormous benefits for a firm in the related knowledge created around the innovation, which can be put to other uses, or in preventing it moving down a fruitless path.

Social, cultural, and political uncertainties

Technology and innovation can only properly be understood in the context of the particular social and cultural environments in which they are developed and used. From the earlier work of Noble (1977) on the development of the automated machine tool to more contemporary analysis of the development of the Linux operating system (Tuomi 2002), the evidence shows that technology is created and used within the context of strong social, cultural, and political influences. Once it is recognized that 'the best technology' is not automatically the technology that wins in the market, and that the way it is shaped and accepted is contingent upon a wide range of complex social issues, increasing the number of influential and unpredictable variables, then uncertainty increases commensurately.

If innovation occurs as a result of the activities of an entrepreneur, it can result from dissonant personal characteristics. Entrepreneurs are often dissatisfied with existing technologies or business processes; they favour change and dislike the status quo. Their entrepreneurship is a means of personal expression and development. They can add to, and benefit from, the amount of uncertainty in an industrial system.[10] They provide what Keynes (1936: 161–2) called the 'animal spirits' that are crucially important for innovation:

Most, probably, of our decisions to do something positive, the full consequences of which will be drawn out over many days to come, can only be taken as the result of animal spirits—of a spontaneous urge to action rather than inaction, and not as the outcome of a weighted average of quantitative benefits multiplied by quantitative probabilities. Enterprise only pretends to itself to be mainly actuated by the statements in its own prospectus, however candid and sincere . . . if the animal spirits are dimmed and the spontaneous optimism falters, leaving us to depend on nothing but a mathematical expectation, enterprise will fade and die.

Keynes' elevation of 'animal spirits' over 'mathematical expectation' in the stimulus to innovation accentuates the uncertainties surrounding it. The issue of the new kinds of leadership skills developing around the use of IvT will be discussed in Chapter 7.

Innovations may have ambiguously positive and negative consequences. As the following example shows, even the most useful and simple of innovations can have negative, and hence risky, consequences. Barbed wire was one of the most important innovations of the nineteenth century. Barbed wire performs the extremely valuable functions of defining space and establishing territorial boundaries. The product itself has the characteristics of all the most celebrated innovations. It is remarkably robust, seen in the way it has been virtually unchanged since its original patent in 1874. It is a highly munificent innovation, with an unceasing variety of use. It is heat-resistant, difficult to bend or break, lightweight, durable, adaptable, easily installed, and cheap to make and buy. It has produced positive benefits. For example, it was instrumental in opening up the west of the USA for economic development. But it has numerous negative connotations. Think of concentration and internship camps, or the trenches of the First World War, or of the dispossessed Native Americans in the west of the USA (Razac 2002). The same innovation has different consequences for different groups: the nineteenth-century Native American saw barbed wire very differently from the settler farmer.

Ambiguities around the value of innovations are seen starkly today in the case of genetically manipulated canola seeds, which are viewed very differently by some crop producers and environmentalists.

The list of innovations that ambiguously provide both substantial benefits and costs include the automobile, perhaps the most important innovation of the twentieth century. It has provided the democratic freedom of cheap, easy travel to millions, and is responsible for a substantial proportion of employment and wealth in many economies. Yet this needs to be contrasted with appalling carnage on the roads and environmental pollution. Fast food is convenient and relatively cheap, but contributes to severe health problems associated with obesity. Email is wonderfully useful, but brings huge computer security risks and clogs the working day. DNA-typing helps catch criminals, but can have negative implications for human rights. Innovations in this sense rely on societal acceptance of perceived risk, and the volatility brought about by the way this differs and varies over time adds to uncertainty.[11]

Uncertainties of time and speed

The outcomes of innovation are significantly complicated by the way time influences success and failure. As the philosopher, Francis Bacon, noted in the seventeenth century: 'He that will not apply new remedies must expect new evils; for time is the greatest innovator.'

Examples of innovations about which perceptions of success have changed over time include the De Havilland Comet, which was the first successful civil airliner and in many ways helped create the commercial airline industry. Little was known at the time of its early success about the problems of metal fatigue and its disastrous subsequent consequences. The Millennium Bridge in London was initially perceived as a notorious failure but its problems were subsequently resolved and eventually moved the technology of bridge design significantly forward (see Chapter 5).

Increasing the speed of production and innovation has always been a preoccupation for firms. In Smith's analysis (1812: 22) of productivity improvements resulting from the increasing division of labour, three factors are identified as being important: the skills of the workforce; the technology it uses; and the speed by which items (what he calls 'species') of work move through the system. The historian of early industrialization, Thompson, shows how the exertion of industrial discipline over a workforce that previously related to seasonal transformations in agriculture was strongly determined by considerations and measurements of time. As he (1967: 69) puts it:

The small instrument which regulated the new rhythms of industrial life was at the same time one of the more urgent of the new needs which industrial capitalism called forth to energize its advance.

The important issue of instruments and their role in the development of science and innovation will be examined in Chapter 2, and we shall be exploring the relationship between instrumentation and creativity throughout the book.

The huge influence of time and speed on the world of work continued into the early twentieth century with 'Time and Motion' studies derived from Taylor's 'Scientific Management', which aimed at developing accurate and scientific measure of unit times in order to exert greater work discipline. More contemporary management preoccupations with time are seen in the evolution of 'lean production' and 'lean thinking', and concerns for being 'first-to-market', or being 'fast-followers'. Books with titles such as *Competing on*

Internet Time (Cusumano and Yoffie 1998) and *Blur: The Speed of Change in the Connected Economy* (Davis and Meyer 1998) discuss the competitive advantages to be derived from speedy innovation. Bill Gates' book is entitled *Business @ the Speed of Thought*. Ownership of patents—awarded to the first to register inventions—can confer significant competitive advantages. IBM, for example, enjoyed revenues of $1.5 billion from licensing its intellectual property in 2001 (Gerstner 2002). First-mover advantages can be obtained by those firms that gain market recognition and position ahead of competitors, or establish beneficial technical standards.

Speed, however, can bring risk. Being first is not necessarily always advantageous. There are numerous examples of companies failing after being first in the market with new technologies, such as EMI with its CAT Scanner and Xerox with office computing, and examples of success in being a follower, such as IBM with its PC and Matsushita with its VHS VCR. There are strong advocates for strategies based on imitation (Schnaars 1994) and very successful companies such as Dell and Wal-Mart are renowned for their strategy of being fast followers (Carr 2003). The frenzy of the dot.com boom and collapse reflected a concern for speed rather than substance, where the idea of being first superseded considerations of whether the technology was proven, markets existed, or the business model was plausible. Indeed, the overheating of financial markets due to speculation on new technologies has occurred with historical regularity (Kindelberger 2001; Perez 2003).

Alternatively, speed can also remove uncertainty. Time compression can enable quicker assessment of the likelihood of success and constrain the effects of those unforeseen developments, through limiting their opportunity to become influential (Mason-Jones and Towill 1999; Towill 2003). The relationship between speed and uncertainty is therefore highly contingent. It may, for example, be highly advantageous to speed up the innovation process when it is routinized and outcomes are relatively well specified. Speed may be disadvantageous when the innovation is disruptive to existing ways of doing things and warrants extensive reflection and learning. An overemphasis on speed would also rest uneasily when the consequences of mistakes are high, as in the design of aircraft or nuclear power plant.

Uncertainty caused by complexity

The sheer complexity of the technological and business environments in which firms operate also contributes to the risk and uncertainty borne by innovators. Complexity occurs because globalization brings potentially many more influential and unpredictable players into an organization's realm of activity. Compliance with government regulations about standards, tariffs, and quotas and the environment that differ broadly between nations and can change quickly adds further levels of complexity to new activities. The vast expansion of knowledge created, as seen in the continuing rise in numbers of academic journals,[12] the increasing amount of interdisciplinary research, and the fusion of different kinds of technologies, for example in biotechnology,[13] extends the 'variety' of potential innovations. Practically, this is argued to increase the range of technical bases firms need to be abreast of in order to compete (Brusoni et al. 2001).[14] Furthermore, various forms of systems impinge upon the operations of firms. Innovation systems, comprising combinations of institutions and relationships, operate nationally, regionally, sectorally, and locally (Lundvall 1992; Nelson 1993; Edquist 1997; Malerba 2004). Production systems around various forms of contractual and cooperative relationships exist between producers and their suppliers (Best 2001). Technological systems, driven by the commercial advantages of scale and scope, and facilitated by open systems computer architecture, emerge with evolving hierarchies of integrators and suppliers. Other kinds of technical systems, with combinations of different vintages of technology, especially in infrastructure and long-term fixed capital, such as the construction of Terminal 5 alongside the existing airport at Heathrow, add to complexity (Gann 2000). All these various forms of system compound the extent to which innovators become reliant and dependent on others, accentuating interdependence and expanding the complexity of the innovation process.

1.7 Conclusions

The essential paradox of innovation is that whilst it is clearly evident, *ex post*, how important it is for corporate and, indeed, national competitiveness and quality of life, it is by no means evident, *ex ante*, which particular innovations will be successful. Numerous uncertainties accompany the process and outcomes of innovation, which combine to make innovation a risky investment. These diverse and multifaceted uncertainties extend from the technical issues associated with unpredictable experimental outcomes, complexity, and systemic integration to notions of timing and social and cultural acceptance.

The fact that so many investments are made in innovation shows that high returns are possible, and also that the alternative—not investing in innovation—is almost certainly riskier. As Francis Bacon noted 400 years ago, if you don't innovate, someone else will. The challenge is to manage the risk—the cost and uncertainty—associated with innovation, accepting that the outcomes of innovation can be highly ambiguous, and that notions of success and failure are not always clear-cut. Managing these uncertainties is a decidedly important matter. As Schumpeter argued, innovation strikes at the very lives of firms, and decisions on innovation ascertain which firms survive and which firms die. As he put it so colourfully, innovation offers 'the carrot of spectacular reward or the stick of destitution'.

This challenge is particularly difficult in circumstances where fast and consistent returns are expected in the financial markets that provide much of the capital for innovation. The requirements of stock markets (Dore 2000) can conflict with the reality of innovation investments, which commonly accrue over the long term and regularly fail to deliver what is expected. It is also difficult where, within the firm, decisions on particular investments involve a rare level of sophistication in risk assessment. As we shall see in Chapter 4, whilst there has been a steady increase in aggregate R&D investments internationally, questions arise about the sustainability of these increases in large companies (Meyer-Krahmer and Reger 1999), and a strategy of continually increasing the scale of investments to mitigate the risks associated with them is only affordable by a few companies, and probably only for short periods. Furthermore, these aggregate data fail to capture international differences in performance: industrial R&D expenditure in Germany, France, and the UK during the 1990s did not match the growth rates seen elsewhere (see Chapter 4).

The alternative solution is to make innovation smarter: to get the proverbial 'more bangs per buck'. Firms make many diverse efforts directed towards this end. Accountants and financial analysts are developing better means to quantify exposure through particular technology investments and to consider the real option values that investments in research provide. Managers are using tools in forecasting and scenario planning to help them consider the risks in innovating, in not innovating, and assessing the damage should competitors innovate first. A wide variety of strategic research partnerships and alliances are now used to mitigate risk by creating scale and scope in innovation investments. Organizational structures and systems are evolving to seek greater efficiency in innovation projects, for example, through 'heavyweight' and 'tiger' teams (Clark and Wheelwright 1993) and the use of 'stage-gate systems' (Cooper 1998).

This book is about another element contributing to efforts to make innovation smarter: the intensification of innovation through the application of IvT to thinking, playing, and doing in the innovation process. Innovation is a strategically important activity and the process by which it is delivered is now a focal attention point for scientists and researchers, engineers and designers, general managers and project and functional managers, and personnel. The traditional boundaries and hierarchies enclosing the innovation process are being broken down.

Technologies used in previously segmented activities are evolving towards integrated technologies to support innovation and reduce uncertainties. Thus, e-science technologies, such as the Grid (see the discussion in Chapters 2 and 4), are creating virtual research communities that involve industry in scientific research.[15] Simulation, modelling, and virtual reality tools are helping designers bridge the gaps between researchers and practitioners, integrating the thinking, playing, and doing in the innovation process. Rapid prototyping is enabling the more active engagement of manufacturing in product innovation. The capacities of search tools, like data mining, to intelligently process vast amounts of data assist the innovation process, from helping scientists in their research to constructing better information about markets. The following chapters will examine in detail the ways in which IvT enables smarter innovation efforts, by organizations and individuals.

None of the changes described will ever remove the need for experimental, trial-and-error processes of learning, driven by intellectual curiosity and accompanied by opportunities created by their very unpredictability and the possibilities of serendipity. Nor should they: routinized innovation will remain an oxymoron. Craft skills should complement and build upon and never be replaced by the opportunities provided in the automated codes of the new IvT. Nonetheless, any methods that make innovation investments more definite in their aim and more economical are certain to be welcomed by private and public sector investors alike. The technologies and new processes described in the following chapters that have intensified the innovation process can, if used effectively in thinking, playing, and doing activities, valuably assist in overcoming some of the uncertainties surrounding innovation.

2   Understanding Innovation

2.1 Introduction

The importance of innovation is well known, yet in many ways 'innovation' itself needs to be better understood. In part this results from terminological confusion. Innovation is sometimes confused with invention: the creation of a new idea and its reduction to practice. The definition of innovation as the successful exploitation of new ideas involves much more than the creation of ideas and includes the ways in which they are developed, diffused, and exploited. Innovation is at once an *outcome*, a new product, process, or service, and a *process* of organizational and managerial combinations and decisions; the two cannot be treated synonymously. An innovation, by definition, is successful (although this may be limited or short-lived, and bearing in mind the discussion in Chapter 1 about the ambiguity surrounding definitions of success and failure). Any innovation *process*, in contrast, can fail to support the successful exploitation of new ideas.

It is possible to think about innovation along a variety of dimensions. What *type* of innovation is it? Is it a product, process, or service innovation (recognizing that the boundaries between them can be blurred and one company's product may be another's process)? What is the *source* of the innovation? Has it emerged from research in a university or from an entrepreneur's vision? Or is it a response to a clearly articulated customer requirement? How *extensive* is an innovation? Is it a minor incremental adaptation or improvement to an innovation in a small component of a system, or a radical innovation, perhaps changing the whole system? Is the innovation new to the firm, industry, or nation, or new to the world? How does the innovation relate to existing technologies, and to what extent does it replace them? What are the *outcomes* of innovation? Are they all positive, and how sustainable are they?[16] A range of widely different questions can therefore be posed around innovation and the cumulative development of understanding requires clarification of the focus of, and reasons for, asking these questions.

Some of the difficulties in understanding innovation come from the specific and differing languages used in, and approaches to, its study brought to the issues by the wide range of academic disciplines interested in researching it. Economists, geographers, psychologists, public policy analysts, historians, scientists, and students of business, management, and organization and innovation studies all contribute to the theoretical and empirical understanding of innovation. Yet, their particular approaches and prejudices make it often difficult to transfer these understandings across disciplinary boundaries. Some economists, for example, may see collaboration between partners in technology development as 'unnatural' and unwelcome in that such partnerships may involve diluting future income streams, redirect scarce managerial talent, and be construed as being anticompetitive collusion. Other observers from strategic management or innovation studies may see collaboration as providing valuable strategic options or as a necessary stimulus to innovation. Some social psychologists may argue that partnerships are a reflection of natural human cooperativeness.

Another problem lies in the innovation process itself which is complex, uncertain, and changing. The innovation process, however, can be and needs to be understood. There are three principles that we believe it necessary to adhere to if innovation—as outcome or process—is to be properly understood theoretically and empirically. Analysts must recognize, in our view, that

1. innovation has to be located in its historical context;
2. innovation is not a discrete event or activity, but results from, and contributes to, a range of systemic relationships and interdependencies;
3. innovation is socially mediated and results from organizational, managerial, and individual practices and decisions.

This chapter uses these principles to place IvT and the intensification of innovation into historical context. It develops a typology of activities and tasks around IvT and indicates their interdependencies with ICT and OMT. The chapter emphasizes the ways in which IvT enables far greater integration of disparate inputs into the innovation process, including those from the science base, customers, and partners, than have previously been possible. The chapter concludes with an examination of the way IvT, like previous generations of technology, depends on managerial and organizational choices. IvT requires the working practices and skills of individuals as they combine the 'code' in the technology with the 'craft' of their knowledge and skills in new, imaginative, and productive ways.

The literature on innovation is large and diverse (see Table 2.1). This chapter draws selectively on key ideas in innovation as they apply to our argument about intensification and thinking, playing, and doing. Box 2.1 offers a brief description of the theoretical basis for our analysis.

2.2 Principle 1: Historical context

The charm of history, as Aldous Huxley tells us, is that, from age to age nothing changes and yet everything is completely different. Schumpeterian historians of

---

Box 2.1 Theoretical and analytical approaches to innovation

There is no existing unified theory that explains the contemporary reality of innovation. The complex and multidimensional nature of innovation makes it difficult, if not impossible, to deliver the explanatory power expected of a theory within a single framework. Nevertheless, a rich collection of theories has emerged over the past twenty years or so in institutional and evolutionary economics, in industrial dynamics and political economy, in thinking about systems and complexity, and in theories of the firm and organizational behaviour, which have significantly enhanced our capacity to explain innovation. The theories drawn upon in this book are not only relatively recent, but also span a number of disciplines. Their integration and synthesis, like innovation itself, is a continuing exploratory effort that entails a considerable degree of iteration with empirical research.

Various strands of thinking have underpinned the emergent awareness of innovation as complex and multidimensional. These include increased interest in the role of institutions in mediating market forces, the importance of collaboration (association) and coordination within an economy, appreciation of the systemic and interdependent nature of innovation, and the differing patterns of development for different technologies, the contribution of learning and trust to economic activity, and, from a business strategy perspective, enhanced understanding of the responses by firms to the challenges of technological change and globalization.

A historical theoretical perspective with contemporary utility is Schumpeterian economics, with its central appreciation that the phenomenon under study is essentially dynamic, involves the historical agglomeration of clusters of innovations that both creates and destroys elements of the economy, and has major consequences for the conduct and performance of the overall economy. Building on the work of Schumpeter, evolutionary economists, such as Nelson and Winter (1982), argue that innovation involves the creation of *variety*, processes of *selection* from that variety assisted by markets (purchasing decisions by customers), governments (as procurers and regulators), and collaborative partners (customers, suppliers, intermediary organizations, such as research associations and consultants), and subsequent *propagation* of innovations, some of which succeed, and are further developed and diffused, and most of which fail. We shall draw on this theoretical approach throughout the book.

In contrast with generic theoretical approaches, Table 2.1 provides some indication of the depth and variety of analytical lenses specifically applied to innovation. These approaches are mostly empirically based and have no pretence of having the explanatory power of theory.

The purpose of the typology is to illustrate the range of research in innovation and to place some of the approaches that we subsequently draw upon into broad categories. Inevitably, analyses span categories and we oversimplify and do damage to the richness of many of the bodies of work; nonetheless the typology is broadly descriptive and helps us distinguish between research conducted into innovation with different lenses of analysis.

---

technological change point to patterns of intense innovation since the Industrial Revolution, characterized by clusters of emerging new technology, patterns of new investment, and associated changes in organization, management, and employment. The pattern remains similar but is manifested in novel ways.

Scholars such as Freeman and Perez (1988; Freeman and Louca 2001; Perez 2003) have identified a series of technological revolutions that have occurred since the mid eighteenth century. These are described in a simplified form in Table 2.2. We have added to this analysis an idealized characterization of innovation which is developed later in this chapter. In addition to the technological changes that

TABLE 2.1   Some of the major analytical approaches to innovation

Major focus	Concept or category of innovation	Key text(s)
Source	Science push	Bush (1946)
	Market pull	Myers and Marquis (1969), von Hippel (1988)
	Coupling model	Rothwell and Zegveld (1985)
Nature and extent	Radical or incremental	Freeman (1974)
	Continuous or discontinuous	Tushman and Anderson (1986)
	Life cycle	Abernathy and Utterback (1978)
	Modular or architectural	Henderson and Clark (1990)
	Dominant designs	Utterback (1994)
	Robust designs	Rothwell and Gardiner (1988)
	Sustaining or disruptive	Christensen (1997)
	Open or closed	Chesbrough (2003)
	Innovation space	Tidd et al. (1997)
	Technology fusion	Kodama (1995)
Type	Product	Cooper (1998)
	Service	Barras (1986)
	Process	Bessant (1991)
System	National	Freeman (1987); Lundvall (1992); Nelson (1993)
	Regional	Cooke and Morgan (2000)
	Sectoral	Malerba (2004)
	Technological	Carlsson (1994)
	Networks	Freeman (1991); Tuomi (2002); Castells (1996)
	Clusters	Porter (1990)
	Complex product systems	Hobday (1998)
Process	Chain-linked	Kline and Rosenberg (1986)
	Innovation journey	Van de Ven et al. (1999)
	Innovation/Technology strategy	Teece (1987); Dodgson (1989); Coombs (1994); Schilling (2005)
	Knowledge management	Leonard-Barton (1995); Nonaka and Takeuchi (1995); Seely Brown and Duguid (2000)
	Operations and production management	Bessant (1991); Womack and Jones (1996)
	Design management	Petroski (1985); Baldwin and Clark (2000)
	R&D management	Iansiti (1993); Gerybadze and Reger (1999)
	Fifth generation	Rothwell (1992); Dodgson (2000)
Outcomes	Technology diffusion	Rogers (1995)
	Technological learning	Rosenberg (1982)

TABLE 2.2. Technological revolutions

Technological revolution	Major elements	New technologies and new or redefined industries	New or redefined infrastructure	Characterization of innovation
The Industrial Revolution 1760–1820 approx.	Handcrafting replaced by factory system	Cotton; iron; machinery	Canals; turnpikes; waterpower	Craft; individual
Age of railways and steam 1825–75 approx.	Massive improvement in connectedness in the economy	Steam engines and power; machinery; iron and coal mining; locomotives	Railways; postal service; global shipping; telegraph; great ports; city gas	Engineering craft; individual
Age of steel and electricity 1875–1920 approx.	Large-scale engineering and electrification of the economy	Bessemer steel; heavy chemical and civil engineering; electrical equipment; canned and bottled food; paper and packaging	Worldwide shipping and telegraph; electrical networks; telephone; great bridges and tunnels	Individual and corporate
Age of oil and mass production 1910–70 approx.	Mass production of cheap goods	Automobiles; cheap oil; petrochemicals; home electrical appliances; refrigerated and frozen foods	Networks of roads; airports; universal electricity; worldwide analogue telecommunications	Corporate
Information and communications technology 1970–	The digital economy	Microelectronics; computers; software; CAD/CAM; new materials	Worldwide digital telecommunications (fibre-optics, satellite); Internet/www	Distributed and open

Source: Based on Perez (2003).

were occurring, innovation has also changed from era to era characterized by a movement from an individual to corporate to distributed model.

These analyses are controversial in some circles, with scholars arguing about the accuracy of the periodicity and the relative contributions of particular technologies (Edgerton 1999, 2004). The controversy is compounded when the argument concerns the relationship between these technological revolutions and the economic cycle (the so-called Kondratiev waves). Nonetheless, we find this conceptualization helpful in a number of respects in understanding IvT's potential development trajectory and consequences.

First, this form of historical analysis sharpens our appreciation of the time scales involved in innovation. Arthur (2002: 6) argues that there is a considerable delay in the realization of the benefits of new technology:

[S]everal decades, usually lie between the technologies that set a revolution in motion and the revolution's heyday. The enabling technologies of the steel and electrification revolution (the Bessemer steel plant and the electric motor and generator) arrived in the 1870s, but their full effects were not felt until well into the 1910s. Watt's steam engine was developed in the 1760s and did not come into prevalent use until the 1820s. Modern mass production arrived in 1913, but did not reach its peak years until the 1950s and 1960s.

In a more contemporary era, the results of the significant investments in ICT in the 1980s and 1990s are only recently being seen in productivity improvements (Lester 1998).

Second, the historical analyses emphasize the interdependence of various kinds of new technology and their continuing relationships with existing vintages of technology. New technologies do not replace existing technologies and investments overnight; periods of coexistence of different vintages of technology can occur. Thus the new generation of biotechnology-based drug discovery processes exists alongside traditional discovery methods.

Third, the importance of enabling infrastructure is strongly emphasized. Canals, railways, roads, electricity networks, telecommunications, and the Internet all provide the basis upon which new products, processes, and services are developed and diffused. Again, there is a time lag between the creation of this infrastructure and the development of new businesses that take advantage of it. Rosenberg (1963a, 1963b) points to the way the development of the US machine tool industry in the mid nineteenth century, which relied heavily on the stimulus brought about by transportation improvements and freight cost reductions in the railways, lagged 30–40 years behind the establishment of the national railway network. IvT can be considered as a new form of infrastructure, specifically developed to create innovation.

Fourth, technological change is inseparable from social change. Each revolution is accompanied by new 'best-practice' forms of organization and new skill mixes in the workforce (Freeman and Soete 1997). We explore some of these changes in Chapter 7.

Fifth, the changes associated with each revolution are ubiquitous: they affect the whole economy, and hence the term 'techno-economic paradigm' (Dosi 1988; Freeman and Perez 1988). The technologies of the fifth wave are not confined to new or 'high' technologies. Their application is also important in areas such as food, packaging, and construction (Gann 2000), and older technologies, such as railways, can be continually reinnovated (seen in the form of fast trains and Maglev).

A historical perspective assists in highlighting the importance of how technologies are adapted in use. It deepens our appreciation of the role of capital goods and machine tools in innovation and industrial development (Rosenberg 1963a, 1963b) and also of the importance of instrumentation in the development of ideas (Crump 2001; Galison 2003). Galison's analysis (2003) of the instruments of time in the physics of Poincaré and Einstein points to the reflexive relationship between ideas and instruments in scientific progress. Critical of the 'endless oscillation between thinking of history as ultimately about ideas or fundamentally about material objects', he (2003: 325) says: 'Clocks, maps, telegraphs, steam engines, computers all raise questions that refuse a sterile either/or dichotomy of things versus thoughts. In each instance, problems of physics, philosophy and technology cross.' Similarly, it was no accident that Faraday was an expert maker of experimental machinery (Hamilton 2003).

An approach to innovation that includes an (albeit more recent) historical element is Rothwell's fifth Generation Innovation Process (1992).[17] Following the categorization described in Table 2.2, the first three generations of innovation process were primarily concerned with the sources of innovation; the latter two generations are more concerned with the process of innovation.

The first generation innovation process, the *science-push* model, emerged following the Second World War. Advocates for big scientific investments, such as Vannevar Bush, argued that large research investments—for example, in nuclear engineering, in the search for cancer cures, and, latterly, in space exploration—would filter down into industrial applications.[18] In Fig. 2.1, science is pushed into the box, which is the firm. The public policy and management challenge in this generation of the innovation process was relatively simple: maintain and increase substantial budgets for R&D. There was a presumed demand for the results of R&D, which was assumed to be the predominant source of innovation.

This simple, linear model of innovation, which was prevalent in the 1950s, began to be questioned and eventually superseded in the 1960s. The growth of large consumer-orientated companies during this period saw the elevation of marketing as a key component of corporate strategies. The growth of consumer movements around, for example, concerns for automobile safety raised

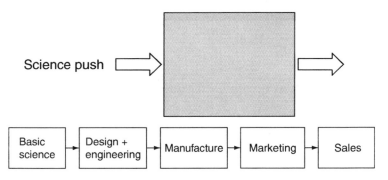

Fig. 2.1 The first generation innovation process: science / supply-driven model

awareness of the importance of customer choice. Also during this period, the growth of corporate planning departments reflected a confidence in the ability to control and direct corporations centrally.

Early research into the sources of innovation, such as the TRACES project at Illinois Institute of Technology, published in 1968, showed the relatively small contribution of universities and government research institutes to important innovation outcomes (although the sample of five significant innovations was small, and another project funded by the US National Science Foundation at this time—project Hindsight—found the contribution in the defence sector at least to be greater, although still subsidiary to 'demand pull').[19] Interpretation of this research at this time infused further thinking about the sources of innovation, and another simple linear model emerged, this time emphasizing *market pull*: the second generation innovation process (see Fig. 2.2). As a result, the policy and management challenges of innovation were again seen as relatively simple: predict market demands, plan, and allocate innovation investments accordingly. R&D was presumed to be responsive to customer demand and innovation opportunities derived from curiosity-driven research were considered of second-order importance.

The 1970s saw far greater sophistication in research efforts into innovation. Projects such as SAPPHO (Rothwell et al. 1974) began to identify not only the importance of key individuals, such as project champions and top management supporters, but also sectoral differences in patterns of innovation. The importance of links with the science base, for example, differed for innovators in chemicals and scientific instruments. Furthermore, research increasingly began to focus on the activities within the 'black box' of the firm and far greater attention was paid to information flow and feedback mechanisms between research and the market. Good communications between sources of scientific and technological information and market intelligence were emphasized and characterized in innovative organizations with jobs described as 'technological

Think, Play, Do

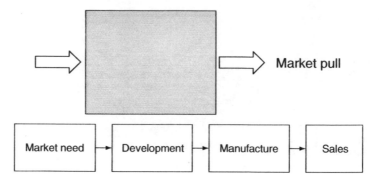

Fig. 2.2 The second generation innovation process: demand/market-driven model

gatekeeper' (Allen 1977). A study at this time of eighty-four important innovations by Langrish et al. (1972: 57), argued that

perhaps the highest level generalization that it is safe to make about technological innovation is that it must involve synthesis of some kind of need with some kind of technical possibility.

The emphasis on complex communications paths was a feature of the third generation innovation process, the *coupling model*, developed by Rothwell and Zegveld (1985) and Kline and Rosenberg (1986) (see Fig. 2.3). The new management and policy challenge of innovation lay in ensuring that companies and government research institutes were aware of the need for, and possessed, good internal and external communications around technological and market knowledge.

The primary change in thinking about innovation in the 1980s occurred as a result of the infusion of learning about innovation success in Japan. Major international research projects, such as the International Motor Vehicle Program, which resulted in the book, *The Machine that Changed the World* (Womack et al. 1990), showed the significant advantages Japanese car manufacturers gained from an innovation process that organized close integration between the research, engineering, production, and marketing functions, with parallel rather than sequential information processing, and the active involvement of customers and suppliers in new product development processes. Although organizational influences on innovation performance had been considered in the academic literature since Burns and Stalker (1961) and Woodward (1965), the 1980s saw a significant expansion in research into the organizational techniques used by successful Japanese firms. They encompassed methods for internal integration, such as quality circles, continuous improvement (*kaizen*), and workflow management (*kanban*), as well as the external integration of customers and suppliers through total quality management and just-

34

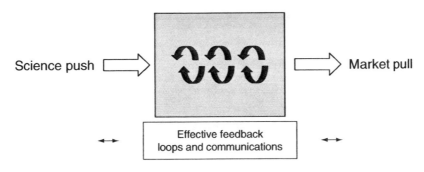

Fig. 2.3 The third generation innovation process: coupling model

in-time delivery systems (known, in combination, as 'lean production'). Japan's product development process at the time was described as a 'rugby team' approach, with different people applying their various skills simultaneously to a shared objective, and contrasted with a Western 'relay race' approach of sequential individual efforts (Takeuchi and Nonaka 1986). Significant investments were made in the skills and training of industrial workers, particularly through training on the job (Dore and Sako 1998).

At the same time, industry and innovation policies in the developed world began to provide significant financial support for collaborative research projects designed to encourage the joint development of new technology, particularly in ICT.[20] Also important during this period was enhanced understanding about the productivity gains to be achieved through advanced manufacturing technology, such as flexible manufacturing systems (Bessant 1991). Although there was considerable difference in performance with advanced manufacturing technologies, particularly in the extent to which their introduction needed to be accompanied with organizational changes and new skills and training regimes, closer integration between the technologies of design, coordination, and production began to enhance innovation performance (Kaplinsky 1984).

As a result of these changes, the management and policy challenge of innovation became much more complex. The fourth generation innovation process—the *integrated* model—involves much more complicated information flows within the firm and with multiple potential sources of innovation (research base, customers, suppliers, and collaborative partners). It requires attention to the difficult management tasks of reorganization around business processes rather than functions through building cross-functional teams and understanding and the use of internal technological integration through intranets and CAD/CAM systems (Dodgson 2000) (see Fig. 2.4). The need to coordinate and manage information and knowledge flows across many actors simultaneously provided the conditions for the development of IvT.

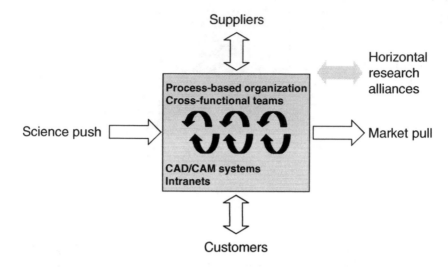

Fig. 2.4 The fourth generation innovation process: integrated model

	Strategic integration	**Technology integration**
Process- and project-based highly integrated organization	Globalization	Technology fusion and synergies; service solutions
Emphasis on knowledge, creativity and learning and supporting skills and team structures	Collaborative networks	
Computer-integrated operations		Innovation technologies
Innovation strategy		

Fig. 2.5 The fifth generation innovation process: systems integration and network model

The fifth generation innovation process, the *systems integration and networking* model is still emergent, and many of its features are still being developed (see Fig. 2.5). Within the firm we see greater appreciation of the role of knowledge, creativity, and learning as sources and outcomes of innovation (Leonard-Barton 1995; Seely Brown and Duguid 2000). Innovation strategies—the identification, development, and use of core resources and capabilities around innovation—are better formulated and implemented. As well as changes within the firm, signifi-

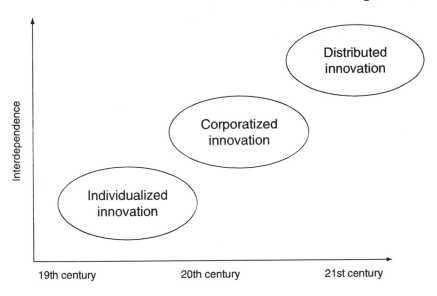

Fig. 2.6 Historical idealized character of innovation

cant changes are occurring in their operating and strategic environment. The level of strategic integration and networking is expanding through the globalization of markets, sources of technology, and partners (Archibugi and Michie 1998; Meyer-Krahmer and Reger 1999). Value is increasingly determined not so much by the ownership of particular assets but by the connectedness of those assets in networks and is realized in new forms of project organization and project-based firms (Gann and Salter 2000). The level of technological integration is increasing through the combinations and fusion of different knowledge sets (Kodama 1995) and value also lies in connectedness of products and services in 'service solutions' (Davies et al. 2003). Of particular relevance to our argument, there is increased use of IvT, or what Rothwell described as the new electronic toolkit, and the systems with which it is interdependent.[21]

Another historical perspective on innovation is suggested in Fig. 2.6. It presents a highly simplified and stylized historical progression in the fundamental character of innovation. It shows a progression from innovation derived from the activities of individuals in the nineteenth century through corporate activities in the twentieth century to what is called 'distributed' or 'open' innovation in the twenty-first century. The move from individualized innovation to corporatized innovation was characterized by the development of Edison's laboratories and the growth of large corporate R&D laboratories in Europe and the USA (Freeman and Soete 1997). The move from corporatized to distributed innovation is still occurring and is typified by the strategies of large companies such as P&G moving from investments in R&D to what it calls 'connect and develop' (described in Chapter 3) and the increasing multiplication of actors investing in R&D (see Chapter 4). In the individual innovator era, there was a high degree of self-reliance in innovation activities. Corporatized innovation required more external relationships with sources of scientific and technological knowledge and market information but there remained a relatively high degree of autarky. Distributed innovation, in contrast, implies significant interdependencies, and it is to these that we now turn.

2.3 Principle 2: Relationships and interdependencies

The second important principle for understanding innovation is that of comprehending its interdependencies: its surrounding mutual dependencies and reciprocal relationships. In the present era of distributed innovation we find two types of interdependence: *strategic* interdependence of firms in what Chesbrough (2003) calls 'open innovation' (see Box 2.2); and *technological*

Box 2.2   Open innovation

With a business strategy focus, Chesbrough (2003) presents the simple and persuasive argument that the process of innovation has shifted from one of closed systems, internal to the firm, to a new mode of open systems involving a range of players distributed up and down the supply chain. He argues that, especially in the new knowledge-based economy, not all the people with bright ideas that a firm might benefit from work for that firm. The next big idea may spring from a maverick start-up or a researcher working for a competitor. Information flows cheaply and instantaneously and talented people can gain access to it from dispersed locations. Chesbrough supposes that smart people may be at once more geographically dispersed and better connected than ever before. They are likely to be highly mobile, taking their talents to whichever firm provides the best incentives, and share the characteristics of what Florida (2003) calls the 'creative class', notably a concern with lifestyle, amenity, cultural diversity, and tolerance.

Some companies' responses to open innovation have been to protect their own R&D in the belief that competitors are intent on stealing their best ideas. These firms, Chesbrough suggests, are following the old paradigm of closed innovation, the old, twentieth-century corporate R&D system based on an assumption that most good ideas come from within the firm and that if you want something done properly, you have to do it yourself (the so-called not-invented-here syndrome). This strategy is based on a model of vertical integration and exclusive control.

Increasingly this isolationism is seen as stifling innovation. The new model of open innovation involves a nimble approach to accessing and exploiting knowledge outside the firm, whilst also liberating internal expertise for others to use. Firms can therefore benefit from the ideas they harvest from outside as well as those they share within their businesses. Information and knowledge-sharing extend to competitors as well as traditional collaborators. This notion suggests importing innovative ideas and exporting intellectual capital. Chesbrough also suggests that many innovative solutions are developed at the boundaries between disciplines, what we call the search for technology fusion and synergies, and the new model of innovation therefore needs to find ways of leveraging this when it may not be possible to own all the capabilities in-house.

---

interdependence between different types and vintages of technology. In circumstances where there is a high degree of interdependence technologies that assist effective communication, integration and management of activities across organizational boundaries are very valuable.

An additional element explaining the move to open innovation, mentioned by Chesbrough, is the way in which firms are realizing that their internally derived R&D project selections may produce worse results than selections resulting from substantial external inputs. As we shall see in the case of P&G, and in companies like GSK, there are distinct advantages in looking mostly outside for R&D projects. These firms are investing in R&D themselves, not only for the internal benefits they bring but also to improve their ability to access external technology, gaining what Cohen and Levinthal (1990) call 'absorptive capacity', which helps them search for and develop ideas from outside.

There are new ways of reaching beyond the conventional boundaries of the firm, tapping into customers, users, and competitors in the search for innovation. Chesbrough's focus is on the business interdependencies in this quest, but there are also related technological interdependencies. The high levels of interdependence in distributed innovation are based upon an excellent ICT infrastructure. Without this enabling ICT infrastructure, IvT could not have delivered the levels of integration of the innovation process they are capable of producing.

Some of the ways in which customers and users are brought into the innovation process through technology are described by von Hippel and Katz (2002: 821) as the 'user toolkit':

Toolkits for user innovation are coordinated sets of 'user-friendly' design tools that enable users to develop new product innovations for themselves. ... Within their fields of use, they give users real freedom to innovate, allowing them to develop producible custom products via iterative trial and error. That is, users can create a preliminary design, simulate or prototype it, evaluate its functioning in their own environment, and then iteratively improve it until satisfied.

These tools vary between specific fields of use, and advancements in IvT are creating opportunities for them to become more powerful, having a more direct influence on shaping innovation choices. From a demand-side perspective, there is a presumption that ideas come mainly from users, rather than from the other sources of thinking, such as the science base, described in Chapter 4.

The possibilities of these major technological interdependencies are illustrated in the quotations below, where some leading thinkers and practitioners describe the ways these technologies can bring customers into the innovation process:

With the power of today's computers to simulate massively complex and nonlinear systems coupled to phenomenal visualisation techniques, the customer can be brought ever closer to the design process. (Seely Brown 2003: x–xi)

[T]he speed and open architecture of this new technology allows us to integrate the diverse processes that make up a complex business in a way that was very difficult to do before. ... Today, we need to be able to go from a creative idea to an assessment of demand, to design, engineering, manufacturing and logistics, all the way through to the relationship with our customers. That's the vision we have for this new technology. (Nasser 2000)

Essentially ... companies have abandoned their efforts to understand exactly what products their customers want and have instead equipped them with tools to design and develop their own new products, ranging from minor modifications to major new innovations. The user-friendly tools, often integrated into a toolkit package, deploy technologies ... (e.g. computer simulation and rapid prototyping) to make innovation faster, less expensive, and ... better. (Thomke 2003)

User toolkits are part of the wider changes in the innovation process brought about by IvT. They help capture detailed information about customer requirements that can be very valuable, particularly in relatively stable circumstances, where incremental innovation strategies are appropriate. In some instances they can lead to users and customers innovating for suppliers, providing new combinations of ideas into the product or service. However, there are some limitations. For example, Christensen (1997) explains that efforts to track the needs of the current generation of customers are of little value when disruptive technologies emerge. Similarly, they may not gain value from improvements in process technology.

In periods of disruptive change the focus of attention for thinking about innovation might more valuably be the science base rather than customer needs. IvT assists the technological interdependencies between research and business through what is known as e-science. The development of e-science technologies is beginning to assist the connectivity of vast, diverse databases and to enable easy access, data interpretation, and knowledge extraction by researchers in universities and industry.[22] An example is provided by the Grid, which is an emergent infrastructure being developed to involve universities in every region of the UK, industrial firms and international collaborators, and supports efforts to create virtual communities of researchers. The UK government describes the Grid as a 'flexible, secure and coordinated resource-sharing infrastructure, based on dynamic collections of computational capacity, data storage facilities, instruments and wide area networks which are as easy to access as electricity in the home' (DTI 2002). Pilot projects on the Grid include testing, diagnostics, modelling, and visualization in aircraft engines, materials design, high performance computing, and protein folding. Rolls Royce, an early industrial user of the Grid, uses it to provide a 'plug-and-play' capability in design and development across the organization. According to Peter Cowley, Chief Scientist, Research and Technology at Rolls Royce, the Grid is an enabler for process improvement in R&D (see Chapter 4 for a more detailed view of e-science).

An indicator of the increasing extent of these interdependencies is provided by evidence from the Cooperative Agreements and Technology Indicators (CATI) database from the Maastricht Economic Research Institute on Innovation and Technology (MERIT). It indicates that the number of international technology alliances has increased significantly since the early 1980s. In 1980, 185 alliances were signed, but by 2001, there were 602 (NSB 2004). This figure refers to the number of equity and non-equity joint research or development agreements, R&D contracts, equity joint ventures, and research corporations. The number of alliances in biotechnology and IT has grown tremendously, reflecting the general growth of scientific and technological activities in these sectors. In biotechnology, the number of alliances rose from 31 in 1980 to 350 in 2001 and in IT, this figure rose from 45 in 1980 to 168 in 2001 (NSB 2004). Although there are considerable year-to-year variations in the data, and the data are collected from a limited range of sources, the overall pattern shows a considerable increase in international technology alliances since the early 1980s and that these new alliances are concentrated in areas of rapid scientific and technological development.

These discussions highlight the importance of Principle 2, the increasingly interdependent and relational character of innovation, both across technologies and organizations. They show the advantages that some organizations are beginning to realize from a more open and distributed innovation strategy.

2.4 Principle 3: Social mediation of innovation

The third principle for understanding innovation is the need to locate it within its social context. Much of the study of the relationships between society and innovation has focused on the relationship between technological change and the organization and nature of work. Such studies have a long history, going back to Adam Smith and Karl Marx. During the 1960s and 1970s, there was a healthy debate on the issue. Some authors at the time emphasized the influence of new technologies in determining work organization (Woodward 1965; Kerr et al. 1973) and workforce skills, with some arguing that new technologies increase skill levels (Touraine 1962; Blauner 1964) and others arguing that deskilling occurs as automation increases (Bright 1958; Braverman 1974). The polarities in the debate were represented by views ranging from those that saw technology emerging as a result of neutral, rational decision-making processes (the best technology won) to those that viewed technological choices as being made primarily to undermine the collective power of labour and to reduce its costs.

Increasing volumes of empirical work in the 1970s and 1980s, which identified the range of contingent factors and the extent of managerial choices around decisions on the development and use of technology, undermined the extremities of these views. New technologies, such as computer numerically controlled (CNC) machine tools, could be used to deskill or reskill, to central-ize or decentralize decision-making (Dodgson 1984). Greater attention was addressed to specific circumstances surrounding particular technologies, and there was a rejection of analyses based on technological determinism or notions of capitalist imperatives.

At the same time an increased appreciation emerged of the social and cultural, rather than political, influences on innovations.[23] Noble's exhaustive historical study of the development of CNC machine tools, for example, began to ask why technological development progressed down one path rather than another. He (1986: 145) decried the notion of the 'objective expert' developing technology and pointed to the way scientists and engineers

come to their work as prejudiced as the next person, constrained by the technical 'climate', cultural habits, career considerations, intellectual enthusiasms, institutional incentives, and the weight of prior and parallel developments—not to mention the performance specifications of the project managers and supporters.

Similarly, he questioned the economic rationalism of businesspeople making decisions about technology, describing them as 'prejudiced, mystified and enthusiastic as ... brethren in the laboratory'.

In his analysis of the development of Linux open systems software—a quintessential socially constructed technology—Tuomi (2002: 9) develops the argument that all innovation is social innovation and innovation is fundamen-tally about social change:

New technologies do not come into the world ready-made. Instead, they are actively interpreted and appropriated by existing actors, in the context of existing practices. A single technological artefact can have multiple uses, and new uses may be invented for old artefacts. Often a product is used in unanticipated ways, and perhaps no one uses it the way its designers expected it to be used.

Tuomi (2002: 20) also describes the role that technological tools play in assisting innovative social practices (see Box 2.3):

Technological artefacts often play an important role in the formation of social practice and transform parts of it from the mental sphere to the concrete material world. Practices, therefore, exist as complex networks of tools, concepts, and expectations.

The success of Linux, he argues, lies in the way the common technological interface of an open system has enabled several 'practice-related communities' to collaborate effectively.

Schrage makes important and insightful contributions to understanding the importance of social and organizational factors associated with prototyping. His models themselves are the central actors in the system, everyone can play with them and the benefits of prototyping tools will diffuse across all sectors

---

Box 2.3 New thinking about prototyping

The idea of technological tools providing a mechanism around which social interactions coalesce in creating innovations can also apply to Schrage's work on prototyping.[24] Schrage (2000) puts prototypes—the ways in which ideas are 'externally represented'—at centre stage in the process of innovation. Often research on innovation has ignored the role of external representations in shaping the way problems are solved and new ideas come about, but Schrage argues that these simulations are central players on the stage of innovation. He describes how product developers engage in 'serious play', improvising with the unanticipated in ways that make it possible to create new value from products. He argues that any tools, technologies, or toys that let people improve how they play seriously with uncertainty is guaranteed to improve the quality of innovation. As Edison put it, to invent, you need a good imagination and a pile of junk.[25]

Schrage's argument is that our focus should not be on how prototypes can solve problems, but on how they can be used to solve problems. He contends, for example, that prototypes should be used in a process of discovering what we need to know and that they should challenge, not confirm, expectations.

His argument comes from the tradition of thinking within the design studies community, which argues that design problems and solutions co-evolve: a problem cannot be stated outside its solution. In a challenge to some recent work within the management tradition on customer needs discussed earlier, he states that it is impossible for clients, even those working with software engineers, to specify completely precisely and correctly.

Rather, models create opportunities for interaction with customers. They allow customers to play—to see new things and try different ways of working. They engage customers and help them see what they really need.

Schrage argues that essentially the purpose of a prototype is to create and unearth choices, and that the best prototypes are those that produce the most useful and important choices.

---

of economic activity. While it is clear that the diffusion of prototyping tools has been considerable across different sectors, their impact depends on the way they are integrated with existing ways of working. In Chapter 5 we show that much of the engineering design process still relies on the 'informed guesses' of experienced engineers, drawing on scientific principles and recursive practice. New tools can help these engineers make better guesses but it is not clear that they will overcome the fundamental uncertainty that pervades the innovation process. Serious play can be fun and helpful but thoughtful and successful engineering is often more a 'hard slog' than a 'leap frog' (Hobday 1998); it involves the combination of craft and code. IvT enhances the ability of designers to play with highly complex and technical calculations, and bring more craft from the designer back into the end product.

Chapter 5 will consider the continuing role of craft skills in what we describe as playing. We will argue that the best way to use IvT creatively is to understand the fundamental scientific and engineering principles of the problems to which it is applied.

Just as thinking and playing around innovation are socially mediated, so too is doing. A classic example of the social choices around technology was seen in the emergence of CNC machine tools in the early 1980s. Essentially, firms had the choice to either attempt to remove the computer programming tasks from the machine tool and place them in centralized programming departments or to decentralize computerized tasks to the machine tool itself. Firms in the same sector, producing similar products with the same technology, made different choices. These choices tended to reflect managerial approaches and industrial relations issues. Eventually, the need for efficiency led more and more firms to incorporate computerized tasks into the role of the machine tool craftsman (Dodgson 1985).

2.5 Conclusions

Analyses of innovation are manifold, which reflects the complexity of the subject matter. Innovation can only be properly understood in its historical context, in the ways it is used in relation to other kinds and vintages of technology, and in respect to the social and organizational practices that surround its development and use. IvT is a relatively new form of technology. There are still numerous questions about the ways in which it will be used to address thinking, playing, and doing and its consequences for work organization. History teaches us that the major impacts of technology on business competitiveness and productivity follow some years, if not decades, after their introduction. We should not, therefore, be looking at the effects of these technologies on the productivity figures just yet.

In contrast with the past, when innovation typically resulted from the efforts of individuals or large corporations, we now live in an era of distributed and open innovation systems where multiple players contribute: individuals, large and small firms, universities, research and technology organizations, and consultancies. This era of 'distributed innovation', when 'experimentation' and 'serious play' are increasing in importance, is underpinned by the generic technologies of IvT, ICT, and OMT. IvT builds upon existing, widely diffused technologies, adding value to massive infrastructural and capital investments.

IvT moves many of the problems of innovation from the real into the virtual world so as to deal more effectively with the uncertainties of the real world and to mitigate the cost of failure. As Schrage memorably put it in an interview, 'it is better to fail in bits than in atoms'. Importantly, as IvT operates in this virtual world, it does not disengage with the real issues and problems of innovation. IvT is used for commercial advantage, gained by, for example, producing better and safer cars that meet new customer expectations. Rather than replacing human craft, ingenuity, and skills with some kind of cybertronics, IvT actually complements these (in all senses) valuable human characteristics.

3 Using Innovation Technology: Procter & Gamble and Arup

3.1 Introduction

This chapter presents in-depth case studies of two companies that have bene-fited from the use of IvT as part of their strategies. The cases describe the evolving innovation strategies of the consumer products company, Procter & Gamble (P&G), and the professional services company, Arup.[26] The chapter is designed to show the importance of IvT in a number of areas and how it

- assists and facilitates the development and implementation of innovation strategy;
- enables effective integration between different players in innovation— customers, suppliers, external sources of knowledge, regulators—and dif-ferent communities of practice inside and outside the firm;
- allows faster and cheaper development of better products and services;
- relies on the use and extension of designers' and engineers' skills and supports a variety of approaches to solving problems.

P&G is a company that has recently embraced a distributed innovation ap-proach. The features of this strategy include some of the changes made by the company to improve communications and understanding across organizational boundaries. The case study examines the ways in which P&G has developed a strategy of substantially increasing the amount of externally sourced inputs into its innovation activities, notably through its position in Internet-based technology markets. P&G's use of IvT is considered in several critical areas, including new product development.

Arup is a company that has grown through diversifying from its structural engineering and design base. It has grown organically, through internally generated new business developments, rather than through mergers and acquisitions. The case study describes new Arup businesses created to use its expertise and knowledge in simulation and modelling tools. The company uses IvT extensively and the case study describes some of the consequences in the ways engineers and designers work and solve problems.

Both case studies are broad-ranging in their scope. They examine IvT and the intensification of innovation within the context of the companies' strategic and organizational characteristics. The cases are primarily descriptive. Their analysis provides input to the following chapters.

3.2 Procter & Gamble

Background

P&G is one of the world's largest and most successful consumer businesses. It operates in almost every country in the world, with net sales over $40 billion and nearly 100,000 employees. Products include world-leading brands such as Pampers, Pringles, Ariel, and Tide. In 2002 three of the top ten new non-food products introduced into the USA came from P&G.[27]

P&G is a substantial R&D organization, with over 6,500 scientists. It owns over 29,000 existing patents, adding another 5,000 on average each year, making it one of the largest holders of US and global patents. Comparable companies in ownership of patents include Microsoft and Intel. Each day, on average, P&G spends around $5 million on R&D and registers eight patents.

P&G possesses strong brands and is always looking for brand growth (Swasy 1994; Dyer et al. 2004). It operates in an extremely competitive, mature, global market, ensuring that the company is always searching for new, innovative ideas. Throughout the late 1990s, P&G experienced lower-than-expected sales growth and attributed this to shortcomings in its ability to produce new products to satisfy consumers' changing needs. No new major product of the scale of Tide or Pampers had been developed for over two decades.[28] P&G recognized that to meet sales growth targets its innovation rate would need to increase significantly. P&G's management also realized that the costs of investments in R&D, technology, and innovation were increasing faster than sales growth, and that this was unsustainable.

However, innovation remains the key to P&G's strategy. Chair of the Board and President and Chief Executive A.G. Lafley has said: 'Innovation is our lifeblood—new ideas and new products that make consumers' lives better, build customers' sales and profits, and build P&G's market share, sales, profits, and Total Shareholder Return.'[29]

Problems within the company included the fact that P&G did not always benefit from its existing knowledge and did not listen to, and learn enough from, the outside world. Gordon Brunner, then Chief Technology Officer and Head of Worldwide Research and Development, was quoted as saying in 2000: 'If we only put to full use what's known, we'd be three times more innovative.'

Using Innovation Technology: Procter & Gamble and Arup

Organization 2005—connect and develop

In June 1999, P&G launched a new strategy to increase growth through innovation called *Organization 2005*. One of the main aims of *Organization 2005* was to stimulate innovation by making P&G's internally focused and fragmented communications more outward and cohesive (Schilling 2005). Brunner and his colleagues wanted to create a culture that connected people and technologies in a more effective way. To emphasize the point, Brunner said that R&D could become C&D—'connect and develop'.

The concept of C&D was fundamental to the *Organization 2005* strategy. P&G was founded on making successful innovative connections. Its business evolved from connections such as that between candles and soap, and the move from the animal fat in soap to the first all-vegetable shortening. This led to discoveries in the emulsifiers and surfactants used today in products such as shampoos and dishwashing liquids. P&G's history was rich with new products innovated by connecting what was not obvious. As P&G's Dr Mike Addison put it at a C&D Symposium in February 2003: 'Innovation is all about making new connections. Most breakthrough innovation is about combining known knowledge in new ways or bringing an idea from one domain to another.' This is characteristic of the 'technology synergies and fusion' elements of Rothwell's fifth generation innovation process (see Chapter 2).

The recognition that the vast majority of solutions to P&G's problems lay outside the company was a critical first step in the development of C&D. Larry Huston, Vice-President of Knowledge and Innovation for P&G's worldwide R&D organization, describes how prior to C&D he discovered that P&G operated in around 150 areas of science. At that time, P&G employed more than 7,500 R&D staff, yet it was estimated that there were approximately 1.5 million researchers around the world working in these areas of science and technology at levels equal to, or better than, P&G's internal expertise. The challenge was both to access this external resource and to change the culture within P&G to encourage and facilitate the necessary searching and learning outside the company.

P&G's strategy for growth through innovation and innovation through building connections is not in itself so new: what is new are the organizational innovations and technological media that assist its implementation.

Organizational changes and connect and develop

Traditionally P&G was protective about its patents and wary of licensing them to outsiders. In 1999, before the C&D programme was introduced, less than 10 per cent of P&G's own technologies were being used in products (Sakkab 2002). The objective of the new strategy for open innovation is to turn more technologies into products. One of the main ways P&G now seeks to do this as part of C&D is to drive innovation through collaboration with external partners in at least 50 per cent of cases. Several organizational initiatives have been introduced to assist the process (Sakkab 2002).

As part of these organizational initiatives, P&G has created a Technology Acquisition Group (TAG). This group is part of the new attitude to licensing at P&G, and its members actively seek out new complementary technologies from external sources. In addition to greater use of its technologies in products, P&G is active in licensing its own technologies to increase its returns on investment.

P&G brought many sources of information for innovation together at *Innovation 2000*, a 'deal-making/technology trading expo', where P&G showcased its most promising technologies. Over 5,000 P&G researchers attended. Those who could not attend were able to take part via Web casting and satellite technology, which acted in the same way as a news TV station with broadcasts, news flashes, and commercials. In addition, P&G distributed cell phones to its employees so they could record new ideas and make new connections for innovation. External suppliers were also invited to showcase their technologies in the hope of making new connections. The event was heralded a success, with over 2,200 ideas for new products and new applications for P&G technologies emerging from it.

P&G also pursued other initiatives, including buying entrepreneurial companies and creating internal seed funds for new product development. Crest SpinBrush is an example of the former. This product was developed by four entrepreneurs. It was initially licensed by P&G, which went on to buy the company and subsequently employed three of its founders. The product has been an outstanding success and returned the company's investment ten times over in only two years.

P&G provides seed funding of $20,000–50,000 for innovative new ideas. Pur Sachet is an example of a product developed through internal seed funding. This product emerged in the company's Newcastle, UK laboratory from a project team hoping to recycle rinse water with detergents in it. The researcher concerned was funded to help with the larger problem of transforming dirty water into drinkable water, and the product, Pur Sachet, which could prove to be a truly significant global innovation, is the result.

Both these cases reveal the success of changes in the organization and culture of P&G. It is prepared to bring in ideas from outside sources, including using the entrepreneurial advantages of small firms, and it allowed a young and relatively inexperienced individual researcher a free hand in the development of the product, in contrast to its past emphasis on high-level supervision for new product development.

Throughout the development of the present case, numerous members of P&G staff referred to the significant cultural changes accompanying the move towards an open innovation strategy. Neil McGlip, Head of Corporate R&D,

Packaging, says: 'C&D is more a way of life than a technological strategy. It is about your mindset. It is ensuring you are open day and night to new possibilities.' According to Larry Huston, such changes in organization require a prior deep cultural change, which in P&G's case took place over decades. The change was assisted by the company first pursuing an intermediate strategy, one in between that of its historical centralized self-reliance in R&D and its current global networking model. During the 1980s, P&G adopted an internal networked model of R&D, with decentralized research activities around its key global markets—a strategy described by observers as 'mutual interdependence' (Bartlett and Ghoshal 1989: 129; 2000). Had this strategy of internal decentralization not already been pursued, Huston considers that the present transition would have been difficult to achieve.

Varieties of Internet-enabled mechanisms have been developed by P&G and are being used to assist in implementing its new strategy. These have, and are playing, an important role in its evolution towards open innovation.

Networked innovation markets

New kinds of 'innovation markets' have developed, as distributed innovation systems become more common, based on the Internet. We describe three examples used by P&G here.

InnoCentive[30]

InnoCentive is an e-business initiative of the pharmaceutical company, Eli Lilly. It describes itself as a Web-based community matching scientists to R&D challenges. Companies register with InnoCentive as 'seekers', posting R&D problems or 'challenges' on its website. Each challenge provides a detailed description of the problem, requirements, deadline, and the amount of a reward, commonly ranging from $10,000 to $100,000. The name of the seeker company is known only to InnoCentive. Scientists around the world can register as 'solvers'. Anyone can view the summaries of posted challenges, but access to detailed specifications requires the solver to be registered. InnoCentive has a science team that can answer questions for solvers and that submits solutions to the seekers. Seekers decide on whether objectives have been met and who is rewarded. InnoCentive receives a posting fee and an amount equal to that of the reward should the challenge be successfully solved.

In early 2004, there were 40,000 people in the InnoCentive network, including scientists from 100 countries.[31] P&G uses the service and has found solutions to its challenges posted on InnoCentive from a patent lawyer in North Carolina, a graduate student in Spain, a US chemistry consultant, a research chemist in Bangalore, India, and a small start-up in Canada. P&G has only one person managing its interface with InnoCentive. As Larry Huston put it: with one person P&G can leverage 40,000.

Yet2.com[32]

To further its C&D strategy for patents and licensing, P&G has partnered with Yet2.com, another Internet-based marketplace for technology. Yet2.com was founded in 1999 by senior managers from Polaroid and Du Pont. Its founding sponsors included P&G, Bayer, Siemens, Dow Chemicals, Caterpillar, and Honeywell. Around 500 companies, including 3M, Microsoft, and Philips, use Yet2.com.

Yet2.com helps 'seller' companies realize the value from their intellectual property and technology, and 'buyer' companies find intellectual property and technology to enhance their resources or to fill gaps. It brokers existing technology and intellectual property. Typically, deals are made between large and small companies, whereby large companies sell technology they think has too small a potential market to interest them or buy technologies from smaller firms that do not have the resources to commercialize them. Yet2.com posts functional abstracts about the technology, which are written as plainly as possible and often speculate on applications of the technology that may not currently be on the market. Yet2.com postings include reference to groups of associated patents. Yet2.com charges a $5,000 commission for its introductions. It is already a significant marketplace, with over 800,000 users.

P&G is an extensive user of Yet2.com. In one instance, Yet2.com marketed a technology from its beauty care division to one of its (unnamed) competitors, and the royalties from this were estimated to have paid for P&G's entire investment in Yet2.com.

NineSigma[33]

NineSigma was founded in 2000, with P&G's assistance. It describes its role as one connecting scientists to companies in order to provide them with an external R&D resource for innovative ideas, technologies, and services quickly and at a cost-effective price. It seeks to match innovation managers with solutions providers to create new technology. It considers itself a leader in finding 'non-obvious solutions', including from outside the industry of the solution-seeker company. In early 2004 it had around forty clients, two-thirds of whom are Fortune 500 firms. It operates what it calls a managed exchange (M:X) service, whereby project leaders meet face to face with clients and assist them in posting request for proposals (RFPs). NineSigma project leaders write detailed descriptions of the problems clients want solved and then manage the collection of proposed solutions from scientists linked on the Internet. It takes on average around two weeks to finalize the description of problems and then three to four weeks to deliver the proposals from the marketplace of scientists. The RFPs are emailed to thousands of scientists around the world.

NineSigma uses a pay-for-performance pricing model. It charges a 'discovery fee' to run each project and a transaction fee as a percentage of the contract established.

P&G tends to use NineSigma for problems that are broader than those for which it uses InnoCentive. By 2004, P&G had used NineSigma for over sixty projects and had a 50 per cent success rate, which it felt was a good return. It is estimated that around 500,000 experts had been contacted regarding these sixty projects.

It is not only large companies that benefit from such intermediaries. In the case of ChromaDex, a start-up phytochemical company with twelve employees, Yet2.com was used to license in a key toxicity screening technology from Bayer AG, one of the world's largest chemical companies. According to the President and CEO of ChromaDex, this technology was essential to the company, it was too expensive to develop, and accessing it through Yet2.com was 'easy'.[34]

Amongst the key management concerns of innovation brokers such as InnoCentive, Yet2.com, and NineSigma are the high level of specific focus and detail required to elicit valuable responses and the trust required in the intermediary. The intermediary role of honest broker involves seekers trusting it not to reveal their identity, and solvers trusting it to submit and attribute their proposal. The benefits for the users are clear: solutions can be sought from a vastly increased range of suppliers and the interfaces and intellectual property issues are managed elsewhere.

Extended labour market

Knowledge workers are not only highly mobile, they are also usually highly paid (see the discussion on knowledge workers in Chapter 7). They can therefore afford to retire early, with some key P&G staff retiring at age fifty-five. P&G has developed a special mechanism, *YourEncore*,[35] for continuing a productive association with early retirees. This mechanism itself also involves partnerships.

YourEncore was founded by P&G and Eli Lilly in 2003. Its aim is to use the capabilities of retirees to build business opportunities for member companies. In 2004 the founding companies were the main users of the service but other companies were able to use it for a higher engagement fee.

For the large numbers of professionals in the USA taking early retirement but still wishing to remain active in business and to maintain their peer networks, YourEncore is a mechanism that allows them to remain connected. By 2004 there were some 160 retirees on the network. They become employees of YourEncore. Each founding member company has a YourEncore relationship manager who works with the client, and the retiree and is responsible for matching the retiree with the client and carrying out all necessary administration. Retirees get paid at the *per diem* rate of their departing salaries. YourEncore has a fee on this rate that pays for infrastructure, staffing, and the management of intellectual property agreements.

Huston, who was instrumental in creating YourEncore, says that one of the unexpected benefits of the service lies in the ways P&G's suppliers have been hiring retirees to create value propositions back into P&G. Their participation helps build the interdependencies between P&G and its suppliers. Huston created the concept of YourEncore, established the business model and cash flows, worked with over twenty-five companies to test the concept, interviewed retirees, worked out compensation plans, and used P&G's lawyers to establish intellectual property arrangements. P&G then gave the business model over to a company in Indianapolis at zero cost, because in Huston's words 'we wanted to be an open innovation network model'.

According to YourEncore's website, member companies utilize retirees for specific scientific and engineering assignments, creative expertise from other companies or organizations, new technology, product and design opportunities, and new creative ideas.

ICT, IvT, and C&D

The C&D project is enabled by the technological advances in the last decade or so, particularly in ICT and IvT. P&G's C&D strategy is founded on the use of technology to connect internal and external resources such as a corporate Intranet and 'smart' reporting systems for knowledge-sharing.

Nabil Sakkab, P&G Senior Vice-President, R&D, explains how the technologies available today provide a modern version of the laboratory lunch table where connections for innovation were made when he first started out in his career. To modernize the 'lunch table', P&G created a Global Technology Council made up of business unit technology directors, corporate R&D heads, and other key R&D decision-makers. Sakkab says the Council explores ways to leverage P&G's technologies and acts as an 'incubator' for research exploration and early-stage new product development (Sakkab 2002).

Members of the global community at P&G can talk to each other through an internal website called InnovationNet. Sakkab claims that InnovationNet acts as P&G's 'global lunchroom'; researchers use this to make connections and share data and information from internal and external sources. There are already over 9 million documents online, and the number continues to grow. InnovationNet also has automated and artificial intelligence support that acts in a way similar to Amazon.com by taking account of users' interests when sending back information on material the user may be interested in and connecting people with the same interests. Sakkab believes that InnovationNet's true contribution to P&G is its ability to accelerate innovation by allowing thousands of innovators across the globe to make new connections, collaborate with co-workers, and cross-fertilize their knowledge in a variety of specialized fields. InnovationNet also provides extranet communications with external business partners and serves as a link to external databases (Sakkab 2002).

The company also uses its intranet for the posting of Smart Learning Reports, with key words for easy search, an AskMe search engine, and another website called DiscoveryNet.

One of the purposes of these Internet-based systems is to facilitate communications within and between 'communities of practice' (Seely Brown and Duguid 2000). P&G contains numerous communities of practice, in physical science, engineering, and production, notably colloids and polymers, organic and analytical chemistry, flexible automation and robotics, fast cycle development, as well as technology entrepreneurship. Part of the personal development plans of researchers is involvement in one or more of these communities of practice.

An important external source of capability developed by P&G is the Technology Entrepreneurs network. This is an extended network of fifty-plus individuals that helps link P&G to external innovation possibilities. The technology entrepreneurs are top scientists and specialists in the technology needs of one of P&G's Global Business Units.[36] They are expert data mining specialists who use the most advanced data mining and visualization tools to search billions of Web pages, scientific literature databases, and global patent databases. Sakkab (2002) says this allows P&G to find the 'needle in the haystack' and link it to business needs. Huston says the 'technology entrepreneurs are really key to the connect and develop strategy'. IvTs are used by P&G in its search for a 'smarter, faster, cheaper' innovation process.

Simulation and optimization techniques are used in the design of logistics networks. Since 1995, P&G has operated under a concept known as the 'Ultimate Supply System', which attempts to tightly couple suppliers through the integration of information, material and products, and financial activities. With 250-plus brands and 120 manufacturing facilities, supply chain management is obviously of considerable importance. The objective of this system is 'to significantly increase sales, reduce costs, increase cash flow and, ultimately, to provide the right product at the right time at the right price to our customers' (Wegryn and Siprelle, undated).

P&G has an internal operations research group called Global Analytics, which uses optimization and simulation techniques for the design of supply networks. These technologies enable the selection of the most effective solution from amongst thousands of options simultaneously to determine a supply chain structure. The advantages of using IvT in this process are described by Glenn Wegryn, Associate Director of IT Business Solutions—Global Analytics at P&G and Andrew Siprelle, President of Simulation Dynamics Inc.:

Simulation modeling allows time-based, execution level events to be represented, analyzed, and understood. Simulation provides a rich environment for experimenting with different approaches to operating strategies that may be effective. Until recently, simulation has extensively been used to examine manufacturing operations for removing throughput bottlenecks, improving operating efficiencies, testing sequences of operations, material handling, etc. More instances of utilizing simulation technology on broader supply chain issues are being reported.

Within the context of supply chains, simulation allows close analysis of inventory positions, their deployment and how they are affected in downstream demand signals, and the reorder policies in place to respond to those signals. Synchronizing planning cycles and production schedules with up- and down-stream supply chain partners, as well as understanding capacity utilization issues in response to closer coupling of supply chains are issues that can be addressed with simulation modeling. (Wegryn and Siprelle, undated)

Product and process design

One of the major ways P&G uses IvT is in its prototyping activities. It aims to develop prototypes as quickly as possible using rapid prototyping systems and rapid tooling in production (see Chapter 6 for a discussion of rapid prototyping).

Here we report the perspective of one of the technology suppliers of IvT to P&G. The way P&G uses simulation and computer-aided engineering in encouraging innovation is highlighted in a case study conducted by one of its suppliers: Silicon Graphics Inc. (SGI).[37] The case study describes how SGI's Origin 3800 supercomputer is used by P&G to create and test prototypes of products and the machines that manufacture them in a virtual state, thereby eliminating the usual requirement for early physical prototypes. It also allows them to simulate the effects of production line changes without building actual equipment.

The case study describes two 'moments of truth' for P&G customers. The first is when the customer decides to buy the product on the basis of its price and perceived value. The second is when the customer opens the product and assesses its performance. IvT is used to help P&G in both. First, it helps evaluate suitable materials, their effectiveness, and the capacity to manufacture them economically. It 'helps to ensure that product containers don't break or crack when dropped, viscous fluids flow easily from their containers, and lids of every type don't leak'. Second, it helps play a role in determining how P&G products function during actual consumer use: how do they perform in the hands of customers? Simulations are used to evaluate how products perform for people with a range of human physical characteristics.

Tom Lange, Associate Director for Modelling Simulation and Analysis, is quoted extensively in the case study. He describes the company's philosophy around these technologies as 'explore digitally: confirm physically'. He says the benefits of this form of IvT are reductions in costs and increases in innovative opportunities. Using IvT has enabled the company to pursue a wider range of creative solutions to meet consumer needs, without having to invest in costly infrastructures. Referring to documented cases where IvT use has saved P&G millions of dollars and months to years in development time, for both products and the machines that make them, Lange is quoted as saying

[V]irtual prototypes provide a timely and cost-effective means by which P&G can determine the 'fit, work and financial sense' components used to evaluate a product before committing to building a physical representation. Virtual prototyping gives us a chance to ask what if, and then test it in any number of ways to determine next steps, if any, moving forward.

P&G also uses simulation-based product evaluation tools, such as virtual-reality shopping malls, to test consumer reaction to its products as opposed to those of its competitors. These tools provide information from factors such as eye movement analysis not easily determined from traditional focus group and telephone product evaluation. Lange also refers to the way in which P&G will continue to make physical prototypes in the latter stages of product development as these 'still carry many intrinsic tactical consumer findings that simply cannot be replaced virtually'.

According to Huston,

the ability to … virtually create the brand story, to virtually create products, to take virtual models and test them interactively with consumers over the Internet … to simulate the storage shelf with that virtual product on it and see whether people buy it … this is the future, the *future*.

IvT and new product development: CreateInnovate

CreateInnovate is a small group within P&G that is an extensive user of IvT. The group produces new packaging to help P&G create brand identity. Packaging is hugely important in consumer product markets as it helps sell products. P&G uses IvT to increase innovation in the packaging and marketing of its products through the use of a visualization suite in order to test representations of package designs with consumers.

CreateInnovate has eighteen staff in Egham, Surrey, and Brussels, and it works with another eighteen non-employees in design and prototyping companies, providing considerable flexibility in capacity. Its objectives are to create new ideas for packaging, and then to develop designs and rapidly prototype them. Its aims are 'to make consumers want to buy P&G products: to make them go wow!'

The group spends a lot of effort brainstorming internally and externally with design houses such as IDEO (one of the world's leading product design houses: see Sutton and Hargadon 1996). The aim of these brainstorming exercises is to bring together in a structured way a number of multi-skilled people with relevant experience to create ideas. Ideas for new packaging concepts are described in text and in sketches, often with the help of sketch artists. This is called the 'ideation' phase. From these rough sketches, 3D CAD models are quickly produced, usually in one or two days. CAD models will be used throughout the entire development and manufacturing process, from initial concept to CNC manufacturing. As the Head of the Corporate R&D, Packaging, and the leader of this group, Neil McGlip says: 'This digital model will live with the product idea until it goes to manufacturing. We only create one model and then play with it.'

The model is then produced and virtual product testing is conducted. Teams of people from around the world look at the virtual model and comment on what they like and what they do not. The image is very close to the real thing. It moves the same way. McGlip observes:

Once it has been created digitally you can show it to people and see what they think. You can change it and tweak it to see if people's attitudes towards it improve. We also make little videos of the products and how they work and then send these to panels of users. There is no need even to create a physical product at this time. For the users, seeing is believing. They sift through various ideas and you can get a quick idea of what works and what does not. Using the new technology helps us get a richer representation of the new idea and almost immediate feedback from users. The whole process takes days, not months. The new tools allow people to play easier. In some ways, the virtual prototypes are like games where users can play with the design, exploring different design options. It provides vivid, accurate representation of the project. It allows you to take 100 ideas and kill the 98 of them that are no good.

Rapid prototyping technologies are used extensively. CreateInnovate uses rapid prototyping machines that were originally developed for Formula One motorsport, where it is essential to be able to create high-precision parts quickly (see Chapter 6). The group works with local rapid prototyping tool developers and tries to share experiences with them about how best to develop prototypes. Rapid prototyping enables designers to quickly get a feel for new components, how they look and feel, and how they fit together.

An example of how the process works in practice is the development of the Tide StainBrush, which is now on the market in the USA. The product idea resulted from the application of C&D principles. The group took the Crest

SpinBrush (a low-cost electronic toothbrush) and tried to see what else could be done with it. One idea that emerged was to use the brush to remove stains. The Tide StainBrush is a battery-powered brush with an oscillating head that helps Tide Liquid penetrate into stains. The fabric-safe bristles rotate back and forth, working the liquid into the fabric and loosening stains.

In total, it took one year from initial concept to full market launch. The process began in October 2002. A CAD design of the Crest SpinBrush was available, but the design needed to be radically altered to make it work as a stain remover. A new grip needed to be created so that the brush could be pressed down upon the stains. It was also necessary to redesign some of the internal mechanical features of the Crest SpinBrush for it to gain more power. The group tried to use or recycle as much of the Crest brush as possible. By December 2002, the first working prototype was developed in-house. It was held together by duct tape but it nonetheless showed that the concept was viable. However, the motor had a tendency to stall when material was rubbed, and the group set out to fix this problem. The CAD files for the new brush were sent to China where 100 physical prototypes of the new product were manufactured. These prototypes were sent around for testing in April 2003. The product worked well in the trials and the decision was made to go for full market launch in August 2003. It was ten months from the initial idea to the product being within P&G internal shops for testing among employees. Once in the P&G internal shop in the USA, the product sold out in a day. This indicated that it might be a popular product in the market. Mass production began in the autumn of 2003 and the product was launched on the US market in December 2003.

Another example of this process is the development of the Swiffer: essentially a dust cloth attached to a pole. Users of the product wanted a liquid system fed into the cloth which made it necessary to develop a pump system. The basic idea in this project was to take the existing product that had no pump and reinvent it. Overall, it took twelve months of design and development to get the product on the market. It involved specialized engineering to make the product work. A new joint for attaching the pole to the mop end had to be developed and a trigger mechanism for releasing the liquid was required. It was also necessary to simulate how fluids flow through the pole and how the cavity inside the mop would fill and react.

The technology used in the group for products like the spin brush and the Swiffer is widely available. It uses entirely off-the-shelf simulation software; there is no in-house software at all. It relies on new modelling packages and standard CAD tools. The company reports no problems in moving the CAD model across different systems.

The use of simulation tools has changed the staffing profile of the group. Previously it almost exclusively hired people with a relatively narrow background in chemistry, biochemistry, or chemical engineering. As it became involved more and more in design, it started to hire staff with a broader range of disciplinary backgrounds, for example, industrial designers and mechanical engineers.

McGlip argues that it is still necessary to perform lots of physical testing on the products: 'You need to drop the package on the floor and see what happens. Does it go splat? Does it really work?' The simulation tools are predictive, but you still need to try it out physically.' His overall evaluation, however, is that the major effect of using the tools has been to compress time scales for creating and prototyping new products.

There are limits to the contribution that IvT can make: it does not provide all the answers to P&G's innovation problems. This is seen in the case of Okido. The Okido project received seed funding from P&G and was developed from a technology that produced heat when exposed to air. The technology used for Okido was traditionally used in products such as pain relief heat treatments for muscular aches and strains. As there were already products like this in the market, P&G provided seed funding to explore potential ways to apply the technology for use in different products and/or markets.

The lead researcher, a chemistry analyst, was provided seed funding to come up with a new product within a year. A cross-functional team consisting of marketing, advertising, and R&D staff was formed. They came up with the concept of a portable, safe, scented candle. The team used CAD and rapid prototyping to come up with product variations. However, a trial of the product to P&G staff via the Internet was unsuccessful. Unsurprisingly, the scented product was not ideal to sell over the Internet.

After significant development costs, the product was scrapped. The company took the strategic view that the market for such candles was too saturated for a new product to make much impact. The costs in dollars and in person-hours could have been avoided by a strategic overview of the potential of the candles market being interjected at the beginning of the project. There should have been a clear market analysis before new product development went ahead. That it did go ahead can, perhaps, be attributed to the view that 'we have the technology so we should do something with it'.

In this case, the use of IvTs may have speeded up the design and development process (its *efficiency*), but it did not assist with the strategic decision of whether it was the right product to manufacture (its *effectiveness*).

Reflections

It is too soon to tell whether these dramatic changes in P&G's approach to innovation will produce the results envisaged in new blockbuster products. Or, indeed, whether the blockbuster product is a thing of the past: the future may lie in more specialized consumer products. What is clear is that the company has become much more successful at accessing external sources of technology and using IvT, which will help it in its innovation and product development strategy. Huston says that the company's goal of leveraging external assets for 50 per cent of its innovations is very ambitious. He argues that the changes are still underway and that in 2004 perhaps 35 per cent of innovations were accessed externally. These changes were occurring rapidly; he estimates that the number of products in the marketplace that were linked to external sources increased from four to fifty in one year and that the pipeline of products with such sourcing looks impressive.

The use of IvT is well engrained in P&G and is being used from supply chain simulations to the design of new products. It has both facilitated greater unity around the innovation process within P&G's organization and enhanced external linkages, which provide new sources of knowledge and better customer involvement.

3.3 Arup

Background

Arup was founded in London in 1946 by Sir Ove Arup. It provides a range of design, engineering, and associated services, and currently has over 6,500 employees in seventy-one offices across fifty countries. Arup is recognized for its concentration of technical and design knowledge. It was involved in some of the greatest building projects of the twentieth century, including the Sydney Opera House and the Pompidou Centre. While working on these and current projects, it has confronted all the major structural and civil engineering challenges by developing highly specialized knowledge of mechanical, electrical, and electronic systems, earthquakes, fire, and smoke, acoustics, and environmental engineering.

Sir Ove Arup was passionate about engineering and his views of how the firm should operate have had a strong influence on its culture. He believed that engineering has a social function and that engineers should seek to use their technical skills to support improvements in social conditions. Ove Arup sought to achieve the ideal of 'total architecture': the unification of all disciplines, actors, and activities into a whole focused toward the delivery of socially useful projects.

Growth in Arup has been almost entirely self-generated. The company started as a structural engineering firm and as it won new projects its capabilities expanded into a wide number of different areas. As the former Chairman of Arup, Bob Emmerson, states: 'gifted people take us in unexpected directions'. It now contains over fifty specialist groups, spanning a range from environmental consultancy to acoustics.

Project-based organization in Arup

Arup works on several thousand projects simultaneously, providing specialist advice to a diverse client base. Most of its work is concentrated in design services for construction, including civil and structural engineering and mechanical and electrical systems for buildings, such as heating and cooling. Arup also has many specialist engineering groups, including Arup Associates, an affiliated architectural practice, Arup Acoustic and Arup Fire, specialist engineering services, and the Advanced Technology Group, which focuses on simulation modelling. Although the construction industry remains Arup's main client, over the past twenty years it has diversified its service offerings into automotive design, product design, project management, and economic and environmental consultancy.

Arup sees its key advantage over competitors as having the ability to combine a wide variety of specialist skills on projects. Reflecting the view of its founder, it aims to become a 'total problem solver', weaving together its diverse skills. Many of its competitors are small, specialized suppliers of design services with fewer competencies across a narrower range of fields. Another advantage claimed by Arup is its ability to recruit talented graduates. Within the firm it is believed that students are attracted to Arup because of its participation in complex and demanding projects and its ability to provide rich work experiences and training, with opportunities for diversification into new businesses. Arup employs 350 students annually.

In some respects, Arup has found itself in a virtuous project-based cycle: the firm wins high-profile projects because of its reputation for problem-solving, and highly skilled engineers are attracted to Arup because of its ability to win complex, exciting projects. But many of Arup's projects require routine engineering. As one staff member commented, his work does not often involve working on prestigious projects but there is enough to keep it interesting. Emmerson remarks: 'We are not doing this to get rich. We are doing it because we are designers. We don't pay well. At Arup, one in five projects is interesting. At other firms, it is one in twenty.' The variety of work, however, creates new opportunities for engineers to work in exciting areas, to find new ways to apply their creative skills. The firm's strategy is essentially to target high-profile, complex products, not only to build its capabilities but also to recruit new talent into the firm and to sustain the firm's reputation for engineering excellence.

As part of this virtuous project-based circle, Arup 'gets problems that others don't get', suggested a senior manager in the firm. Arup has gained a reputation for 'delivering difficult projects', and 'creativity in problem-solving', and for working with leaders in their fields. In part, the strength of Arup's reputation is based on close, personal relationships amongst architects, clients, and Arup staff. These relationships have been built from working on past projects and also by the high levels of recognition of Arup's abilities.

Arup actively seeks to originate projects. Emmerson states that Arup does not want to wait for work to come to it. If it waits for the work to come in, then it is unlikely to win enough interesting work opportunities: 'We have to create interesting work.' Arup wants to offer something different to its clients. Emmerson says that if Arup becomes averse to risk, it is finished. 'Arup cannot compete on the same ground as everyone else.' It has to seek opportunities to innovate.

There are numerous problems for managing innovation caused by the way work is organized in the construction industry. Specialist independent firms join together in a team that usually disbands at the end of the project. The project-based nature of activities means organizations working in the sector often struggle to learn from project to project. Projects are often one-off and task-oriented. Learning in one project is rarely fed back to the other areas of the organization, as project teams operate semi-autonomously and outside the boundaries of the firm (see Gann and Salter 1998). Furthermore, design activities are often undertaken under severe time constraints and this lack of time acts as a barrier to innovation. At any one time, for example, Arup is working on thousands of projects across the world, and each regional or divisional office operates with a large degree of autonomy. The organizational and technological means by which Arup deals with some of these problems will be discussed in the following examples of Arup projects and businesses (see Chapter 7 for further discussion of the project-based firm).

Arup's diversification strategy

The growth of Arup has been accompanied by an increasing number of specialist groups within the firm. Many of these new groups developed inside the body of an existing team, and as project leaders in these groups saw new market opportunities to develop a specialist service offering, they spun out a new team. Central management recognizes the de facto independence of these teams. Senior managers in Arup have adopted a 'let a thousand flowers bloom' strategy for the management of these groups, and the company is decentralized. They feel that attempts to impose central control of these groups might weaken their development and argue instead that they should be left to get on with developing their own markets and skills.

The tradition of limited control has led senior managers to state that 'you can't tell anyone what to do' inside the firm. The management style adopted is similar to that found in many professional service firms employing highly creative people (McKenna and Maister 2002). Emmerson claims:

People do things on their own regardless of any corporate five-year plans. Office growth has been based on someone getting a job in a new area and then starting up an office. There was no strategy to go global or to develop offices in particular areas. The growth in the firm is organic. We have made a few acquisitions here and there, but mainly our growth has come from people inside the firm and developing new skills.

Emmerson says that 'Arup is really a federation of 124 different companies'. Each group within the firm pays a central overhead but then has considerable operational autonomy. Integration between the groups is maintained by agreements among group leaders to work together and to share resources. Central agencies inside the firm also provide a number of services, such as financial control and reporting, and human resource management. There is also an overhead for central R&D activities. However, many of the groups retain their 'own' funds to develop their capabilities and to expand into new areas.

The emergence of a new capability in Arup has often resulted from experience of working on particular projects where specialist and unique skills and technologies have been developed. These capabilities are honed and transferred to other projects as the market for them expands. IvT lies at the heart of many of the new specialist groups in Arup and much of its specialized simulation software has been developed in-house, or in close collaboration with software firms. An example of this diversification process using IvT is described later in the case where Arup was hired to explore the potential impact of a crash of a train carrying nuclear waste, and the way this evolved into a design business in the automotive industry.

Managing knowledge in distributed engineering networks

Arup's approaches to design, innovation, and problem-solving in engineering are similar in many respects to other engineering firms. Some of the approaches to sharing knowledge and generating ideas are similar to those observed in P&G where the InnovationNet and 'global lunchrooms' were devised to improve linkages between experts within the organization in different locations. Project-based firms like Arup also rely heavily on external actors and frequently collaborate with other organizations in their innovative activities (Tether and Hipp 2002; Salter and Gann 2003). Much of the search for new ideas is driven by the requirements of new and existing clients, often requiring deep interactions, which lead to new knowledge being created collaboratively with other specialists, clients, and suppliers (Den Hertog and Huizenga 2000; Bettencourt et al. 2002; Miles 2003; Dougherty 2004). In this respect, firms like Arup act as open innovators, collaborating with many different partners to develop an idea, and brokering new ideas between different industries and contexts (Hagardon 2003). Much of Arup's capabilities to solve problems are based on the abilities of employees to develop and nurture their own professional networks and to build up their personal knowledge and capabilities inside and outside the firm (cf. Gallouj and Weinstein 1997; Tether and Hipp 2002). Much of the knowledge is often developed through 'recursive practice' and remains situated in activities through which people accomplish their tasks (Constant 2000). The practice requires 'artful competence', learning how to apply principles of the profession to unique situations while making do with limited resources (Dougherty 2004). It is partly because of the *ad hoc* nature of search and selection mechanisms that firms in consultancy practices, like Arup, have been leaders in developing and adopting knowledge management systems (Elder 2003; Gault and Foray 2003).

The development of a formal 'knowledge management' strategy in Arup began in late 1990s. Arup directors were sceptical about 'business process re-engineering' and what they saw as other management fads at the time. They were interested in knowledge management because of its perceived benefits for managing groups of professionals working in dispersed locations in project-based activities. Over the firm's fifty-year existence it had built up experience on more than 100,000 projects and needed to find new ways of tapping into its historic and current knowledge. Moreover, other pressures were contributing to the need to improve its use of engineering knowledge. Arup was growing and diversifying. Some of its engineering activities were being subcontracted offshore and it was facing new forms of competition. Its business environment was becoming more litigious and the need to make rapid decisions was creating extra stresses. At the same time, the nature of innovation was also changing, involving a wider range of specialists working concurrently on delivering projects. The volume of information engineers needed to access was also growing, as was the gap between individuals' existing knowledge base and their capacity to absorb new information. Arup faced the challenge of developing a new approach to knowledge management whilst preserving its past record of consistently delivering complex projects. The development of knowledge management followed three distinct stages.

The first involved developing a case for supporting knowledge management. In 1999, the Arup Board seconded Tony Sheehan, then working in Arup R&D, to spend six months developing recommendations for an Arup knowledge management strategy. Arup already had well-developed knowledge management activities because, as an engineering consultancy, its work involved knowledge creation, capture, and transfer. It had developed a well-resourced internal library, an internal journal, intranet and a variety of other tools. Although these activities were not labelled as knowledge management, they were extensive and some had been in operation inside the firm since its inception. Arup thought, however, that the firm could use ICTs in new ways to share expertise across its dispersed and global organization. As a result of his experience of working in Arup R&D, Sheehan had a network of contacts around the world and was able to draw upon these to assess what type of approach to adopt. His framework involved three elements: people, processes, and technology. In each of these there were five phases of development, involving learning about tools, thinking about the Arup context, developing cases and gaining sign-off, integrating and demonstrating benefits, and identifying self-sustaining activities.

The second stage saw the delivery of knowledge management through small pilot projects. The challenge here was to take the framework developed in the first stage and translate it into action, without the new system being imposed in a top-down manner (which may have caused a reaction against it). At this time there were many smaller knowledge management projects in different parts of the business, some very small, but others involving many members of the firm. Through these small projects a list of opportunities for further development became evident.

The third stage involved widespread implementation and this required considerable political positioning for the initiative. There was a strong inclination amongst many in the company to re-badge what was already being done as knowledge management. One example of an existing system that was re-developed was Arup People, a corporate 'yellow pages' of expertise. At the time, much of the knowledge about who knew what in Arup was unknown. The list of experts created by the R&D department was London-based and involved the 'the usual suspects'. This needed to be broadened to the whole organization and made accessible to people anywhere if the firm was to make better use of its historic and current know-how. Arup did not want to impose a strict format or a peer review system to judge people's skills. Rather it developed the corporate yellow pages as a collection of individual Web pages. Individuals were given the opportunity to describe their own skills and capabilities. They were asked to provide three sets of information about themselves: (a) a list of their skills; (b) areas where they gave presentations to external bodies and associations; and (c) areas of developing interests and hobbies. An interesting consequence of the third item occurred when an administrator logged her hobby of equestrianism. It transpired that she was a successful event rider and had deep knowledge of equestrian courses. She has since worked on more than twenty Arup projects for the design and construction of equestrian centres.

Each entry contains three boxes of free text. The overall information is searchable, but the style and format of the entries is decided by the individual. People also list their contacts, so the network of expertise is cross-referenced and expands through the 'snowball effect'. Because the information in Arup People is not validated, it comes with a 'buyer beware' label. Given this environment, there is considerable social pressure not to overclaim. Indeed, one manager said that if someone claims a skill that they do not have and they are exposed, it can be 'ritual humiliation time'. The system therefore grew in a self-regulated manner.

Another major area of Arup knowledge management was the development of 'skills networks', of which there are more than ninety. Some are focused on traditional engineering disciplines, such as structural engineering, while others focus on underpinning technologies of design, such as CFD simulation tools. The Skills Networks act as a key mechanism for problem-solving and shares ideas about practices and new technologies. Each Skills Network is organized slightly differently, often with different websites, tools, and practices. Most members of Arup belong to more than one network. There is some concern that the Skills Networks may become insular and fail to pick common problems across different engineering disciplines. Arup has tried to remedy this problem by creating new networks when key issues emerge, spanning a range of skills areas. One example of this was the creation of an Extreme Event Skills Networks in the aftermath of 11 September 2001. This new network brought together expertise from across the range of Skills Networks to focus on the development of new engineering solutions to extreme events, such as fire, terrorism, and earthquakes.

To build a project-to-project learning tool a search engine was needed that could quickly assemble useful information from unstructured data sources. Arup sought a technology to scan through huge archives of different types of data, including drawings and text, in order to find potentially useful information and links for use in current projects and technical problems. Arup eventually teamed with Autonomy, a small Cambridge University start-up business that had expertise in searching unstructured data. A tool was developed that could statistically analyse packets of text in these databases, searching inside text and drawings to provide information that people had either forgotten existed or that was too difficult to access by other means.

Innovation in Arup

A key part of Arup's innovation strategy is to 'piggyback' research alongside everyday projects. This strategy is possible because the firm is involved in a variety of different, complex projects. Its reputation for engineering excellence means that it is often presented with problems that competitors do not get, which provides both a challenge and an opportunity. The firm consciously attempts to use the challenges in these projects to develop new technical expertise and expand its research capabilities. Complex projects allow the firm to access and explore new areas of technology. Clients pay for these research projects because they are essential to fulfilling their own goals, but the lessons of the research are adopted more widely within Arup and provide a key source for developing new ideas and business opportunities.

In its area of business—the built environment—firms like Arup play a role similar to the design, engineering, and R&D departments in firms like P&G. Much of its business is technology development and applied research for production processes managed by subcontractors. Unusually for an engineering services firm Arup has a central R&D unit. This unit plays two different roles inside the organization: primarily to provide technical support to project teams, and secondarily to help develop new business areas and engage in future thinking, building various future options for the business. The R&D group divides its efforts between what it calls the '3N': *Now*, technical support for continuing projects; *New*, adding value to the business through introducing new ideas; and *Next*, looking at long-range future possibilities. Problem-solving on existing projects accounts for roughly 80–85 per cent of the group's time and effort. Working on the introduction of new ideas accounts for around 15 per cent and thinking about longer-range ideas around 5–10 per cent. The latter is usually done in close collaboration with university research groups.

Knowledge is captured and developed in several ways. The R&D group is designed to assist in turning one-off problems into more generic sets of knowledge. Staff have typically been with the company for a long period and usually know where to look for expertise in the organization when particular problems emerge, thus actively maintaining a network of experts. This is seen in the case of the Millennium Bridge, discussed later.

The organization of the work of the engineers also facilitates innovation. Designers act as 'practitioner researchers' (see Chapter 5), conducting research both to solve practical problems and to turn this knowledge into future competitive advantage for the firm. The process of engineering design usually involves searching for appropriate solutions. Within Arup, designers see their activities as being divided between creative and operational design, both of which can be a source of innovation. Creative design involves developing new concepts, structures, and activities. Operational design is more common and it involves the practical business of getting a design to meet with standards, safety, and other regulatory conditions. The design tasks differ between projects and, over time, within a project. Designers clearly recognize that creativity is not limited to creative design but can be applied, making designs fit standards for safety and environmental performance. The ways in which designers used IvT to assist creativity is described below.

IvT and innovation in Arup

Arup has invested heavily in ICT and IvT to undertake its 'total problem-solver' role. Investments in these technologies support direct design activities, such as the development of simulation models, and communication across the various parts of the geographically dispersed firm. In the following sections a number of 'mini' case studies are presented of the ways in which IvT is used in, and its impact upon, projects and businesses in Arup. The use of IvT to help solve the problem of the notorious wobbly bridge in London is described as a means of finding solutions to complex problems. Its use in retro-design of the acoustics in the Sydney Opera House shows how technology builds cumulatively. This case is also an illustration of the way Arup has historically used technology as a means of diversification. This is clearly illustrated in the case of crash test simulation. The way the company approaches the management of its extraordinarily rich knowledge is examined in the case of its use of the autonomy system. A lengthier case is presented on the way Arup uses IvT in its fire safety design activities, where the impact of this technology upon regulators is described.

Developing solutions: fixing a wobbly bridge

The London Millennium Bridge, linking the Tate Modern Gallery and St Paul's Cathedral, was the first pedestrian bridge across the river Thames in more than 100 years. The bridge design was awarded through a competition aimed at producing an innovative, modern approach. The winning team involved collaboration between Foster and Partners architects, the sculptor, Sir Anthony Caro, and Arup engineers: the team spanned at least three different communities of practice. Working together, they created a minimal design to give pedestrians a good view of London, free of traffic and high above the river. The bridge spans 325 m and is a complex structure, only 4 m wide, with an aluminium deck flanked by stainless-steel balustrades, supported by cables on each side so as not to infringe upon important, protected views within the city. The bridge's span-to-depth ratio is 63:1, around six times shallower than a conventional suspension bridge. The environmental credentials of the bridge are that it is car-free, creating little pollution in use. The design team used IvT to achieve this. They drew upon lessons from other bridges around the world and they built sophisticated computer simulations to test their designs.

The result was heralded as a beautiful architectural, engineering, and sculptural contribution to London. The bridge opened on 10 June 2000. As part of the celebrations, 80,000–100,000 people walked across it. When large groups of people were crossing, however, greater than expected sideways movements occurred, and it quickly gained notoriety as the 'wobbly bridge'. A decision was taken to close the bridge only two days after its opening in order to fully investigate the problem and take remedial action. This led to embarrassment for the design team and incurred costs. Reputations were at stake and engineers were castigated in the press and media for not checking the 'footfall amplification problem', which occurs when groups of people walk across bridges.

The engineers had in fact tested for these potential problems and were puzzled as to why the bridge moved so much. Arup communicated the problem to their worldwide network of design offices, using the Internet. An international search was undertaken for a diagnosis and solution to rectify the problems.

Three research units were set up and worked together simultaneously. The first was brought to London from offices around the world and was instructed to test the bridge and discover where the problems lay with the original computer model. They found no problems with the model. The second group was selected from external organizations judged to have the best expertise in diagnosis and problem-solving in bridge design. Working in tandem with the Arup teams, the external groups played an important part in finding the solution. University research groups from Cambridge, Sheffield, Imperial College, and Southampton were commissioned to run tests on crowd behaviour patterns on bridges. The third team worked on the design of new dampers to be installed to absorb shock and reduce lateral movement. Young engineers were encouraged to think laterally about the problem and the team came up with a potential solution two months after their exploration began.

During this process, Arup's engineers found a paper on the 'lateral excitation of bridges' in an academic seismic engineering journal. The paper qualitatively described the phenomenon but did not quantify it. Other searches found similar problems on a heavy roadbridge of a very different structure in Auckland. In developing the design of the dampers, which eventually overcame the bridge's wobble, lessons were learned from the car and rail industries and their use of shock absorbers.

Using inputs from these diverse sources, the problem of the wobbly bridge was solved. Whilst the problem was a temporary embarrassment for the companies involved, the process of finding a solution brought considerable benefits for them and for bridge design in general. Arup published their results on its website, placing their findings in the public domain for others to use and facilitating learning from project to project.

The simulation technology used in the design of the bridge, bringing together the engineers, architect, and sculptor, was used in finding the solution. It was an important tool in the extended coordination of the international teams and the university research groups. As a result of finding the solution new knowledge about bridge design was created. The posting of this knowledge on Arup's website demonstrated new capabilities in the company and opened market opportunities for it. The tools of IvT were successfully applied to learning from failure.

Reinnovation: the Sydney Opera House

The design and construction of the Sydney Opera House (1956–73) was a milestone in the development of Arup's reputation for engineering capabilities.

The project became synonymous with the ability to innovate, solve problems, and design elegant solutions. It was the first of a number of major projects the firm has become known for, and the building is an icon of twentieth-century engineering and architecture. Thirty years later, it is being refurbished with the involvement of a team of structural and acoustical engineers from Arup, drawing upon the original design models and mathematical solutions. The team is able to integrate its approach to the refurbishment, exploring structural and acoustical options concurrently, using sophisticated software programs. The aim is to significantly improve the theatre's acoustics. Acoustical engineering is a relatively new discipline compared with structural engineering, and Arup is one of a number of internationally recognized firms with the capability to model and simulate acoustical performance.

The Sydney Opera House project originated in a 1956 design competition, attracting wide international interest from 933 architects, 230 of whom submitted designs. In 1957, Jorn Utzon's design was chosen. At that time, Utzon was a little-known Danish architect with a naval background, having worked on yacht design. His scheme was regarded as a difficult project to deliver, given its scale and ambition, and because its structural engineering had not been thoroughly thought out. Shortly after, a team of Arup engineers won the structural engineering design contract led by an expert in mathematical modelling. The team spent three years exploring options for the roof shell structure, culminating in the now-famous 'dissection of an orange', supported by a precast, post-tensioned concrete structure. It developed a structural analysis computer program, which was used to an unprecedented extent. It was one of the first large-scale applications of computing in building structural design, which led to many subsequent developments in the technique. The experience led to extensive developments in structural software programs, and on that basis, Arup developed its own CAD system (CADRAW) as well as a form-finding and analysis package.

This case illustrates the ways in which Arup has throughout its history used technology in the production of highly innovative structures, leading to the development of new technologies, and the ways in which technological opportunities can grow cumulatively: once the electronic data exist, refurbishment, or reinnovation, is possible through the use of IvT.[38]

Diversifying capabilities: crash test simulation

Crash test engineering is an example of growth in technological capability and business opportunities associated with IvT. It illustrates how the company diversified into new markets. Work in this area began in the early 1980s, when Arup was hired by the UK's Central Electricity Generating Board to explore the potential impact of a train crash involving transportation of a nuclear waste flask. The project was led by John Miles, who completed a

Ph.D. on simulation of vibration control in the late 1970s, at a time when computing power was limited, but the opportunity of using computers for simulation was expanding rapidly. Following his Ph.D., Miles had worked with Arup for a couple of years designing structures with protection against earthquakes, before joining an automotive engineering company. Arup invited him back to work on the crash test project. It involved building a simulation of the reaction of the train container to an accident or derailment. The simulation model was verified in a dramatic physical test in which a British Rail locomotive was driven at 160 km/h into a bright yellow flask, which survived the impact. The work involved the use of a software package, LS Dyna, a non-linear finite element code that proved particularly useful for dynamic analysis. It resulted in new knowledge about vehicle and materials design, simulation and testing, and the emergence of a new process of computer-aided engineering (CAE) for crash testing.

The expertise gained from this work has evolved in at least two directions. First, in Arup's traditional business of structural engineering for building design, where simulation of vibration control due to earthquakes and wind on tall buildings grew with the expansion of simulation capabilities in Arup's London office. New orders were received to assist in design of buildings in earthquake zones, and Arup extended their simulation capabilities by deploying experts in their Tokyo office. Second, in what was for Arup, completely new markets in the motor vehicle industry.

During the 1980s, design requirements in the automotive sector were changing partly as a consequence of more stringent safety legislation. The cost of physical prototypes was considerable, and the delay in receiving results held back improvements in new product development in the industry. Demand for design testing expanded and new work for leading motor vehicle manufacturers resulted in the formation of the Arup Automotive Design Group. But, until the 1990s, most simulations were generally used at the end of engineering processes to verify the results of physical tests, mock-ups, and prototypes, because the technology of simulation was expensive and inflexible. There was little opportunity for results to be used in fundamental redesign, although engineers sought to replace routine physical prototyping with the CAE models. In 1996, FT-Arup™ FE-Model Series was launched, a finite element analysis (FEA) computer program developed in collaboration with First Technology Safety Systems of the USA. The software provided accurate predictive occupant simulation of the behaviour of dummy models. It enabled simulation tools to be used earlier in design activities in quite new ways, augmenting and changing design processes.

Markets for Arup's Automotive Design Group grew as expertise expanded, focusing on engineering safer cars for occupants and pedestrians. Arup Automotive's safety integration specialist, Bhavik Shah states: 'The approach enables manufacturers to perform a higher number of design iterations in a shorter timeframe and therefore at lower cost, with the net result that we can help manufacturers produce vehicles that are more "pedestrian-friendly".' (Pedestrian fatalities account for around 25 per cent of deaths on Europe's roads.)

In 1999, Arup acquired a vehicle styling company, Design Research Associates, to exploit opportunities of integrating safety engineering design with vehicle styling. The capacity to integrate styling and engineering is rare among consultants, and according to Neil Ridley, one of its engineers:

It means we can produce breathtaking designs that will work as engineering structures. ... Clients use us because we bring different ideas than their in-house resources, which tend to be more focused on the mainstream issues. We are particularly strong on early feasibility. Manufacturers come to us to find out if it is worth taking an idea forward.[39]

Ridley estimates that this technology has reduced typical new product development programme times by about six months. But some scenarios are too complex to simulate reliably on a computer to the precision required. New development effort is focusing on applications such as air bag sensing; ensuring that air bags only deploy when they are required to do so. This has to be physically tested in about fifty different situations, including driving a car into a gravel trap or pushing a loaded shopping trolley into it. This is difficult to replicate on a computer, even for the best modellers. Ridley's aim is to reach the stage where manufacturers can dispense entirely with prototypes. This, he says, would reduce the development programme time by another six months to between twenty-eight and thirty months:

We can take drawings from a stylist, look at the available volumes for absorption and stiffness and quickly determine if the space is going to work structurally or whether something in the body shape is going to have to move.

This is particularly attractive to manufacturers who are moving towards the design of cars for niche markets based on the modification of platforms where there are likely to be lower volumes in production against which development costs must be offset (see the discussion of automotive production in Chapter 6).

Arup's Automotive Design Group employs about 140 staff based in three traditional motor industry centres in the West Midlands (UK), Detroit (USA), and Japan. Results emanating from this work include new vehicle and pedestrian safety developments such as non-aggressive front-end styling, deployable bonnets, crushable headlamps, softer bumpers, breakable bonnet hinges and latches, and collapsible front grills, many of which are manufactured from an array of novel materials. Using IvT, Arup engineers simulate these impact tests to an extremely high level of accuracy. According to Shah:

Designing a new vehicle is a complex engineering task involving many compromises. The fact that we can use computer modelling in more and more areas of vehicle design has meant that a typical four-year development programme can now be condensed down to three.

Playing with fire

Amidst the analysis of the horrific events of 11 September 2001 in New York is the salutary information about the loss of life caused by shortcomings in the design of the lifts and stairwells of the World Trade Center. In the North Tower an estimated 1,360 people died above the point of impact. The hijacked aircraft had destroyed the central core of the building, where all the stairs and lifts were located, leaving no way out for those on floors above. In the South Tower, all barring one staircase were destroyed. Staircase 'A' remained intact and eighteen people ran down it to safety. Another 600 people died above the point of impact in the South Tower.

The great height (over 1,360 feet) of the Twin Towers, which at one time were the tallest buildings in the world, required exceptional strength to cope with New York's ferocious winds. The design involved a mesh structure at the periphery of the buildings and a central core of lifts and stairs. The central core was created so that people could be transferred quickly to all levels of the building. The design was of three separate lift systems: fast non-stop lifts led to sky lobbies, where people conveniently transferred to frequently stopping lifts to their destination floors.

Designers of the buildings had presciently considered the potential impact of aircraft crashing into the buildings. However, they had estimated the impact of the then ubiquitous Boeing 707 and considered that the buildings could survive such a crash. The aircraft that crashed into the Twin Towers were the larger and faster Boeing 737s. Designers had made no allowance for the impact of burning aircraft fuel, which buckled the floor supports and led to the collapse of the mesh structure supporting the building.

To add to the tragedy of those who died in the impact zone and the floors above, it is also believed that congestion in the stairwells of the Twin Towers caused many fatalities. People lost their lives on floors below the crashes by simply being unable to evacuate the buildings promptly. Further loss of life was caused by the inability of firefighters to reach the levels of the building that were on fire as they had to climb the stairs against the flow of the people attempting to escape.

IvTs are being used in architecture and engineering, notably by companies like Arup, to ensure that such loss of life is minimized in future crises in tall buildings. Simulation techniques can readily model the impact of differing kinds of projectile and the behaviour of individuals and crowds in fires. The behaviour of metals and materials and their design configuration can be tested for stresses without physical prototyping. There is much that can now be done in companies like Arup through the use of technologies unavailable to the architects and structural engineers of the World Trade Center to make buildings safer and more resilient without compromising on convenience and economy.

Arup Fire

Arup Fire is a group of over 200 engineers with offices in eleven different locations in five countries. It specializes in fire engineering services, including fire modelling, escape and evacuation, fire detection and alarm, fire strategies, and smoke modelling.

Arup Fire was founded in 1998 with a staff of four specialist engineers in London. Originally, fire engineering was located in Arup's R&D department but, with the emergence of new market opportunities and in accordance with the company's diversification strategy, it was possible to set up a separate specialist division. The creation of Arup Fire was led by Peter Bressington, who developed a plan for an expansion of the fire group. Arup Fire expanded quickly. By 2000, there were around twenty engineers working in London, while offices were soon opened in Manchester, New York, Hong Kong, and Australia.

Arup Fire works closely with other parts of Arup, with almost 60 per cent of the work performed for projects within the company itself. The ratio of external and internal work undertaken by Arup Fire is shaped by its own view of its role inside the firm. Bressington believes that by bundling fire engineering into other projects Arup is able to increase the value of its service offering. It allows other areas of Arup engineering greater possibilities to find more innovative solutions because they are able to draw on the expertise of Arup Fire engineers as their designs are emerging.

The growth of fire engineering in Arup is intimately connected to changes in the way fire is regulated in the UK and elsewhere. In the UK in the late 1990s, there was a shift away from prescriptive code-based regulation towards performance-based regulation. In the old model, there was only limited opportunity for fire engineering to develop as a service. Fire engineering was the responsibility of architects and designs were organized around the requirements of the statutory codes governing egress and entry into the building. With the shift to performance-based regulation, however, it became possible to work outside the codes, allowing much more flexibility in the designs available to architects, engineers, and their clients. Under the performance-based regulations, if the designers could prove that a design provided a high level of fire safety, the design would be approved by local fire control agencies. As Bressington states:

We can't make a prescriptive code flame-proof—it's not possible to design these extreme events out, so instead we look at specific scenarios. A better understanding of building performance, such as focusing on how people would be able to escape from lifts in an emergency, will have more bearing on building safety than simply changing codes.

Essential to the process of gaining approval for a new building is convincing fire prevention and control staff that the design would be safe not only for the occupiers of the building but also for emergency services personnel. Gaining approval for a design involves meetings between the designers and local planning and fire authorities.

To demonstrate the safety of the design, Arup Fire engineers rely on multiple simulation and modelling tools. Bressington states that it is 'using modelling as a pre-emptive design tool, rather than a way of analysing what happens after a fire has already happened'. Using the simulation tools 'makes the scenario more realistic and is a much clearer way of seeing and analysing flow and the positioning of exits'.

The Evac model

Much of Arup Fire's work focuses on fire hazards in tall buildings with the goal being to get as many people out of a building on fire as fast as it is possible. Egress in a tall building is extremely difficult: stairwells can become jammed with people leaving the building and emergency staff attempting to gain entry to the high floors of a fire. Travelling down stairs from high levels can take a long time and be dangerous, while disabled people might be unable to climb down forty flights of stairs in an emergency. People at high levels often need to queue to gain access to the stairs.

Arup Fire engineers have come up with a radical solution to the problem of egress in tall buildings: they use elevators. By pressurizing the elevator shafts and blowing the smoke and fire out of them, elevators can provide a means of escape. A key part of the development of the elevator evacuation strategy is the use of simulation models of the movement of people in tall buildings. One of these models is called Evac. It shows the number of people on each floor and how they move down and out of the building over time. The model also shows whether these people assemble before evacuation. This simulation is essential to overcome the long-engrained lessons of 'in case of fire, do not use the elevator', and of the spectacular failures of lifts to evacuate people successfully in some notorious fires.

After 11 September 2001 many of the residents of London's tall buildings were concerned about safety and evacuation. Arup Fire was approached by the facility managers of the HSBC Canary Wharf tower to examine its fire strategy and to determine whether it was appropriate. Arup Fire engineers had been deeply involved in the development of the building and had developed its fire strategy, and the client was now seeking assurance that their building was safe. Using the Evac model, Arup engineers investigated the HSBC tower. They used their model to think about, and play with, different possibilities for the building and found that if people followed the traditional strategy of walking out of the building via the stairs it would take 22 minutes to remove everyone from the building. In contrast, if elevators were used, everyone could be evacuated from the building in 12 minutes. The added advantage of the elevator strategy is that it enables disabled people to escape from buildings at the same time, and makes employment of disabled people in high buildings less risky for the individual and employer.

The use of elevators in fire strategy has had a significant impact on the design of new buildings. On the higher floors, workers are advised to congregate in the lobby in front of the elevators, so the floor plan of the buildings must accommodate a large number of people there. The elevators must also arrive at the right floors for the evacuation from the building. The Evac model allows Arup Fire engineers to play with different design options, including lobby and stairwell size, speed, and number of elevators, and the behaviour of people as they wait for elevators to evacuate them. Each of these possibilities is developed by engineers with experience of extreme events and deep knowledge of the materials and behaviour of people in fire situations.

The elevator strategy for fire evacuation from tall buildings is not simply about changing technology: it requires considerable retraining for staff working in buildings. People need to be taught that elevators can be the keys to survival in case of fire.

Fire and structures

Fires do not always undermine the steel structures of buildings. Steel is an extremely robust material for construction and its use dominates commercial buildings. Steel frames will often bend but maintain their structural integrity, even in the case of long and hot fires, but the relationship between fire and steel structures has until recently been poorly understood. As a result the conventional strategy in the UK has been to treat all steel beams in the building with fire-retardant materials—a very expensive and time-consuming task that usually takes place on site. Traditional tests of steel structures involved heating up a beam until it melted to see at what temperature the material became unstable. This strategy does not locate the steel beam in the context of an integrated structure of a building, and the theory behind it fails to explain why many buildings are able to stand even after an extreme fire, and even though many of the steel elements were not treated.

Using a new generation of structural modelling, Arup Fire engineers have begun to develop an approach to design that takes account of how different steel beams interact with one another and hence shape the strength of the structure. This approach emerges from one of Arup Fire's research collaborations with universities: a co-supervised Ph.D. from Edinburgh University. The modelling begins once the plans and design of the building have been agreed: Arup Fire engineers set up a digital mesh representing the structure of the building, including the dimensions of the structure, beams, and slabs.

The model provides a 3D picture of the building. The power of this tool is not limited to visualization, but also allows the engineers to simulate the deflections and forces within the structure under different fire events. 'We can see how the structure behaves and whether it is failing or not failing because of fire.' The model thus allows Arup Fire engineers to think about new ways of protecting a building during a fire.

In one project, for example, the Arup Fire team was able to use the model to change the design strategy for the protection of steel beams, as it showed which beams needed to be protected and which could be left unprotected with no harm to the structural stability of the building. By removing the need to protect all of the steel, the team reduced both the cost of construction by £250,000 and the amount of time needed on site during the construction process.

The model was also extremely useful to insurers, allowing them to shape their policies towards buildings more accurately. Insurers are interested in the effect of localized, small fires, and in this case asked the Arup Fire team to explore the impact of a small fire on the structure. The model showed that they had little or no impact. This ensured that if there were a small fire in the building itself, there would be no need to remove all of the structural steel after the event. Insurers could then revisit their estimations of the cost of repairing damages after a fire.

The model is also visually elegant, appealing to clients and regulating authorities. Working with the Advanced Technology Group within Arup, the Arup Fire team is developing a more visually refined version of the model.

Using Arup Fire's model requires great skills. As an engineer put it: 'You would have to be comfortable using FEA models. You need to be quite an experienced modeller to do it.' The use of IvT needs extensive, new skills, and the implications of the technology for engineers and designers are discussed in subsequent sections.

A key element in the development of the model has been interactions with regulating authorities, meeting with the fire brigades, clients, and insurers to discuss what they were going to do. Fire regulating authorities can be conservative and wary of non-code-based designs. Control authorities were used to seeing information presented in tables and figures, the standard language of fire engineering. Winning support for the new model from the authorities involved a long series of meetings and presentations. The City of London sent ten district surveyors to ask the Arup Fire team questions about the model. They probed the concepts behind the model and how it works. One Arup Fire engineer commented that 'it was worse than a Ph.D. viva'. The regulating authorities also sent the fire plan to a UK university for peer review.

The STEPS model

Nicole Hoffman, a fire engineer at Arup, has been instrumental in developing a simulation model of fire evacuation. After leaving university, where she gained several years of experience in academic research on fire modelling, Hoffman entered the private sector in 1996. She began work at Mott MacDonald in its simulation group, focusing on ventilation in railways and doing simulations of fires in tunnels and railway stations. Hoffman was the lead engineer in the development of the Simulation of Transient Evacuation and Pedestrian movements model (STEPS)—a 3D model of the movement of people through a building. Although STEPS was originally developed by Mott MacDonald, a competitor of Arup, it has become one of the most important simulation tools used by Arup Fire.

Previous models of movement of people in buildings were crude tools. They assumed that people walked in straight paths, Hoffman argues, not allowing people to overtake others, and that all people moved at the same speed. In the models, the engineer would specify where people would turn to leave the building. Hoffman felt this approach was insufficient and thought engineers could do better. Using her background in mathematics, she approached it as a logic problem and thought about the sequence of decisions of individual agents and developed a long-term vision of what could be done. She was tired, furthermore, of printing out floor plans and drawing 'stupid little lines' through them to tell where the smoke was moving.

STEPS models the movement of people under both normal and emergency conditions. It produces real-time 3D simulations of the movement of people through a building in easily understandable graphical form. This allows the results to be interpreted by 'non-specialists and designers alike, helping to identify natural bottlenecks and preferred exits, as well as testing evacuation routes and timings for different kinds of emergency'. STEPS is validated by comparison with designs based on building code standards and can calculate evacuation and travel times in accordance with recommended methods and codes. At the same time, its advanced visualization techniques give the 'user access to people movement information at a much more intuitive level allowing more direct optimization of design'.

Arup Fire used STEPS in the design and development of the Turin ice hockey stadium for the 2006 Winter Olympics. In this case, the fire engineers needed to think about how different uses of the building might shape the behaviour of people during a fire. In the STEPS model, agents move as individuals, yet a major public event like a hockey game is a social event, with many families and groups of friends moving together. Arup Fire explored the implications of this group movement for the design of the building. They found that group movement considerably altered the way people move out of a building in the case of an emergency and that the building's fire strategy needed to respond accordingly. In partnership with Mott MacDonald, they were able to create a new feature in STEPS for group movement. Using the model, many revisions were made to the architects' design, reshaping exit doors and the location of stairwells.

Engineers import geometric data from a variety of design tools, such as AutoCAD files, to the model, and specify features of the people inhabiting the building. The model allows characterization, including the number, width, depth, and height of the people in the building, and engineers to specify the patience, walking speed, and familiarity of people in the building environment, providing a more realistic description of how people move in buildings both in extreme events and in normal circumstances. The model provides a 3D fly-through allowing engineers to look at snapshots both in time and in cross-sections of the building.

Simulation and regulations

Models are only useful to their full potential if their use is acceptable to regulators and statutory authorities. The nature of the conversation between the authorities and the designers changed with STEPS. Once the authorities saw people moving through the space, Hoffman says, it was a 'revelation' for them. On some of the early projects, fire authorities would gather around the model just to see it, and when it was not available their disappointment was 'palpable'. For Hoffman, this is the crucial aspects of the model. It conveys 'an awful lot of information and lifts off a lot of boring calculations into a pictorial idea'. The simulation frees people from tedious 2D plots and turgid descriptions of how smoke moves. 'Now they can see it in technicolour and moving animation. It is just so much more powerful.' The model builds on people's ideas of 'playing computer games'. For Hoffman this sense of play and visualization of boring data was always at the heart of the model.

Reflections

Arup provides an example of the ways in which IvT can facilitate diversification around a technology base. In some respects, Arup is becoming a 'software house' for the development of new simulations of buildings and structures, including acoustics, lighting, heating, and movement of people. As well as using its extensive expertise in this technology to help build other businesses, some of the IvT is being used as a business in its own right. Arup has launched a new business called Oasys, which emerged out of the growth of Arup's in-house capabilities in software development. It offers a range of suites of software for design, including computer-aid design tools, document management software, structural and geotechnical analysis tools, and FEA packages. Specialized simulations are connected to other specialized simulations.

Arup's expertise can be used in a wide range of areas and much of the discussion here has focused on disastrous events. Unfortunately, there is no shortage of extreme events that engineers, clients, and insurers need to think about. According to Arup Director, Faith Wainwright (2003), virtual modelling is used to understand complex phenomena relating to life safety in extreme events and extreme environments. These include:

- a tanker crashing into bridge support;
- vehicle impact on bridge parapet (crash models include air bag activation and impact on passengers);
- street viaduct collapse;
- impact of icebergs against oil platform supports;
- floors of building becoming overloaded because of falling debris due to disaster on upper floors;
- analysis of spread of toxic gases in a building.

Future accidents or events cannot be defined precisely, so engineers must explore many different scenarios. Modelling techniques assist engineers in asking the essential 'what if' questions, providing answers that are valuable for the everyday as well as the extraordinary.

The use of models in fire engineering has changed the skills needed (or held) by engineers. Hoffman argues that the models require highly skilled operators. At the beginning, she says, models came out from the research field and the people who used them had a very good understanding of how they worked. Once they became more widely used, however, they became more standardized and off-the-shelf. Now anyone can buy them and use them. There is now a danger, in her opinion, that inexperienced users misuse the models and generate results that might make sense of first impressions but can be misleading. Because the operators lack deep knowledge of the models, they may not even realize they have made a mistake (see the discussion on this problem in the Leaning Tower of Pisa case in Chapter 5).

Hoffman argues that CFD modelling is a very skilled job. 'You need to know an awful lot. The more sophisticated the model becomes, the more you need to understand the background to the model.' Although the models are themselves fairly robust and appear to make the job easier, she argues that you cannot give this job to the untrained. Hoffman used the analogy of a car mechanic: 'When you take your car to the mechanic you want to know that you are going to get it back in one piece.' Unskilled operators cannot see the deeper patterns underlying the numbers. They cannot see the mistakes. For Hoffman, the numbers speak. She says:

If you look at a picture, the computer graphics is already an interpretation of the numbers. You are already losing a certain amount of information. You need to know the numbers. If you put a decimal point in the wrong place, then everything will go the wrong way around. The equations are very sensitive to the input data. You can all of a sudden have the model spur off into another direction with meaningless answers.

3.4 Conclusions

This chapter has discussed IvT and the intensification of innovation in two very different types of company: consumer products and professional services. In both cases, IvT has been instrumental in assisting their innovation strategy and their overall strategic development.

In the case of P&G, the use of IvT has assisted the company in its C&D strategy of increasing its receptivity to external sources and markets for technology. IvT has helped integrate different communities of practice through information exchange, and knowledge search and representation. It has also assisted consumer feedback into its new product development activities in new ways, quickly, cheaply, and thoroughly.

In Arup, IvT has created opportunities for groups of employees to start up new businesses in accordance with the company's diversification strategy. It has also helped integrate the inputs from various important players in projects, notably regulators, assisted by its capacity to represent complexity simply. In both companies, IvT has reduced the cost and increased the speed of innovation.

Although the technology has been a powerful tool in the realization of competitive strategy and in the more operational management of developing new products and services, both companies continue to emphasize the importance of embodied knowledge and expertise. P&G's Technology Entrepreneurs, and Arup's highly experienced network of experts in its R&D group exist to transfer knowledge and experience from one part of the organization to another. The importance of these embodied skills, built over many years of experience, is shown in the case of Hoffman and in the practice of the P&G manager: 'exploring digitally—confirming physically'.

Both cases have highlighted the importance of considering organizational and cultural change as much as technological change in innovation. Technology and organization coexist in innovation: they are two sides of the same coin.

4   'Think'

4.1 Introduction

When Galileo pointed his telescope towards the sky, he became part of the rich history of the relationship between the instruments of science and scientific development. This chapter examines the role of IvT as a new form of instrumentation and scientific infrastructure, exploring its relationship with scientific and engineering thinking. IvT provides scientists, engineers, and researchers with instrumentation that enables them to explore ideas, conduct new types of experiments, and think in new ways about creating innovations in a cost-effective and quick manner. IvT increases the variety in the technological options available to firms. Through its ability to facilitate the collaborative production of knowledge and to represent knowledge in a more comprehensive manner, it brings science and the innovator closer together.

The chapter examines the broad context in which increased thinking occurs: expanded education and research systems, and extensive internationalization and collaboration, both increase the opportunities for thinking about innovation. The chapter analyses the intensification resulting from applications of IvT: modelling, simulation, data search and data mining, virtual reality, and artificial intelligence. It argues that IvT can produce significant economies and greater accuracy in experimentation and problem-solving activities. It describes the way this technology provides a common platform for research, which assists thinking and the representation of ideas across disciplinary and organizational boundaries, creating yet more opportunities for innovation. Science, engineering, and innovation are, in our view, increasingly linked through the developing application of IvT. It is also resulting in the production and creative use of vast amounts of data, the management and interpretation of which requires sophisticated new thinking. This thinking can be assisted by the code engrained in computer power but depends upon the craft skills built on human knowledge and insight, intuition, and serendipity.

Throughout this chapter we shall refer to thinking primarily in relation to science and research. Thinking occurs throughout the innovation process, however, and we do not imply any sequential progress in thinking, playing, and doing: all occur simultaneously, although a firm or an individual's efforts may concentrate particularly on one activity at any one time.

4.2 Instrumentation

Scientific thinking produces new instruments and relies upon their use for its further development. Babbage's dream for his Analytical Engine—a computer—was its application to science. As he wrote in 1832:

The whole of the developments and operations of analysis are now capable of being executed by machines. ... As soon as an Analytical Engine exists, it will necessarily guide the future course of science. (Babbage 1989)

For the historian of scientific instruments, Crump (2001), it is the design and production of scientific tools that has continually extended mankind's creativity and the frontiers of science. He argues that the 'new science' of the sixteenth and seventeenth centuries triumphed largely because of the instruments available to it, particularly the telescope and microscope. The subsequent history of science, he contends, is allied to the development of such instruments as thermometers and chemical balances, spectroscopes, vacuum pumps and X-rays, particle counters and accelerators, semi-conductors and microprocessors. Using the example of what he calls the 'exact sciences' (i.e. physics), he argues that the pace of development of these is related to the 'apparatus' needed to explore hypotheses: 'the physicist wants to see facts fit theory ... to be confirmed by experiment and observation ... apparatus must become more sophisticated and innovative, accuracy in measurement and counting is at a premium' (Crump 2001: xvii).

As well as the major input provided by these instruments and tools in scientific and engineering thinking, they also provide one of the most important outputs. Contemporarily, the computer, the World Wide Web and the laser were all developed to help scientists answer their research questions. Indeed, one of the key benefits of publicly funded research has been the creation of new instruments (Salter and Martin 2001).

Many interdependencies exist between the development of instruments and new thinking since the use of available instruments has a profound impact on the conduct of both experimental and theoretical science. Einstein, in his role as a Swiss patent officer, was deeply engaged in examining patent applications for electric clocks and distributed electrical time signals, thinking practically alongside his development of the theory of relativity. As Galison puts it, in the development of science, philosophical speculation and technological invention are inextricably linked.

New instruments create new methods and different ways of seeing the world. The electron-tunnelling microscope, for example, allows us to 'see' and manipulate atoms in nanotechnology (Jones 2004).[40] The development and use of X-ray crystallography by Rosalind Franklin and Maurice Wilkins at King's College London played a major role in the discovery of the structure of DNA by Crick and Watson. In January 1953, Wilkins had innocently shown Franklin's famous Photograph 51, with its stark cross of black reflections to Watson, who was visiting King's; and in February 1953 Max Perutz, then at the Cavendish Laboratory, had let Watson and Crick see his copy of the Medical Research Council's report summarizing the work of all principal researchers, including Franklin's. It was only after seeing the results of experiments with these new instruments that Crick and Watson were able to gain the crucial insight that led them to the double-helix structure of DNA (Watson 1968, 2004; Maddox 2002).

In his history of the development of the laser, Robert Townes, who was awarded the Nobel Prize for Physics for his research in this field, relates how the theory and practice of lasers developed hand in hand. He describes his experience of using wartime radar equipment to conduct basic research at Bell Labs, and how other laboratories at the time benefited from cheap war service scientific instruments. Townes writes how he purchased a few klystrons[41] from a sidewalk vendor in lower New York and applied them to his work on molecular spectroscopy. His wartime experiences with instruments were crucial to his subsequent development as a scientist:

The wartime detour had given me a rich and crucial experience with electronics, with electromagnetic generators such as klystrons and magnetrons used in radar, and with practical engineering. (Townes 1999: 48)

This apprenticeship was important for his development as a scientist as 'it takes time to get clever with instruments, and experience counts' (Townes, 1999: 48). This quotation illustrates much about the impact of IvT on the development of science, engineering, and innovation. Crump appears to be correct in his analysis of the importance of instruments, particularly regarding their contribution to the accuracy or definiteness of experimentation, but their relationship with research advances are much more reflexive than he implies. It is the complex iterations and the combination of the 'code' encapsulated in instrumentation, with the craft of the theoretician and experience of the scientist brought about by long apprenticeship, that lead to progress. The technology needs to be used by thinkers skilled in theory and method, aware of cognate disciplines, and capable of thinking laterally.

The ways in which IvT can assist creative thinking are encapsulated in the following brief illustrative discussion of a continuing internationally collaborative research project in skin science.

The brief example of skin science shows how IvT can affect thinking about scientific research and its conduct. As we said in Chapter 1, IvT can contribute

> **Box 4.1 International collaborative thinking: skin science**
>
> Two scientists, Professor Annette Bunge from Colorado School of Mines, and Professor Martin Berzins from Leeds University School of Computing, met whilst enjoying their hobby of rock climbing. Bunge's expertise lies in the simulation of the flow of oil through rock. Berzins' expertise lies in writing numerical simulations for the representation of various systems, from the evolution of jellyfish to the deformation of cogs and gears in machinery. They realized that their skills could be combined to study how chemicals permeate human skin and develop a model of the skin that takes into account the microscopic details often absent in existing models.
>
> The benefits of this joint research could lead to more accurate assessment of safe levels of chemicals such as those found in pesticides, to the development of new drug delivery mechanisms through skin patches, and to a better understanding of skin trauma such as burns.[42]
>
> In the example of this collaboration, IvT simulation and modelling techniques used in one area of science have been transferred to, and combined with, others and can provide a medium for shared understanding and creative developments. Communication between remote researchers is assisted by computing systems that provide the infrastructure for transferring data and information rapidly, cheaply, and securely (across international borders in this case), and the software that allows more effective data search and management. A website for skin permeation researchers has recently been developed.[43]

to the conduct of the innovative thinking needed for new science, engineering, and product and service development in many ways. These include most notably a critical contribution to

- the creative use of the vastly increased amounts of potentially useful data being produced by research through advanced search and mining tools and services around the processing of this data;
- the development of sophisticated and cheap modelling and simulation techniques that assist accurate experimentation and testing;
- increasing the speed of experimentation and problem-solving, which is particularly important in some areas of science and engineering, as data is being generated faster than it can be analysed;
- improving the capacity to represent knowledge in a broadly comprehensible and more readily transferable manner, enabling better interdisciplinary research. Improved representation of information depends upon software designed to assist the visual display of results (e.g. heatmaps) and people good at analysing changing patterns;
- increasing the ability to add value through ICT infrastructure, enabling more effective collaboration on common platforms and protocols, such as open source and Linux.

IvT in the form of powerful computers and advanced graphical interfaces is helping researchers understand highly complex physical phenomena and is providing the base for significant, new science-driven innovations.[44]

4.3 The expansion of research and education

The major investments occurring in research and education across the world have led to a rapid and historically unparalleled expansion of scientific and engineering thinking. The education system is now highly international and open, enabling a flow of students, academics, and researchers across countries. The new research system is also international and is increasingly collaborative, as well as being highly competitive between nations and institutions, and between the public and private sectors. These changes profoundly affect the extent and scope of 'think' activities, in particular extending the scale and range of potential contributors to a distributed innovation process.

Education

The growth in science and engineering capability worldwide from 1970 to the present is unprecedented. With the economic and social transformation of China and other Asian countries, the number of scientists and engineers has been doubling every ten years since the 1970s. Even amongst advanced industrialized countries, recent growth in science and engineering has been considerable. In 1975, 39,800 engineering students graduated from US universities. By 1998, this number had increased to 60,900. In Asia, including China, India, Japan, Taiwan, and South Korea, growth in science and engineering has been explosive. In 1975, Asia produced 92,780 graduate engineers. By 1998, this number had increased to 372,900. These patterns of growth are consistent across both the natural sciences and social sciences (NSB 2002).

The substantial growth in scientific and engineering capability can also be seen at the level of doctoral training. The total number of science and engineering doctorates completed in the UK, the USA, France, and Germany almost doubled from 27,400 in 1975 to 54,900 in 1998 (NSB 2002). Amongst Asian countries, the growth in doctoral degrees was even more dramatic. In 1982, only 13 doctorates were awarded in China. In 1999, 10,200 were awarded. In South Korea, the number of doctoral degrees has grown from 557 in 1975 to 5,600 in 1998. Japan has also seen dramatic rise in the number of doctoral degrees, from 4,800 in 1975 to 14,000 in 1998.

Education systems have become increasingly internationalized in the sense of student origins. There were over 514,700 foreign students studying in US universities in 1999/2000, of which 54,466 came from China. The total number of foreign graduate students in the USA was 225,400 in the same year. The UK, the Netherlands, France, Australia, and Canada have also received large numbers of foreign students. Many of these students choose to reside temporarily or permanently in the country in which they were educated, and many advanced industrial countries have created more flexible and welcoming immigration policies for foreign citizens studying in their universities. The USA gives people holding doctoral degrees permits to stay. Close to 70 per cent of all foreign citizens who study in the USA plan to stay there after they finish their education (NSB 2002).[45] In the UK, the government has sought to loosen immigration rules to allow students to remain there after completing their education. In Singapore, students from China are asked to stay for five years after their education. Many of these scientists and engineers carry with them key skills that they may eventually transfer from the countries in which they were educated (and may have worked) to their home nations when they return.

Science and engineering in the labour force

An increasing share of the labour force is involved in scientific and engineering activities. In 1999, there were 2.1 million scientists and 1.4 million engineers working in science and engineering occupations in the USA. There were also 13 million trained scientists and engineers employed throughout the US labour force and over 480,000 of these had doctoral degrees (NSB 2002). The share of the labour force engaged in research, including the conception and creation of new knowledge, products, processes, methods, and systems, among OECD countries also increased in the 1980s and 1990s. In 1981, 1.7 per cent of labour force was researchers. By 1997, the share of researchers in the labour force had increased to 3.1 per cent (Salter et al. 2000).

Total investment in R&D

Investments in 'thinking' accounted for by research expenditure constitute an important share of economic activity. Across the OECD, the level of R&D expenditure increased from $400 billion in 1993 to close to $600 billion in constant (purchasing power parity, PPP) dollars in 2001 (OECD 2004). Within the OECD, R&D expenditures account for 2.2 per cent of gross domestic product (GDP). Investment in R&D has been steadily increasing since the middle of the 1960s, but from 1995 to 2001, R&D expenditure in the OECD rose by 4.5 per cent in real terms annually, indicating an increasing investment in 'thinking' in the economic system (OECD 2004).

Much of this growth in R&D expenditures has been driven by increased industry investments, especially in the USA with considerable growth from $96 billion in 1990 to $166 billion in 2000 (in 1996 constant dollars) (NSB 2002). However, several European countries, including Finland, Ireland, and Sweden, have also seen large real increases in industrial R&D. Similarly, Asian countries, such as South Korea, Taiwan, and Singapore expanded their investments in R&D (OECD 2004). In this period, however, the growth in industrial R&D in the large western European countries, like Germany, France, and the UK, has grown modestly.

An increasing proportion of industrial R&D funds in the USA and elsewhere is being invested in basic research. In 1990 in the USA, 5.6 per cent of industrial R&D was invested in basic research and this increased to 9.1 per cent by 2000. The growth in industrial support for basic research performed in universities and colleges also expanded from $815 million in 1990 to $1.3 billion in 2000 (in 1996 constant dollars) (NSB 2002). Growth in such funding is also seen in European countries, like Switzerland. Most of the growth of basic research in these countries has been concentrated in the business sector (OECD 2004). These patterns of funding indicate a growing pattern of interaction between public and private R&D providers, which is important for industrial innovation (Mansfield 1998).

Research system

Gibbons et al. (1994) argue that the nature of knowledge production is shifting toward a new mode, with greater collaboration and transdisciplinarity, and with research being conducted 'in the context of application'. They argue that in this new mode the distinction between what is public and private in knowledge production has become blurred, if not irrelevant. The traditional view of public and private research is based on the distinction between publicly funded research and business-funded R&D. Pavitt (1998), echoing the earlier views of Price (1986), argued that, 'basic research mainly builds on basic research ... and technology builds mainly on technology'. The difference between the two kinds of research is related to the *purpose* of each. Publicly funded basic research is designed to produce codified theories and models to explain and predict reality, while business-funded research and development focuses on the design and development of useful and profitable artefacts (Pavitt 1998: 795).[46] In many respects, however, this distinction is much too simplistic in that it underplays the overlapping, interactive nature of science and technology and of thinking, playing, and doing in the innovation process. Furthermore, it fails to account for the increasing number of citations to academic papers in patents described below, reflecting the increasing integration of science and technology.

There is now an increasingly fuzzy boundary between public and private research activities. Some publicly funded research is proprietary, focusing for example, on projects related to national defence, whilst some privately funded research takes place in institutions that are similar to publicly funded research laboratories. Some private research organizations offer incentives for academic publication and considerable freedom for individuals to pursue their intellectual interests, often in collaboration with their peers in other organizations. Examples of these types of private institutions include Xerox's PARC centre (Brown and Duguid 2000; Florida 2004) and biotechnology firms, such as Celltech (Dodgson 1991). Just as private sector knowledge producers have started resembling those in the public sector, the reverse is also happening. Increasingly, university researchers may try to capture the benefits of their research through patents or spin-off companies, as well as through more traditional academic means and channels (Henderson et al. 1998; Lambert 2003). Such changes are not always welcome and this development has raised concern about the maintenance of the valuable and traditional role of the university (Bok 2003).

Price (1963) suggested that the number of journals tends to double every 15–25 years as a result of the natural expansion of the research system—an estimate that has turned out to be fairly accurate. Growth in the numbers of academic and non-academic journals since the 1950s has been extraordinary. In 1900, there were less than 700 different academic journals. By 1950, there were 3,000, while by 1970 this number had increased to 7,000. In the most recent year of record (2000), there were 17,000 peer-reviewed academic journals. At the same time, there has been widespread growth of non-academic journals. In 1900, there were around 10,000 of these journals. In 1950 and 1970, the numbers increased to 40,000 and 85,000 respectively. In 2000, there were over 165,000 of these journals (Mabe and Amin 2001). The long-term trend in growth in the number of journals is not simply a product of the use of ICT, as the expansion began long before the advent of the PC and Internet. Research shows a strong correlation between the number of researchers and the number of journals (Mabe and Amin 2001). The growth in the number of journals reflects the increasing size of the pool of scientific and engineering thinking available to support innovation.

The increasing power of knowledge production systems, and one of the results of the expansion of such thinking activities, can be seen in the rise in the total number of scientific papers from the world science system. May (1997) found that from 1981 to 1994, the world's output of scientific papers increased by 3.7 per cent per year, corresponding to a doubling of total world scientific output every nineteen years. Between 1981 and 1985, the world's leading scientific nations produced over 2.16 million papers. However, from 1994 to 1998, the number of papers increased to 3.42 million, illustrating the increase in quantity of scientific output. Given that such figures do not include the contribution of developing countries, the growth in the number of publications may be even more dramatic than they suggest. Along with the rise in the number of papers has been a rise in the number of citations in their papers. In total, between 1981 and 1985, there were 7.4 million citations in scientific articles by the world's leading scientific nations. Between 1994 and 1998, this figure increased to 15.7 million (Salter et al. 2001). This is evidence of the way ideas are built upon the work of others and shows how thinking grows cumulatively.

Data from a variety of sources reveal the increasingly collaborative and international character of research in both the public and private sectors. The number of multi-author scientific papers has been rising since the early 1980s. Between 1981 and 1985, 42.3 per cent of all scientific papers by the world's leading scientific nations had multiple authors, yet in the period 1991–95, 58.1 per cent of all scientific papers had more than one author (Salter et al. 2001). Smith and Katz (2000) show that between 1981 and 1994 the number of world scientific outputs involving multiple institutions grew from 33 per cent to 50 per cent, and in the UK in 1994, 88 per cent of all papers from higher education institutions involved collaboration, with 55 per cent involving more than one institution. Collaboration is pervasive and appears to be expanding across all fields of research. This collaboration is assisted by the use of technology in creating virtual research communities.

The science system is also becoming increasingly internationalized. From 1981 to 1985, 20.3 per cent of the papers of the world's leading scientific nations were the product of international collaborations. But in the period 1991–95, the share of international co-authored papers rose to 31 per cent (Salter et al. 2001). Within Europe, in 1998, international co-authored papers represented between 30 per cent and 40 per cent of all papers published. In both Japan and the USA, the number of co-authored international papers has increased from 6 per cent and 9 per cent in the early 1980s to 13 per cent and 16 per cent in the early 1990s (NSB 1998).

Industrial firms are increasingly publishing scientific papers in public journals to disseminate the findings of their research (Hicks 1995). By the mid-1990s the scientific output of large industrial firms matched the output of a medium-sized university. The incidence of university–industry joint publications has increased at the same time as the number of industrial publications has grown. Calvert and Patel found the numbers of university–industry joint publications in the UK increased from 499 in 1981 to 1885 in 2000. The increase in joint publications occurred in all fields of science (Calvert and Patel 2002). Overall, the rise in joint publication activity indicates increasingly collaborative thinking between universities and industry.

These increasing linkages can also be seen in industrial patents. By examining the front pages of 400,000 US patents issued in 1987–94, Narin et al. (1997) were able to trace the 430,000 non-patent citations contained in them, of which 175,000 were to papers published in the 4,000 journals covered by the Science

Citation Index (SCI). For 42,000 papers with at least one US author, they determined the sources of US and foreign research support acknowledged in the papers. Their findings show an increasing number of scientific references cited in patents. Over the same six-year period, the number of citations to academic research in US patents tripled. This referencing would seem to indicate a significant increase in the flow of knowledge from US science to US industry, and observers have suggested that industrial innovation is becoming more and more dependent on academic research (see Mansfield 1998). US government agencies were frequently listed as sources of funding for the research cited in these patents. Narin et al. (1997) suggest that this indicates a strong reliance by US industry on the results from publicly funded research. This is more important in some sectors. Hicks et al. (2001) found that most of the increasing interdependency between public research and private innovation is concentrated in the health and information technology sectors.

IvT is playing an important role in the expansion and use of pools of ideas and talent. It can connect research skills with new techniques, which are radically changing teaching and learning through the use of games and simulations (cf. Foreman 2004). Given the growing size of the knowledge pool as illustrated in the above statistics, it requires greater capacity on the part of individuals and organizations to absorb potential innovative ideas, as they come from increasingly diverse sources. The rise in the number of knowledge producers and in the information they produce creates the need for more powerful searching, data mining, and visualization tools to guide and support thinking. IvT allows individuals to search, mine, and represent the system with greater effectiveness and less effort.

We shall now turn to the contributions to thinking made by IvT by means of a number of case studies. First, however, there will be a brief examination of an important technology underlying these new developments: the e-science facilitated by Grid technologies.

4.4 A new infrastructure: the Grid

The World Wide Web was born out of the needs to support communication between scientists in enquiry-based research at CERN in Geneva (Hafner and Lyon 1996; Gillies and Cailliau 2000).[47] But scientists' needs for powerful computing and communication networks continue to drive the development of new technical infrastructure. As mentioned in Chapter 2, the Grid in the UK is an example of an evolving technological platform for e-science. Definitions of Grid technologies vary from connecting supercomputers together to mass utilization of idle time of personal computers (such as the Search for Extra Terrestrial Intelligence project: SETI@home). In the USA, these systems are known as cyber-infrastructure, or cyberscience (Nentwich 2003). The Grid technologies to which we refer are defined by the directors of the e-Science Core program in the UK as being the 'middleware' infrastructure, including software enabling construction of virtual research organizations (Hey and Trefethen 2003b). This middleware includes shared resources: computers, data, facilities, and people. The focus on middleware that enables dynamic interoperability and the visualization of systems extends the utility of Grid technologies beyond 'big science' applications, such as astronomy, into industrial and commercial applications. The aim of such a platform is to enable 'different communities to come together and create robust, secure, virtual organizations to attack new and complex problems, exploiting a wide range of distributed resources' (Hey and Trefethen 2003b). It is notable that the UK Department of Trade and Industry made a £20-million contribution to the 'Core Program' of the Grid initiative, expecting it to be matched by industry. By 2003, £30 million had been contributed by over fifty UK and US companies.

One of the major contributions to innovation of Grid technologies is the capacity to deal with the magnitude of data being created by researchers. Enormously increased amounts of potentially useful data are being produced. As Hey and Trefethen (2003b: 1811) say, 'the volume of e-science data generated from sensors, satellites, high-performance-computer simulations, high-throughput devices, scientific images and new experimental facilities will soon dwarf that of all of the scientific data collected in the whole history of scientific exploration'. They use the example of the European Bioinformatics Institute in the UK, which currently contains 14×10^6 entries of 15×10^9 bases with a new entry received every 10 seconds. Its database tripled in size in less than one year. The extent of the problem of managing this data is shown by the Sanger Centre at Cambridge, which in 2003 hosted 20 terabytes of key genomic data, and that data is increasing fourfold annually, whilst the computer power required to analyse the data is only doubling in capacity. Simply put, without IvT such as advanced searching, mining, browsing, and representation technologies much of this data would be useless.

The capacity of Grid technologies to make vast compilations of data useful is seen in the case of Rolls Royce, which makes nearly half of its revenue from maintenance and servicing its engines in aircraft, ships, and power stations. In the airline industry it sells the capacities of engines, in their power per hour, rather than engines themselves, and effective maintenance improves the availability of the engines for service. The quicker the company becomes aware of problems, the quicker they can be resolved without affecting revenue streams. Advanced warning of problems allows better planning and avoids passenger delays. The company is part of a collaborative e-science research programme with four universities and two other firms called Distributed Aircraft Maintenance Environment (DAME). It aims to demonstrate how the Grid and Web services can facilitate the design and development of systems for diagnosis and maintenance. It will collect information from Rolls Royce engines in use all around the world (which accumulates at a rate of 1 gigabyte per flight), and then develop tools for their analysis.

Grid computing could have broader implications for Rolls Royce's range of collaborative projects with its major partners, Boeing and Airbus. Peter Cowley, chief scientist at Rolls Royce's Research and Technology Division, is quoted as saying that projects with these partners are often short-term, with four of five running at any one time, and that the Grid could help build continuity and links between them. He says: 'We want to build integrated systems across a partnership, and then unplug and plug in others for each new project and perhaps grids can help us do that.'[48]

We now turn to a case study of the use of IvT in one of the world's great pharmaceutical companies.

4.5 A large firm perspective: GlaxoSmithKline

GSK was formed on 27 December 2000 through the merger of Glaxo Wellcome and SmithKline Beecham. The result was a world-class research-based pharmaceutical company with an estimated 7 per cent of the world's pharmaceutical market by sales.

GSK's therapeutic focus covers the central nervous system and anti-infective, respiratory, and gastrointestinal/metabolic concerns. It is a leader in vaccines and has a growing portfolio of oncology products. GSK also has an over-the-counter (OTC) portfolio, which includes brands such as Panadol, Zovirax, Gaviscon, Ribena, and Lucozade.

In the 2003 financial year GSK had sales of £21.4 billion ($35.2 billion) and profit before tax of £6.7 billion ($11 billion), and on average was the largest company by capitalization on the UK stock market.

Rising R&D costs and reduced R&D output

Like most pharmaceutical companies GSK has huge capital costs associated with the production of new drugs. The key cost elements are:

- R&D: Within the industry it was estimated that the average drug in 2003 cost $800 million to get to market, more than twice as much as in 1987. In recent years, GSK has seen its R&D costs rise as a result of, amongst other factors, the increased scientific opportunities that have emerged from the Human Genome Project and associated research;

- long lead times before sales are made: The process between drug discovery and testing through to approval from regulatory bodies such as the US Food and Drug Administration can take 12–15 years;
- sales and marketing expenses: Sales staff for some drugs can number several hundred persons.[49]

GSK spends £1 billion a year on R&D just in the UK, which is the home to 40 per cent of GSK's global R&D effort.

The merger between Glaxo Wellcome and SmithKline Beecham resulted initially in an estimated annual cost saving of £1.8 billion. However, according to some analysts, the cost-saving potential of the merger has now been fully realized. The lack of future cost-saving opportunities combined with an increase in cut-price generic products on the market competing with GSK's current crop of blockbusters (defined as products whose revenues exceed $1 billion, e.g. Augmentin, an antibiotic) thus make it increasingly important for GSK to maintain and increase growth through new drug development.[50]

In 2001, GSK went through an R&D restructuring with the research function splitting into six autonomous Centres of Excellence. Each of the centres is focused on a different therapeutic area, such as treating cancer or AIDS. Part of the rationale was to create a more entrepreneurial environment where scientists compete for funds.[51] The company has also signed a number of major research collaboration deals with biotechnology companies, including Nobex and Exelixis.

IvT and drug discovery

IvT is also an important stimulant in the search for new drugs and in their design. The Human Genome and Human Pathogen Genome projects have resulted in many new potential drug targets. The development of technologies such as high-throughput chemistry and automation of screening have coincided with the need to increase the rate of compound identification associated with these new opportunities (Watson 2004).

Tachi Yamada, Chairman of Research and Development at GSK, says GSK's aim is 'to become the most productive research and development organisation in the industry. One way GSK R&D will achieve its goal is by transforming drug discovery through the use of high-throughput technologies and automation in discovery research'.[52]

The use of IvT appears to have widespread support within GSK's research organization. Tachi Yamada at GSK says: 'Our systematic high-throughput approach will improve productivity and allow us to reduce the time it takes to bring a drug to market by as much as 2 years.'[53]

Box 4.2   Simulation and process intensification in drug discovery[54]

At the simplest level, the fundamentals of the drug discovery process have remained unchanged for many years. Novel compounds are designed, then prepared by chemists and assayed (tested) against biological targets. Hypotheses of the relationships between the structure of these compounds and their biological activity are developed, and the cycle is repeated. In recent years, however, new technologies have had a dramatic impact on the throughputs of both preparation (high-throughput chemistry) and assay (high-throughput screening) capabilities. A decade ago, a chemist might have made fifty new compounds per year. The same chemist can now prepare many thousands of compounds per year, with obvious implications for the quality and speed of hypothesis development. This new IvT has freed skilled scientists to spend more time being creative instead of performing tedious, repetitive practical procedures.

Preparing compounds is a multistage process, including synthesis, work-up, purification, quantification, and quality control. Furthermore, in pharmaceuticals unlike some other mass production industries, every product (compound) is unique, so it is not always possible to predict exactly which downstream processes will be required following synthesis. For such a complex production operation to proceed efficiently and effectively, suitable technologies need to be developed for each of the stages. Understanding how these technologies fit together and how they might impact other parts of the process is critical for success and, where possible, weaknesses should be identified before major investments are made.

Discrete event simulation has proven to be an effective tool for understanding the interplay between the process stages as individual components (technologies) are changed and as the number of entities (compounds) passing through the system increases. A particular strength is the ability to model parameters that fluctuate over time by using statistical distributions rather than the fixed values, which might be employed in a spreadsheet-type analysis. Variations are difficult to avoid in a high-throughput chemistry process and include the varying size and frequency of synthesis campaigns, the unpredictability of downstream requirements, and the time required for acquisition and interpretation of analytical data. Simulation allows GSK to explore the effects of different possibilities prior to implementing them in the 'real world'.

An example of this is seen in the use of preparative high-performance liquid chromatography (HPLC), which is used for the purification of compounds following synthesis. This procedure separates a solution of the compound (along with its impurities) into a number of fractions, some containing pure compound, others containing the impurities, and others perhaps still containing a mixture. Aliquots[55] from each fraction must be transferred to a microtitre plate for analysis. The analytical results enable the chemist to judge which fractions contain the desired compound at sufficient levels of purity. These fractions are then combined and the solvent is evaporated.

GSK desired an integrated robotic solution that would replace the repetitive manual stages of liquid transfers. Additionally, integration of an automated evaporation process would give the advantage of unattended overnight running of this time-consuming stage. Hence the final robotic set-up would include automation for liquid handling, storage of compound and fraction solutions, and transfer of samples to and from an automated vacuum centrifuge for evaporation. A simulation study was initiated with the goal of assessing the required capacities for each of the elements described above under a range of possible throughputs. Simulation was the ideal tool as there was considerable fluctuation in the daily input rate of fractions into the system, as well as in the time taken for chemists to make decisions at various intermediate stages, and the number of fractions requiring recombination for any particular compound.

Some very useful insights were gained from the model. A system configured with a single evaporation unit was shown to be optimal for giving a balanced utilization of all components.

This was contrary to the anticipated requirement for two or three such units and resulted in a significant cost reduction. The model also demonstrated adequate capacity to recover from the queues that would inevitably develop during periods of shutdown for routine mainten-ance. Some improved working practices were also highlighted that minimized the number of fractions in storage at any time.

This and other applications of discrete event simulation have demonstrated the effectiveness of the technique in understanding the operation and requirements of new systems and processes prior to their implementation—a result of increasing importance as drug discovery processes become increasingly automated and integrated across functions.

Peter Goodfellow, Senior Vice-President, Discovery Research, R&D, GSK, says: 'Automation is an enabler of our scientific strategy and skilled scientists are vitally important to these new technologies. If we make more of the right molecules, we can make more drugs, faster and cheaper.'[56]

Brian Warrington, Vice-President for Technology Development, Chemistry, says his team at GSK use simulation technology to help them understand the drug discovery process so they can improve it. Ian Hughes, a member of the Technology Development team says that a key change in the way scientists work is that 'the new automated processes free skilled scientists to spend more time being creative (thinking) rather than performing tedious practical procedures, and this further enhances the output quality of the processes.'

IvT is contributing to improvements in GSK's 'pipeline' of new potential products. In December 2003 there were thirty more all-new compounds in the pipeline than in October 2001, with the number of programmes in Clinical Trials Phases II and III rising from twenty three to fourty four. The number of Phase I trials increased from ten in 2001 to twenty in 2003. The GSK pipeline of eighty potential products is one of the industry's largest.[57] These product statistics compared favourably with the world's number one pharmaceutical company, Pfizer.[58]

Given the way that scientific understanding of the highly specific nature of diseases is improving through, for example, the Human Genome Project, it is possible to speculate on the continued efficacy of the blockbuster drug, and the need for individualized drugs, taking into account idiosyncratic molecular and genetic requirements.[59]

One of the characteristics of IvT is that the assistance it provides to thinking is not necessarily expensive or difficult to access, and has a range of applications in the public as well as the private sector. This is clearly seen in the following case study: an example of IvT in public policy planning.

4.6 A public policy perspective: the transport congestion charge

By 2002, average road speeds in London had fallen to such an extent that travelling by car was slower than making the same journey by horse-drawn carriage 200 years earlier. In Britain as a whole, it is estimated that hundreds of millions of hours are wasted each year as a result of congestion on the roads. This congestion was inevitable and getting worse. Since the early 1980s there had been negligible growth in road capacity, whilst traffic was growing at 3 per cent a year. It was estimated that between 2002 and 2010, traffic would increase by 25 per cent.

Finding a solution to growing congestion is a pressing social, economic, and environmental problem. It is also a political problem: apart from the resulting economic inefficiencies, politicians are wary of the growing frustration of 30 million motorists and potential voters.

In February 2003, London took the lead in attempting to address the problem by introducing a congestion charge for automobile entry into central districts. The scheme, which was widely criticized in the press before its introduction, is considered successful, with traffic being reduced by up to 30 per cent at peak times. The government and motoring organizations have closely monitored the outcomes of the London scheme with a view to national charges to reduce congestion. The decision to proceed with the congestion charge followed creative thinking using IvT.

The Centre for Transport Studies at Imperial College London was asked in 2001 by the Independent Transport Commission to conduct a research project into national congestion charging in England. The main aim of the project was to identify the road speed and financial revenue impact of such charges. The project made the assumptions that charges would vary according to usage levels and would reflect levels of traffic congestion, road maintenance, accident, and environmental damage costs.

The project faced technical and representational difficulties. How do you generate the data, then represent it and make it comprehensible to decision-makers and opinion-formers?

The model had to account for nine different types of transport and 8,500 different parameters (region, time, etc.) in a national database. To build this interdependent matrix reflecting such complexity would require large processing power and a detailed set of iterating underlying equations. The results of the project needed to be presented to a target audience of government ministers, press, and lay-people. The data generated by 9 × 8,500 outputs had to be easily understandable.

The capacity for the amount of data required to describe the current traffic situation throughout the UK seemed beyond the capability of any off-the-shelf software package. The team leader, Professor Stephen Glaister, therefore considered using a high-level program language, such as Pascal, which he had used in the past to solve similar problems. The magnitude of the data, however, made this nearly impossible because of the amount of coding required.

Glaister then examined the capabilities of Microsoft Excel, the world's most popular office spreadsheet package used conventionally for financial reporting and basic statistical analysis. At this time Microsoft launched an advanced version, Excel XP, which had twice the capacity and many more capabilities than its predecessor. It proved particularly valuable for the project in its ability to iterate, which is the crucial element in producing convergence into a solution and simulating random disturbance. Glaister contends that without this version of Excel the whole project would have been more difficult and taken longer to complete, and that such computing capabilities have allowed us to do things that would have previously been unthinkable.

The team hypothesized mathematical relationships, describing how cells would change as the parameters change. Various data were already available for use but some needed to be collected, for example, on bus and train users.

With the numbers crunched, the project team decided to represent the Excel XP output by using a software package called MapInfo, which produces a heat map related to geographical information. Heat mapping is a common form of visualization to represent the relationships between complex data. The colours on the map represent the predicted increase in speed and decrease in traffic compared to existing circumstances if a national congestion charge were implemented. MapInfo was used to relate Excel output to various forms of geographical information, including electoral ward boundaries. Like Excel, MapInfo had recently become much more powerful and was compatible with XP. The integration of the two packages, however, required the significant software skills possessed in the project team.

Apart from representing the changes in road speeds caused by congestion charges in an easily comprehensible form, the project produced other benefits. In particular, the graphical representation of the data allowed patterns to be seen more easily. National congestion charging involves the transfer in aggregate of relatively large sums of money from road users. The project output showed the extent to which finances would be transferred out of different regions. For example, government ministers talked about a revenue neutral system in which regional 'losers' and 'winners' would balance out in fiscal terms. By looking at the map it was obvious that the losers would be concentrated in urban zones and winners in rural areas. Such redistribution, however, would conflict with another element of government policy of moving resources into urban regions for inner-city regeneration. The details of these flows were not obvious until the maps were produced. The model thus helped government make allocation decisions. Where a politically sensitive issue like a new tax is concerned, the ability to use the technology to represent the data simply to sceptics and critics is an invaluable tool for communication and involvement.

As well as producing the model, the project also undertook some simulations. For example, the team examined how buses interact with other traffic. They found that they could understand the general properties of the system by using visual simulations of the buses represented by coloured dots.

The technologies used in this project enabled its fast completion on a relatively small budget; the project lasted around eighteen months and its total budget was £50,000. A major follow-up government study into the issue was announced in 2003.

The existing knowledge and skills possessed in the research team were essential to the project's success. The integration of the two software packages, which in the event combined so successfully, was always feasible technically, but required high-level software skills and constructive imagination in realizing they could be combined. Furthermore, Glaister refers to the way he relied heavily on past experience of this kind of economic modelling to guide him on what the essential economic features were and to judge what compromises and simplification had to be made in order to get the model to work in a useful way.

4.7 Data creation, searching, and mining

Data mining has traditionally been used to automate repetitive recognition tasks around statistical analysis and cataloguing. However, it is also increasingly being used in the discovery of new scientific knowledge. Langley (2000) refers to examples of its use in astronomy (for classifying stars and galaxies in sky photographs) and planetology (for recognizing volcanoes on Venus). It is also used in the creation of knowledge about markets and in areas such as financial services. An area of science in which it is critically important is functional genomics, where robots generate data about genetic material, and data mining is used to extract useful knowledge from that data.

Box 4.3 illustrates some components of the new craft skills that we shall be discussing in later chapters. Much research in computer science is directed towards the development of semantics and ontologies to help manage knowledge, and allow for automatic processing and discovery of relevant information. Cell tomography images, for example, can be tagged and annotated with database information. The construction of these systems not only requires extensive scientific knowledge but also sophisticated understanding of how scientists search for information.

Box 4.3   Using data mining in cell biology

Data mining is being used by a University of Queensland researcher, Rohan Teasdale, to extract information contained in the genomes of mice and humans about how cells work. He believes that database mining combined with traditional cell biology allows a more intuitive approach to identifying information to give greater understanding of the crucial role that different cell membranes play in physiological processes. Cell membranes and the proteins embedded in them are essential mediators of the transfer of material and information between cells and their environment, between compartments within cells, and between regions of organ systems. Transporting newly synthesized proteins to different cell membranes is a fundamental cellular process. Its disruption has been linked to diseases including cancer and high cholesterol. Understanding the normal function of cell membranes helps the fight against such diseases. According to Teasdale:

'By combining database mining with cell biology we will develop reliable computational prediction methods allowing us to identify membrane proteins in the mouse and human genome and predict their location in the cell. Additionally, these predictive strategies can be confidently applied to different research projects by other research groups on a genome-wide scale. ... In the field of computational biology we are amongst the first to critically evaluate our computational predictions experimentally, while in cell biology we provide the degree of confidence necessary for experimental scientists to critically evaluate the worth of the prediction.'

Teasdale contends that this synergistic approach, combining experimental evaluation with computational methods, will build significant collaborations within his university, nationally, and internationally.[60]

The contribution of IvT in data management includes faster testing of results. There have been, for example, huge advances in the speed and capacity of analytical equipment used in chemistry and chemical engineering. Automated testing has become common. This is faster and more reliable than traditional processes of analysis where chemists had to crystallize substrates through numbers of steps, before being able to analyse the results. Analysis is now much faster than was previously possible.

According to one of Britain's leading chemical engineers, Professor Dame Julia Higgins, IvT has taken away much of the drudgery of research. When Higgins started her work as a physical chemist she needed to consult the Chemical Abstracts. These were large documents of formulae and proofs contained in rows of shelving in the library. She spent a lot of time searching and referring to these (the ones she needed were invariably the heaviest ones on the top shelves!), as she had to track down all previous known literature on a particular reaction. Now this work is done almost instantly on a desktop computer linked to the Internet, saving time and energy for more fruitful and productive work, and for more important, creative thinking.

Professor John Darlington, Director of the London e-Science Centre, says the Grid enables all sorts of information to be 'woven' together. This includes large amounts of different kinds of data—literature, databases, images, operational and instrument data—with many different applications. The information to be brought together is often highly complex, interrelated, and volatile. It is heterogeneous, including algorithms and implementations, and communities of researchers and service providers. One of the key characteristics of information weaving is the high degree of autonomy it gives to the user to use it specifically as is wished, which in turn is highly dependent on the new craft of semantics and ontology. IvT enabling the 'weaving' of technology allows greater liberation to individual exploration and thought. An example of this was shown in Arup's use of the Autonomy search-engine in Chapter 3.

Modelling and simulation

Modelling and simulation tools are used extensively by researchers, from climate modelling to computational biology, genomics, and proteomics to financial simulations.[61] They have highly practical implications: from assisting commodity option pricing in the City of London to considerations of future prices for soybeans at the Chicago Board of Trade to rainfall prediction for Australian farmers. In the latter case, in work undertaken by Professor Kevin Burrage and colleagues at the University of Queensland, rainfall recorded at 8,000–10,000 weather stations across Australia on a weekly basis for over 100 years have been interpolated on 5-km grids. The results helped develop a software package for farmers' decision-making, which, in the driest continent on earth continually plagued by drought and flood, has some potentially significant benefits.

Another way in which modelling and simulation can help researchers is seen in chemical engineering. Modelling physical properties can save time in what is called 'scaling-up' in chemistry. Scaling-up is the process by which, once observed, a particular phenomenon (reaction) is scaled up to a larger size to test whether the same conditions apply at the new scale. This is a common process used by chemical engineers in working out the viability of moving from lab-bench to mainstream production. Scaling-up usually involves a series of steps, and parts of this process can be simulated. It is possible to gain enough information from initial experiments to build a model and simulate outcomes, enabling some of the steps to be skipped. This saves time and money and enables bigger investment decisions to be made earlier in the process from experimentation to commercialization. The problems of scale-up are found in a range of sectors, including biopharmaceutical production. Nevertheless, validation and calibration of models still often depends upon physical testing at different stages of scale-up.

In some fields it is not possible to carry out physical work until a model has been fully tested. IvT can assist in providing the confidence in models before expensive and/or sensitive work begins. For example, Professor John Burland's work on the mechanics of tunnelling-induced ground movement and ground stabilization had important applications in stabilizing the Leaning Tower of Pisa (see Chapter 5), and providing data for temporary works to stabilize the famous tower of the British Houses of Parliament, Big Ben, prior to the construction of a new underground rail line beneath it. In neither of these cases would the building authorities permit physical work until conceptual models had been fully tested.

4.8 Visualization

Visualization technologies, such as virtual reality, are used in a wide range of creative thinking activities, from the representation of ecosystems to drug design to medical research and training to urban development simulations.

Virtual reality is used extensively in healthcare. It is used widely in surgery-related and anatomical training and can be used in diagnosis through, for example, representing heart strain or the growth of polyps. One example of the extent of its value in doing things that previously could not be done is in the clinical assessment of psychological disorders. Virtual reality is now used to enhance the experiential learning outcomes of medical students by simulating the visual and auditory hallucinations of patients with psychosis (Banks et al. 2003). This visualization has benefits for scientists as the created environment can be used as a structured and repeatable trigger for neurophysiological examinations of the central nervous system and may assist in understanding the intra-cerebral pathways of psychosis, thereby helping to unravel the mysteries of illnesses such as schizophrenia (Banks et al. 2003). Virtual reality also represents an improved medium that for the first time helps clinicians experience what patients' hallucinations feel like. Virtual reality is now helping psychotic patients clearly express the nature of their experiences, thereby facilitating better care.

Visualization techniques are useful in enhancing human perception of complex data through pattern recognition. Essentially, visual images create opportunities to see patterns more easily (see Tufte 1983, 1997). When the analysis of outputs is very complex, for example in the representation of environmental problems, virtual reality can be highly useful. In one example of this, virtual reality is being used to model an actual reef, showing both the growth of hard and soft coral and the behaviour and motion of fish (Jeffrey 2003). The tool helps researchers develop models and interactively examine their results, to educate people about reef ecology whilst entertaining them through demonstrating their beauty. Technologies are improving so rapidly in this field that it is nowadays possible to receive sophisticated visual representations on mobile devices, such as Personal Data Assistants.

4.9 Artificial intelligence[62]

Since the publication of Herbert Simon's pathbreaking work *The Sciences of the Artificial* in 1969, the development of mathematics to study complex systems in areas as diverse as genetics and economics has expanded in parallel with growth in computational power (cf. Simon 1996). Artificial intelligence, sometimes known as 'expert systems', has been applied to scientific discovery in a wide range of disciplines, including mathematics, astronomy, metallurgy, physical chemistry, biochemistry, medicine, anthropological linguistics, and ecology (Langley 2000). According to Langley (2000), artificial intelligence is used in all elements of the scientific process, including problem formulation, representational engineering, manipulation of data and algorithms, and evaluation and communication of science. He provides the examples of its use in the development of stellar taxonomies from infrared spectra, prediction of carcinogenicity and mutagens, understanding metallic behaviour, and producing quantitative conjectures in graph theory, temporal laws of ecological behaviour, structural models of organic molecules, and reaction pathways in catalytic chemistry.

The robot scientist

An exemplary case of the potential of IvT in scientific thinking is reported in King et al. (2004), in an article in *Nature* on the development of a 'robot scientist' for functional genomic hypothesis generation and experimentation. These researchers developed a robotic system to carry out cycles of scientific experiments. The system

automatically originates hypotheses to explain observations, devises experiments to test these hypotheses, physically runs the experiments using a laboratory robot, interprets the results to falsify hypotheses inconsistent with the data, and then repeats the cycle. (King et al. 2004: 247)

The robot scientist is applied to understanding the functional genomics of yeast, and particularly in the automated determination of the function of its genes from strains in which one gene had been removed.

In the biological experiments that automatically reconstruct parts of the model (involving genes, proteins, and metabolites), the researchers showed that 'an intelligent experiment selection strategy is competitive with human performance and significantly outperforms, with a cost decrease of 3-fold and 100-fold (respectively), both cheapest and random-experiment selection' (King et al. 2004: 248).

The robot scientist has so far only been used to rediscover the role of genes in known functions in order to test the efficacy of the new machine. The researchers plan to extend the system, however, to uncover the function of genes whose role is currently unknown, and are actively considering its use in drug design and quantum control of chemical synthesis.[63]

4.10 Interdisciplinarity

Whilst there cannot be interdisciplinarity—productive thinking conducted across different academic disciplines—without disciplines, much exciting work in science and technology is conducted at the interfaces of different fields of research. The importance of interdisciplinary work can be seen in the way that few Nobel Prizes have been awarded to researchers working within the confines of particular disciplines; most have been given to those who adventure across boundaries.

Hollingsworth et al.'s (2005) study of major breakthroughs in biology found that the types of institutions producing breakthroughs are very different from the types of organizations that specialize in highly productive 'normal' science. They defined major breakthroughs as a 'radical or new idea, the development of a new methodology, a new instrument or invention, or a new set of ideas' and found that the potential to achieve these break-throughs are shaped by a particular institutional context and environment (Hollingsworth et al. 2005). Diversity itself does not ensure pathbreaking thinking.

It is the diversity of disciplines and paradigms to which individuals are exposed with frequent and intense interaction that increases the tendency for creativity, and for breakthroughs to occur. Working in an interdisciplinary environment without intense and frequent interaction among members of the work group does not tend to lead to new ways of thinking (e.g. major discoveries). (Hollingsworth 2005: 13)

As Gunner Mydral once stated, 'problems do not come in disciplines'. It is the capacity of IvT to assist communication and understanding across disciplines that provides one of the new technology's major benefits. The role of IvT in breaking down barriers, and assisting with the 'technology fusion' we described earlier as being an important element of the fifth generation innovation process is examined here by considering the future of engineering as a discipline. We draw on the work of Rosalind Williams at Massachusetts Institute of Technology (MIT), and especially her experience there as Dean of Students.

Williams (2002: 44) distinguishes between science, where the fundamental unit of accomplishment remains the discovery, and engineering, where the fundamental unit of accomplishment is problem-solving.[64] But she refers to the increased amount of 'techno-scientific trading' between science and engineering in new areas, and in the role of a 'common digital language' that is readily transferable across all parts of MIT. She refers to the work of Castells (1996: 30), who contends that

biology, electronics, and informatics seem to be converging and interacting in their applications, in their materials, and more fundamentally, in their conceptual approach. ... Furthermore, the current process of technological transformation expands exponentially because of its ability to create an interface between technological fields through common digital language in which information is generated, stored, retrieved, processed, and transmitted.

Williams (2002: 47) argues that, in the form of a common digital language, technology dissolves the familiar boundaries of engineering:

It also lifts engineering, once the most down-to-earth of professions, from its familiar ground of materiality, endowing it with a new and ghostly lightness of being. Fewer and fewer faculty members in engineering actually make things or build things. More and more work with symbols and models.

She uses the examples of MIT's civil engineering faculty that designs not structures but software systems to manage construction, and argues that just as civil engineering has migrated from structures, mechanical engineering has migrated from machines. Many younger mechanical engineers are designing programs to replace machines, using electronics and computers to assume functions previously performed by more conventional mechanical systems. She provides the anecdotes of one junior faculty member, saying that he uses computer graphics as an 'imagination amplifier', and another, explaining that he uses the computer not as a calculator but as a laboratory. Here we see IvT facilitating thinking, playing, and doing and also enhancing the porosity of their boundaries.

Such changes are not without considerable organizational stress. From the perspective of the student, Williams refers to the curricular equivalent of Moore's Law: every eighteen months the amount of information one would like to cram into the head of a student doubles. From the perspective of the faculty and its disciplinary and professional allegiances, she quotes a member of faculty saying that 'it seems to me that we have long ago given up training our students as "professional engineers" in most departments. We are really training technology innovators'.

To cater for the new breed, engineers increasingly need to be interdisciplinary; to work with scientists, and academics from management, humanities, and arts; and, of course, to work across different engineering boundaries. In Williams' analysis, engineers are migrating to a concern for systems or for design, both of which are essentially interdisciplinary. This migration is not

> **Box 4.4   A visionary past**
>
> MIT, a powerhouse of US training in science and engineering, has long had an enlightened view on its approach to education, a view with considerable relevance today and for new generations of scientists and engineers developing and using technology such as IvT and learning to work in interdisciplinary ways. In the *MIT Bulletin* of 1954–5 it was said that the aim of its School of Humanities and Social Studies was to 'impress upon the student how important human relationships are in any society, and to develop in him the first-rate human and social values which must accompany technical competence if an individual is to make his maximum contribution as a citizen' (quoted in Friedmann 1961). The curriculum reflected these values. All students in the first two years of their four-year science and engineering degrees undertook core courses encompassing history, philosophy, and literature. Their focus was on problems rather than solutions and the development of an attitude that education was something they *have*—to use continuously and develop—rather than something they *have had* (Friedmann 1961: 147). The courses in humanities and social sciences extended throughout the full period of students' degrees: in the final two years of study, students had the option of taking two humanities and social science courses out of the four they needed to complete without their training as a technical specialist being in any way compromised (Friedmann 1961: 147). Students could choose from fields including history, literature, modern languages, music, economics, political science, international relations, labour relations, and psychology, and each field had a wide choice of courses.
>
> MIT's experiment to 'break down the opaque curtain which has needlessly separated technologists and humanists' (MIT document 1955, quoted in Friedmann 1961) is just as, if not more, relevant for the contemporary challenges of thinking about science and technology and the organization of university departments.

easy and Williams refers to a crisis in engineering resulting from an identity crisis in engineering education. It could well be, and we shall speculate further upon this in Chapter 8, that this kind of crisis will occur across many more disciplinary and functional groups as IvT becomes more widely diffused.

IvT will not inevitably and comprehensibly break down disciplinary barriers. Existing modes of education and the psychological, social, and political pressures of professional identification that limit and constrain membership will continue to create boundaries. IvT can, however, facilitate more effective thinking and collaboration across disciplines than ever before.

4.11 Conclusions

Increasing levels of education and research, scientific and technological capability, internationalization, collaboration, and greater numbers of journals and patents help create a powerful system to support the efforts of firms and individuals to think about new innovative ideas and opportunities. There is simply more talent, ideas, and information available to innovators than at any previous period in world history. With the rise of the Asian economic and educational systems, particularly in China, it can be expected that the pool of ideas and talent will become even greater and probably more specialized, requiring new management expertise to synthesize results between different disciplines.

IvT is increasingly used in scientific and technological research. It aids a wide range of activities, and is leading to an intensification of thinking activities in the sense of being able to do more, faster, and better with relatively less resources. The long history of the close interdependence of scientific development and instrumentation is entering a new phase, built on powerful computers, Grid-like networks, and the tools of modelling, simulation, data mining, virtual reality, and artificial intelligence.

The consequences for scientists are still unravelling. Lessons have already been learned. Langley (2000), for example, argues how artificial intelligence has learned from earlier failures, which emphasized the automation aspects, and attempted to replace humans in the system. The approach now is to use artificial intelligence to assist researchers to combine the code in the technology with the craft of the skilled individual. As King et al. (2004) contend, the increased automation of science is both inevitable and desirable: it not only enables new experiments to be conducted at reduced cost, but it frees creative thinkers to make the high-level leaps at which they excel. The challenge for developers of IvT is, as put by Langley (2000), to increase the synergy between human and artificial scientists by modifying discovery systems to support their interaction more directly. Langley (2000: 407) says:

This means we must install interfaces with explicit hooks that let users state or revise their problem formulation and representational choices, manipulate the data and systems parameters, and recast outputs in understandable terms.

The challenges include ways of building upon past experience, valuing intuition and inspiration, and facilitating the removal of the 'opaque curtains' between disciplines and organizations.

In an education and research system that is distributed and international, IvT operates in an environment that is conducive to problem-solving. By expanding the width and depth of comprehensible search activities, IvT helps thinkers find new combinations. It helps them operate more effectively at the boundaries of their competence. From the perspective of industry, this technology extends the boundaries of distributed innovation practices into the scientific research base in universities and research institutes.

5   'Play'

5.1 Introduction

The architect Frank Gehry is known for his highly sculpted designs, epitomized
by the Bilbao Guggenheim Museum. Gehry plays with ideas when selecting the
optimum shape for his buildings. He does this by iterating between sketches and
physical and computer-generated models in order to make choices about shape
and form. Gehry trained using drawings and physical models. He is a craftsman
who loves to work with his hands, sculpting shapes in a range of materials such as
cardboard, clay, and plasticine. For him, computers were initially alien, representing a medium that constrained creativity and expression. But his designs were
difficult to engineer and build. It usually cost too much to convert the sculpted
models into constructed artefacts. Then, in the early 1990s, James Glymph, a
production engineer from the automotive industry, joined Gehry's workshop in
Santa Monica, bringing with him knowledge of digital design tools and production logistics. He began to harness the power of advanced computer modelling
and simulation to engineer Gehry's designs, turning them into viable buildings.
An iterative process evolved in which Gehry was able to play with different
options, retaining control over design choices. The story of Gehry's work described here succinctly illustrates the use of IvT for making choices, selecting
from a range of possible design options by enabling engineers and designers to
play with solutions. Commenting on the use of this technology, Gehry says that it

provides a way for me to get closer to the craft. In the past, there were many layers
between my rough sketch and the final building, and the feeling of the design could get
lost before it reached the craftsman. It feels like I've been speaking a foreign language
and now, all of a sudden, the craftsman understands me. In this case, the computer is
not dehumanising, it's an interpreter.[65]

Gehry and his design team are involved in many activities within the 'think,
play, do' schema, from developing original ideas for a building to operationalizing them in construction processes. But, as we shall see in the case study later
in this chapter, much of what makes Gehry innovative is the ability to play. The
example demonstrates how to take ideas from the mind's eye and prepare them
for action and implementation. Chapter 4 explored the use of IvT to aid

thinking about problems in enquiry-based processes, such as in experimentation and the generation and discovery of new knowledge. The main focus of this chapter is the link between thought and action. It shows how IvT can be used to support selection processes, help make choices, and shape outcomes in what Schrage calls 'serious play' (see Chapter 1). It builds upon analysis of the use of IvT in new product development in P&G and in engineering design in Arup described in Chapter 3.

Many firms and organizations recognize the need to develop ideas from which new value will flow, but most find it difficult to choose which options to take. For designers this is their stock-in-trade. And it is the ability to play with ideas through collaborative and iterative processes involving other experts and specialists that leads to choices being made. This selection environment ultimately limits the range of possible ideas that could be implemented, and thereby limits risk and uncertainty before further, expensive development work takes place in the 'doing' phase of innovation (see Chapter 6).

In this chapter we show that using IvT enables firms to play more rapidly and at lower cost. Iterations can occur more swiftly as scientists, technologists, engineers, and designers are able to share knowledge and data, working concurrently on different aspects of an idea or problem. They manage control over work stages and different versions of projects and processes electronically. The cost of changing designs before physical production is started can be reduced enormously. Clients and customers using IvT can be involved in new product and service development at a much earlier stage, thus enabling them to participate in making choices about designs. They can experience possible outcomes—physically or virtually—before expensive decisions are taken. The ability to use IvT to play with choices can therefore increase efficiency and create more accurate, lasting, and appropriate solutions. There is a focus on engineering design—one of the most important activities in innovation, and also on innovation in architecture and the built environment, which is perceived as being highly traditional, but is actually illustrative of the range of new innovative practices built around the possibilities of IvT.

The selection and choice-making aspects of 'play' relate closely to design processes. The chapter begins with a summary of the role of design in innovation. The difficulties of measuring design and the role of 'play' in innovation are discussed. Design practices themselves are changing to accommodate opportunities offered by IvT, and these emerging design practices are explored in the following section. Case studies are presented to illustrate facets of 'play' in different sectors, illustrating the ways in which selection takes place using IvT. The first case—'playing with models'—illustrates the use of models for problem-solving in engineering design and shows the ways in which engineering choices were made in finding a solution to save the Leaning Tower of Pisa. Three further case studies show different ways in which designers 'play with technology', including analysis of Gehry's work processes, a study of Polaroid's prototyping process for a new digital camera, and the use of simulation by Ricardo engineering. The use of games technology is also discussed in serious business decision-making in the military, health and education sectors, and the entertainments industry. This section also explores how users can play more directly in decisions about new products and processes. The chapter ends with a discussion of new design practices, examining the benefits, challenges, and limitations of IvT and the possible dangers in its use.

Box 5.1   Measuring play

It is difficult to use conventional R&D measurements—in basic research, applied research, and experimental development—for any of the categories of 'think, play, and do'. Nonetheless, in Chapter 4 we discussed basic research data related to think activities, and there are also connections between applied research and experimental development and what we describe as play. Significant problems remain in using these measures.

Applied research and experimental development covers all expenditures of firms up until the point of the first working commercial prototype. Given the ability of IvT to simulate, rapid prototype, and iterate between different stages of design, development, and manufacturing, it is hard to establish this end point of R&D. The *Frascati Manual*, the OECD's guidebook on the collection of R&D statistics, has long recognized the difficulty of finding the cut-off between R&D and subsequent innovative activities. Indeed the *Frascati Manual* states that the line between experimental development and the other stages of the innovation process is 'fuzzy' and will 'vary from industry to industry' (OECD 1992). The cost of innovation expands, moreover, as they move towards the market and experimental development accounts for a high percentage of R&D expenditure. The innovative activities that firms engage in beyond experimental development or after the creation of the first working commercial prototype can also be progressively expensive, time-consuming, and risky.

At the root of the *Frascati Manual* is the 'first-generation' model of innovation process (see Chapter 2) with its assumption that investments in R&D create greater opportunities for innovation by increasing the ready supply of economically useful new products and services. The innovation process, as we know, is far more complex than this.

Given these shortcomings, it remains difficult to measure the costs of play. Whatever the merits (or deficiency) of R&D as a measure of innovative input, the level of expenditure of industrial firms on the third component of R&D—experimental development—is considerable, and the extent of this expenditure is broadly indicative. Industrial firms in the USA spent $47 billion in experimental development in 1972 and $66 billion in 1982. By 1992 expenditures rose to $92 billion and by 2002 this reached $130 billion (all figures in 1996 constant prices) (NSB 2004). These patterns of growth can also be seen in a variety of OECD countries, notably Finland, Ireland, and South Korea.

Another partial measure of play activities relates to expenditure on design. The UK government estimates that UK firms spent £26.7 billion on design services in 2000 (DCMS 2001). These design services include expenditures on brand identity, corporate identity, new product development, interior and external design, and design departments within industrial firms. Most of these design activities are performed in-house with close to 55 per cent of large firms in the UK reporting that they have an internal design department (Design Council 2003). There is, however, a large and diverse design services industry in the UK with 3,000–4,000 specialist design consultancies. Between 65,000 and 80,000 designers are employed by UK industry to perform design activities (DCMS 2001; Design Council 2003). Design services are estimated to account for £1 billion of UK exports.

5.2 The practice of design

Design and engineering are central to the innovation process and play a key role in the way new products and processes are developed. The main characteristic of design and engineering problem-solving is that it draws on ideas generated in 'think' and connects them to operations in 'do' thereby uniting the innovation process.

IvT enables designers to play this important integrative role in the new innovation process but there are many necessary changes associated with its use. Before we begin to examine the role of IvT in 'play' we need to understand how engineers and designers actually work and appreciate some of the problems with existing practice.

Combining theory and practice

Previous studies of design and engineering emphasize the differences between scientific and technological problem-solving (cf. Constant 1980; Vincenti 1990; Simon 1996; Perlow 1999). Whereas the former primarily concerns the development of theories and predictions about the physical world, the latter normally starts with a functional requirement and seeks to use scientific principles and technological components and systems to help achieve desired goals. In this view engineers and designers work differently from scientists by working closely with a variety of actors in the innovation process such as users to help understand the functional requirements and goals of the task they are undertaking. They tend to be practical, pragmatic, and goal-oriented (Nightingale 1998; Pavitt 1998). The stark differences outlined here, however, ignore the important practical components of science and the theoretical basis of engineering, and furthermore do not account for the ways in which IvT is blurring the boundaries between scientists and technologists.

Design and engineering involves the preparation and application of an elegant and efficient choice of solution to a problem or opportunity. The knowledge that designers and engineers use for these purposes grows incrementally, but 'traditional' knowledge such as the Second Law of Thermodynamics remain an essential element in problem-solving routines and methods. Furthermore, engineering relies on a set of 'heuristics' about problem-solving that is framed by the technological trajectories the engineers are working within (Dosi 1988). Whilst engineering and design knowledge draws from scientific principles it also relies heavily on 'rules of thumb', 'informed guesses', 'routines' and 'norms' of problem-solving that are built up through education and experience with real-world problems. Engineers and designers learn to use practical, iterative approaches in their education, which often combines a problem-oriented approach with theory about physical properties, and draw upon a vast body of knowledge about how things work to solve their design problems (Vincenti 1990). Even seemingly simple designs can draw upon both routine knowledge used in 'normal' design and less well-defined knowledge carried out in 'radical' design activities. Constant (1980) refers to the development of *recursive practice*, a slow and steady accretion of engineering knowledge about how things work and how they fit together, involving judgement and intuition about which potential solutions to select for analysis.

Social factors

The decisions engineers and designers make are based not only on physical and technical factors but also social, economic, and sometimes political parameters. Furthermore, social and informal culture, and networks and patterns of communication remain of great importance in engineering and design (cf. Allen 1977). Project work is commonly carried out in diverse, multidisciplinary teams that span a number of different organizations (see Chapter 7). Team members communicate by sketching and telling stories about related design and engineering projects to help develop solutions. Studies have shown that designers and engineers need time for face-to-face interaction and time to work alone (Perlow 1999; Salter and Gann 2003). This balance between the need for interaction and solitary work creates deep and structural tensions in organizations that are often reflected in heavy workloads, late nights, and cycles of heroics and overwork (Perlow 1999) (see the discussion of creative workers and workplaces in Chapter 7).

Modularity

Simon (1996) argues that for engineers to solve complex problems they need to break them down into modules or small parts. By decomposing tasks engineers are able to focus their work on an area of manageable complexity and apply their techniques and capabilities to a narrow range of tasks while leaving the remaining problems to other groups. In this way engineers are able to divide tasks across many different subteams and units and increase both the efficiency and effectiveness of problem-solving.

The concept of modularity and the design rules that flow from it help create a structure for managing decomposed design processes (Eppinger et al. 1990) (see Chapter 6 for further discussion of modularity). In environments where modularity is the guiding principle in design, innovation often involves new combinations of existing technologies applied to a specific problem. Some designers and engineers work as systems integrators, choosing components and technologies and specifying the interfaces between different systems combining new components with different vintages of technology (Baldwin and Clark 2000; Brusoni et al. 2001). As we shall see in Chapter 6, modularity has its limitations, but even when it is highly appropriate engineers and designers still require a deep knowledge of different technologies and components and how they fit together.

Sequential processes

Traditionally, design decisions are attained sequentially, making them slow, exclusive and progressively expensive. Large amounts of resources can be consumed before decisions are taken to change course or not to proceed at all. In some sectors, like the built environment, this process was successful in producing the occasional spectacular, one-off, innovative result. But more often than not sequential decision-making failed the expectations of clients and frustrated architects, engineers, and suppliers, whilst fuelling the coffers of lawyers in legal wrangles that ensued over responsibilities and performance when things went wrong. In these cases it was almost inevitable that the value added through design was diminished. Whether or not a high-quality result was produced depended on luck and the coincidence of good intentions on the part of all the participants (Gann 2000). Similar problems can be found in traditional product development processes in which choice and selection of options may not be possible until expensive physical prototyping and development work has been carried out.

Traditional work organization and skills requirements

The built environment provides a useful example of the problems of traditional design and engineering practices found in many industries. The skills used for designing buildings, for example, are highly codified, with several years of education needed before practice is allowed. In this traditional model there is a rigid division of labour where professional boundaries are strongly demarcated. Everyone knows his or her place and work has to progress in a particular procedural manner. Promotion is based on movement up a graded scale in relation to responsibility and experience. Many firms operate as partnerships in which seniority and experience are often valued above innovativeness, novelty, and creativity, and remuneration is standardized for routine and substitutable tasks. Competition among design firms is often price-based as there are few differences between most traditional design, engineering, and product development practices. There is little or no upstream and downstream integration in this business model.

Design often involves multidisciplinary, and sometimes large, teams of engineers and technicians as collocation enables different engineers to successfully work together in solving problems (Gann and Salter 2000). These teams, however, spend much of their time routinely producing drawings and checking small but important details. Edison's dictum that 'innovation requires 1% inspiration and 99% perspiration' applies. Problem-solving is largely paper-based, with sketching being the preferred method of communication in the development of solutions. Although firms working in the built environment were early adopters of computers they have generally been used for simple, repetitive tasks, and in some firms CAD is likened to a fast and expensive eraser. The design and engineering system is bounded by quality checks and professional practices including the use of regulations and guidelines. Engineers use mathematical models and designers make expensive physical prototypes. There are few possibilities for cross-fertilization of ideas nor to relate to the initial body of ideas in the 'thinking' phase of a project or process, and links to marketing personnel and clients are also limited. Opportunities to interact with those responsible for operations—'doing'—are equally limited with few connections to suppliers and specialist producers. There are few feedback loops in this linear, sequential process.

5.3 Emerging practices of design

The organization and structure of design and engineering practice described above has particular implications for the ways in which professionals work individually and together, and shapes the ways in which knowledge is developed and transferred. As we shall see in the following case studies, IvT influences all these issues. The development of models lies at the heart of design and engineering knowledge and underpins the ways in which people play with solutions, thereby altering traditional practices.

'Playing' with models

Ted Happold, the structural engineer and designer working with Arup on the Sydney Opera House in the 1960s, articulated the importance of modelling in developing solutions, observing that

the solution is conceived as a model, initially a mental model. This is developed and communicated in a variety of ways: description, drawings, physical models (representational or form-finding), analogous models, mathematical or computer models. It is only by developing the model into a communicable form that the concept becomes imaginable and can be evaluated. (Quoted in Groak 1998)

Simulation and modelling have always played a central role in engineering problem-solving. Models provide a mechanism for engineers to learn about artefacts before and after they have been built. Physical prototypes are expensive and time-consuming to create but they play an important function in developing and verifying design decisions. Models enable engineers to examine different options and weigh the choices of structural elements, materials, and components against one another.

In 1976, Happold established the consulting engineering and design organization, Buro Happold, which by 2004 employed more than 700 engineers working in twelve countries. His insight into the process of designing a solution to an engineering problem links the creative process of ideas generation with its development into a model that can be played with or evaluated. The iterative notion of selection and verification has resulted in a description of designers as 'practitioner researchers' because of the ways in which they research and solve problems (Groak and Krimgold 1989). Practitioner researchers operate as a bridge between ideas and practice, linking artistic, imaginative, and creative elements with practical, realizable outcomes. This involves a demanding set of capabilities because as John Makepeace, the furniture designer and maker, notes:

An artist sets a different benchmark from a maker. A maker will want to get it right ten times out of ten. An artist has more elusive targets. One success out of ten will suffice, with the other nine pieces acting as sketches, prototypes and support material along the road to that significant artistic result. (Quoted in Myerson 1995: 195)

An important part of this process is the way in which ideas are represented so that different designers and engineers can 'converse' using visualizations. The way in which designs are represented at different stages in their development directly relates to how choices are made in developing a solution (Groak 1998). Groak suggested that representations are among the principal tools for exploring, manipulating, and conjuring possible solutions. He cites a range of representational techniques from the invention of mathematical perspective by Brunelleschi and Alberti to mechanical drawing of third-angle projection used in production drawings in many industries today.[66] Different representational methods provide designers and engineers with different perspectives on particular problems and their solutions. These views allow what Groak called a 'playfulness' in investigation because they can show a whole range of non-obvious things that may be important and interesting. He foresaw future design and engineering practice supported by a set of methods and tools that would allow designers to participate in greater interaction with users, clients, and other specialists, enabling designers to confront problems with 'more brains, less brawn'.

Designers learn by playing with representational forms, sometimes creating their own physical analogue models such as the hanging chains used by Gaudi to verify the structure of the Segrada Famillia in Barcelona at the turn of the nineteenth and twentieth centuries. These models provide far more information than can be sketched and calculated using paper and pencil. Groak (1998) provides an example of how design engineers play with solutions using models to create a dialogue between representations. In the design of a complex curved surface, he cites the use of a stocking-net model to define high and low points in a structure. A pre-tensioned rubber membrane was produced from this, moving the rubber parts to the system points defined in the previous model. Plaster casts were then taken from these and a 'dressmaking exercise' was carried out to assemble pieces to make the curved surface. A 1:10 model was made demonstrating how the structure could be produced in full scale. Groak argues that it would be extremely difficult to manipulate drawings and 2D sheets to achieve the same result. Another example provided by Groak is Alvar Aalto's use of point sources of light to represent movement of sound around a space. Auditorium acoustics have subsequently been modelled using this technique. Computer models explore acoustic properties that are used in conjunction with recorded sounds superimposed within the computer model in a process of 'auralization', enabling designers to simulate the sounds in different parts of a planned concert hall. Whilst the use of ray-tracing has made acoustics more accurate and predictable, judgement is still required to interpret the results to enable designs to satisfy different user groups (Hough 1996). This example illustrates the mix of physical and digital modelling that takes place when designers develop a solution.

Building the model: the Leaning Tower of Pisa

An example of the use of IvT in combination with traditional engineering knowledge and practice can be found in the solution to the problem of instability in the Leaning Tower of Pisa. The tower is about 60 m tall, weighs 14,500 tons, and has foundations with a diameter of 19.6 m. In 1990 the foundations inclined due south at about 5.5 degrees to the horizontal and the seventh cornice overhung ground level by about 4.5 m. For most of the twentieth century the inclination of the tower was increasing. The rate of inclination in 1990 was twice that in 1930 and an instantaneous buckling failure of the masonry could have occurred without warning. Computer modelling of the tower helped produce a solution that prevented its collapse.

The tower was constructed as a hollow cylindrical bell tower for the cathedral. Construction began in 1173, progressed to about a quarter of its final size by 1178, and then stopped for about 100 years. Work recommenced in

1272 and the tower reached the seventh cornice height in 1278. Work to add the bell chamber took place between 1360 and 1370. Had the construction work taken place in a continuous fashion, the tower would have collapsed due to unstable ground conditions. The two long pauses in activity, however, provided time for the ground to harden and resist the load of the structure.

Stabilization of the tower was achieved by means of an innovative method of soil extraction, which induced a small reduction in inclination not visible to the casual onlooker. Implementation of this remedial work required computer modelling and large-scale development trials with an exceptional level of continuous monitoring and daily communications to maintain control over the project (Burland 2004).

The leader of the project to prevent the collapse of the Tower of Pisa was Professor John Burland, currently Emeritus Professor in Soil Mechanics at Imperial College London. Burland's research interests lie in the mechanics of tunnelling-induced ground movements and their progressive effects on build-ings and mitigation. His involvement in the work on the Leaning Tower of Pisa lasted for twelve years, from 1990 to the end of 2001. He spent on average two days per month on the project at Pisa and three to four hours per day back at Imperial College. Burland uses models extensively in his work, notably his research on the potential impact on thirty buildings of the construction of a new underground line in London.

The engineer is modelling all the time. You do not do anything without modelling, whether this involves some simple conceptualisation or a highly sophisticated model. Before doing anything on Pisa, we knew it was on the point of falling over, very delicate. We had to develop a good physical or numerical model in order to investigate stabilisation measures. It was unthinkable to go in and try anything without it being well and truly underpinned by modelling.

The issue that initially exercised Burland in his work in Pisa was how to validate the model. He spent the first year learning about how the tower was built and what the original builders did as they corrected the lean during its construction. He had to become an architectural historian with an understanding of what the original builders had been doing so as to reproduce the history of the inclin-ation of the tower. This then provided his team with a deduced history of behaviour that could be used for validating a model.

Professor David Potts, Head of Soil Mechanics at Imperial College, and Burland spent a long time developing numerical models of the tower with different degrees of sophistication, checking to see if they correlated with their version of history. A model of the tower was built on a computer checked against the historical research. Burland and Potts were able to get a very close fit and as this had never been achieved before it gave them confidence in the model.

The team then began to temporarily stabilize the tower and further refined the model on the basis of this work. In 1993, 600 tons of lead were very gently and progressively placed on the north side of the tower using precise measurements. The tower responded extraordinarily closely to the predictions in the model.

At least six permanent solutions to the tower's lean had been previously devised and these were evaluated on the model. Each solution had its supporters, many of whom were very dogmatic about what could be achieved and how it should be done. The model showed that their implementation would in each case cause the tower to fall. The model was therefore very useful in testing these ideas before the eventual solution of soil extraction was decided upon. Modelling showed that in principle the technique of extracting soil would work.

The basis of the model used by Burland and his team goes back to sophisticated models of soil behaviour that emerged from Cambridge University in the 1960s. Potts had years of experience with these non-linear, incremental plasticity models at Imperial College. The computer techniques have to be extraordinarily rigorous to ensure that what you are doing is converging towards correct answers. According to Burland there are many programs that are unreliable because the computational procedures are not right. Potts uses a very large package called Imperial College Finite Element Program (ICFEP) which is the only program of its kind and is owned by Imperial College.

The reason Burland uses the word 'modelling' rather than 'simulation' is because physical models are used extensively in his field of soil mechanics. This is especially the case where complex properties need to be understood. For example, soil exhibits a very complex mechanical behaviour, and physical and computational modelling is used in order to understand this. He describes the general lessons that emerged from his experience of using modelling at Pisa as being the need to understand as much as possible the history of the project. In this case he had to understand the existing building going right back to its design and construction to explore what is going on physically. The case illustrates the value of modelling, the extreme caution required in their construction, and the benefits of links with the research base in universities.

'Playing' with technology

Design and engineering practices are changing markedly with the use of IvT, which combines paper-based, physical processes with new, virtual digital processes. In many cases this results in the use of both physical and virtual design environments that complement traditional approaches. The emerging design process embodies the capability to move fluidly between ideas and it can be more inclusive than previously, involving a range of participants—customers, suppliers, collaborators—who interact simultaneously by shaping and selecting from different choices. Yet design and engineering like innovation itself is often a highly uncertain activity. Mistakes can be common and the costs of failure can be high.

The drivers for introducing IvT include reducing costs and improving accuracy. Simulation and modelling technologies can help designers better understand and play with physical properties and behaviour before they construct artefacts and systems, allowing them to 'learn before doing' and to experiment with different technologies and components (cf. Pisano 1997).

The specific technologies that enable designers and engineers to play in this way have emerged from a range of different sectors and applications underpinned by advances in computing power and improvements in visual and other interfaces. CAD tools and computer games are at the core of these technologies. In many design and engineering environments, selection and choice is aided by access to databases and the use of data mining tools including navigation and visualization facilities. But there are as yet no definitive ways to classify the types of IvT to support 'play' in design and engineering. Some systems are multifunctional, others are highly specialized. Many support 'thinking' and 'doing' as well as 'playing'.

IvT helps engineers manage complex, multidisciplinary, and collaborative projects by providing the means through which various forms of integration can occur. If, as Simon (1996) suggests, engineers solve complex problems by breaking them down into smaller components, IvT can assist in analysis at the decomposed level and in the reintegration of those components. It helps ensure that there is technical compatibility and provides cost-effective ways of manipulating and playing with potential solutions informed by the requirements of systemic integration and interfaces. Other examples of IvT supporting design and engineering include expert systems that help guide good practice and decision-making processes in product development and concurrent engineering, and methodologies and tools for managing information flows in design and engineering, such as the Design Structure Matrix (Eppinger 2001).

One of the key challenges using this technology is how to achieve holistic simulations. A possible solution in some cases is the use of avatars: digital representations of people in simulated, virtual environments with embedded personal attributes that allow responses to be assessed in many different physical conditions such as sound, humidity, temperature, lighting, and colour. These can be interpreted for different parts of the body. As we have seen in Chapter 3, such techniques are used in work on vehicle crash worthiness where, instead of destroying expensive cars and crash test dummies, a computer model generates an avatar, a simulation replacing the dummy. This tool can model specific types of injuries caused by crashes.

When used in an appropriate manner IvT enables designers and engineers to play with different attributes such as functionality, build quality, and impact, and perceptual impacts such as the effect of design on the mind and senses (Gann et al. 2003; Whyte and Gann 2003). In doing so, it opens new opportunities for non-professionals to participate in making choices and design decisions. The design system has the potential to become more fluid; thinkers play at doing, doers think, and clients can be involved in decisions on thinking and doing.

An increasing proportion of design work is being carried out on computer rather than on paper, although most engineers are still heavy users of paper (Salter and Gann 2001). Computer programs are used to assist in many aspects of routine, 'normal' design in stable environments. The automation of routine tasks can improve accuracy and predictability in areas such as air movement, acoustics, lighting, thermal comfort, energy consumption, safety, and utility. At the same time the development of 'radical' design options can be supported using these technologies, because IvT can produce new information about functionality, build quality, and impact that was previously impossible to access: what Zuboff (1988) calls 'informating the process'. The use of IvT, for example, can reveal aspects of the basic behaviour of a material or system that traditional design methods, craft judgement, and decision-making had no means of representing and interpreting.

Many digital design tools are easily affordable and readily available. They can support designers to do more than they could in the past, more quickly. IvT provides the basis for digital models that assist in abstracting physical phenomena and allow designers to experiment, simulate, and play with different options. This is leading to a new culture of modelling and simulation in which traditional sequential practices of design are being opened to more concurrent diagnostic enquiry (Schrage 2000).

Designers routinely use techniques to overlay one option or part of a design upon another. These methods are used to explore, play games, and critically select optimal solutions. IvT is used here to support the processes of playing with solutions. Some of these technologies have evolved from developments in the computer games industry and a growing array of software tools have been developed to support processes of selection and analysis, from Ashby's materials selection charts—which are now available as digital tools using computer visualization interfaces[67]—to software for structural analysis. Thousands of programs are available, many of them originating from in-house software packages developed by designers, engineers, or researchers with specialist knowledge in particular areas of design selection and analysis.

Some of the ways in which IvT is being used to 'play' in design and how this changes processes of design is described in the following case studies.

Box 5.2 Playing with serious games

Many of the technological advances seen in the realms of simulation and representation have derived from the game industry: the world of platforms like Nintendo's Game Boy, Microsoft's X-Box, and Sony's Play Station, and programs such as Grand Theft Auto and the Sims. This is itself a substantial market: games software sales alone reached $7 billion in 2003. Games are everywhere, they are found on computers, mobile phones, and the back of aeroplane seats. Games technology contributes significantly to the entertainment industry, from gaming machines to cartoons and special effects in films. But there is also a 'serious games' element to these developments found in education, military, and health applications amongst others.

Consider the expense and risk in training pilots. Simulators, such as those produced by Thales Training and Simulation, create a virtual environment where pilots can train on instruments to fly at night and land at every major airport in the world virtually and realistically at limited cost and zero risk. Pilots can learn to make choices with feedback loops that improve decision-making, which in future may be life-saving.

The military has long known the value of games. Jose Vargas, writing in the *Washington Post*,[68] argues that the Pentagon is estimated to spend $4 billion annually on simulation tools and software, and has developed a number of popular games, like Full Spectrum Warrior and America's Army, to train soldiers. The latter game apparently has 4 million registered users. The popularity of such games is unsurprising given the fact that the average age of the US half-million-plus armed forces is twenty: the Game Boy generation.[69]

Games technology is used in the training of surgeons, helps managers learn about team building, assists currency traders make better decisions through repeated simulations, and can be used to teach children about science.

The architect: Frank Gehry

Frank Gehry's best-known works include the Guggenheim Museum in Bilbao, Spain (1991–7), the 'Ginger and Fred' office building in Prague (1992–6), the Weatherhead School of Management, Case Western Reserve University, Ohio (1999–2002), the Experience Music Project, Seattle (1999–2000), and the Walt Disney Concert Hall, Los Angeles (1989–2004). These gesture-based buildings would have been technically difficult, if not impossible, to realize before the late 1980s because it was not easy to model the fluid surface shapes and engineering structures using traditional CAD systems. The vision of the building for Gehry's clients could not be realized without a new kind of technology application.

Gehry's work is based on highly sculpted, geometrically complex forms, created through an iterative process of physical and computer modelling. His practice invested in a CATIA system in 1990 having observed its use in producing curved shapes at Chrysler automobiles and in the design of Boeing's aircraft. This system was introduced as part of a radically new approach to design, development, and construction, managed by James Glymph, an expert in production process design. The new approach created the opportunity for Gehry to be involved in more of the overall design process than had previously been possible. He made the physical, sculpted shapes by hand. Scale models were then produced from these by Gehry's assistants and scanned into 3D computer models using a digitizer—a medical plotter—originally designed to record the shape of the human head for brain surgery. The digitized forms are manipulated using CATIA software on IBM RISC 6000 machines, providing the ability to accurately model and engineer every spline and node point in a building. This was an advance on the polygonal rendering techniques used in most CAD systems in the 1990s. More physical models are then created for design verification using rapid-prototyping machines, including a Helysis rapid-prototyping solid modeller (see Chapter 6 for further discussion of rapid prototyping). Once the final design has been agreed, electronic design data can be transferred digitally to various specialist fabricators working in steel, stone, glass, titanium, and composite materials. The design office works closely but 'remotely' with suppliers and subcontractors to reduce costs and improve buildability.[70]

This process was used successfully to coordinate the production of idiosyncratic designs using standardized components such as the façade for the Ginger and Fred office building. It was also used to produce buildings made of discrete, bespoke parts such as the steelwork structure in the Guggenheim Museum. The process of designing and producing the Bilbao Guggenheim Museum involved designs from the CATIA software program being automatically translated into geometric databases and digitally transferred from Santa Monica in California to the steel fabricators' BOCAD CNC software in northern Spain. The approach eliminated traditional sequential steps in the process such as developing working and shop drawings. Each unique piece of steel was bar-coded and erected on-site using a laser surveying system linked to the CATIA model for positioning. The use of tape measures on-site was unnecessary.

This process required a radically new approach to architecture and construction. As Glymph expresses it, the company wants to achieve 'a fundamental reshuffling of the roles, responsibilities, and compensation structures for participants across the industry as a consequence of the digital revolution'.[71] The Gehry example combines physical and computer modelling to improve production processes in the design and construction of complex building forms. The system assists in providing predictability from the use of repetition in manufacturing without sacrificing form in overall design. It shows how shared databases can be used as an essential tool in new integrated design and production processes by different specialists located in different countries. The result is a radical change in design and construction that places the designer within the team at the centre of the process, enabling better value to be provided to clients. The designers' responsibilities are increased because they generate the database around which everyone else works and on which different options are played with.

The design office is at the same time placed in closer relationship with contractors, suppliers, and subcontractors. This approach blurs the traditional distinctions between where architecture and engineering stopped and con-struction started: tasks are divided differently from those in the traditional design–construction process. Thinking, playing, and doing overlap, and sup-ported by the same IvT tool kit are conducted concurrently. Moreover, the process enables better measurement of performance improvements when the project is implemented, for example in the number of change orders and defects in manufacturing, and on-site assembly, which reduces the need for cutting, adjustment, and defect rectification.

In its formative stages the development of this radically new approach clearly required the patronage of innovative clients who were prepared to underwrite the risks of innovation, such as Walt Disney.

As a result of its success in using these technologies the Gehry practice established a company in 2002—Gehry Technologies (GT)—to 'raise the level of technological fluency within architectural practice'. According to James Glymph, the CEO of GT, faster, cheaper computers make it feasible for firms of all sizes to use the digitally driven process that Gehry follows in his practice, and the process is suitable for a variety of project types, and not just the high-end cultural buildings for which Gehry is known.[72] GT collaborates with IBM and Dassault Systèmes, the American Institute of Architects, the Civil Engin-eering Research Foundation, and MIT's Media Lab.

A further indicator of Gehry's success is the number of new commissions the practice has received for high-profile museums, galleries, concert halls, and other publicly visible buildings such as university libraries.

The Gehry example shows how IvT enables architectural design to become reintegrated within the total design and construction process. But it may also assist thinking about the design of space in relation to social uses in a variety of different markets. The organization of space is seen by some architects as being of equal importance to the physical development of space itself. This requires an understanding about the use of design, not merely to provide space for what organizations think they do at the moment but for a much more active involvement in design as an agent of organizational change to improve per-formance in users' business processes. The ability to 'play' with options on digital systems in collaboration with users may result in more efficient, effect-ive, and attractive buildings.

A new Polaroid camera[73]

In the late 1990s, Polaroid sought to develop a new digital camera that would print passport pictures. The primary market for the new product was profes-sional photographers. Polaroid estimated that some 12 million portrait pictures for passports were taken each year. The idea for the new product came from Polaroid sales agents talking to passport photographers.

The new camera had to be lightweight, flexible, and ergonomic. It would need to be able to print quickly and at a high quality both passport and large-size pictures. It would also need to print identical or different pictures of individuals on the same film. The camera was to possess advanced photographic technologies such as sonar rangefinders, bounce flash capabilities, and a high-resolution printer. The liquid crystal display had to be relatively large and of high quality to help the customer decide on the particular picture in memory to be printed.

The first stage in the development of the camera was to determine the size and design of its motherboard. This motherboard needed to contain all the necessary components in order to make the camera function, including its visual processor, memory chip, power coupling, and printer drivers. The size of the motherboard was regulated by the nature of the components, all of which were standard and off-the-shelf. The design of the motherboard was done in-house through the use of an electronic circuit design tool that identified the location of different electronic modules and drew circuit connections across the board. This design tool produced a first virtual design, which was then passed on to a specialist manufacturer to make a physical version of the motherboard to Polaroid's specification.

Polaroid's designers began to build up a full working prototype of the new product, placing different elements such as handles and the location of the printer paper discharge around the motherboard. They began by using a series of roughly made paper-based prototypes. Users were invited to comment on various ergonomic options and prototype configurations. An initial shape was agreed and designers then used a CAD program to translate the physical model into a digital model or virtual prototype. The designer added different elements into the model, incorporating modules with different features and functions. The CAD software found a number of clashes between the different modules. By revising and iterating the features of the design the designers completed a working virtual model. This model was passed to manufacturing and external suppliers for production of the first working prototype.

It was discovered in trials of the new prototype that the quality of the printed picture was poor because of the appearance of small lines. After an extensive period of testing it was found that the location of different components on the motherboard was creating interference. The memory chip for the digital picture processor was very sensitive to electrical interference from other components on the motherboard, such as power coupling. As a result, the motherboard was redesigned and the modules were moved around to maximize the space between the digital picture processor and the power coupling. The new electronic layout for the motherboard was sent for external manufacture and incorporated into the final product. The product has been successfully launched in a variety of models on the market. Another new MiniPortrait

Camera for retailers was launched in 2003. Overall, it took one year from the original conception of the product idea to full launch.

The Polaroid passport camera case shows how IvT increases the speed, flexibility, and economy of the design process. The problems in the mother-board design could be quickly addressed as the circuit connections could automatically be redrawn following the realignment of its various components. Designers were able to play with different solutions. The virtual representation of the prototype enabled clashes between components to be identified and redressed prior to the production of the first physical prototype. As a result, a new product family for a major market based on new designs around existing technologies and components was developed in one year.

Designing a new bra[74]

Bras are big business. It is estimated that in the UK the bra market is worth £850 million and in the US market, $4.6 billion. The modern bra has as many as forty-three components, including pulleys, airbags, advanced plastic moulds, and silicone-filled inserts. According to *The Economist*, it has long been a small miracle of engineering.

In the late 1990s the bra manufacturer, Charnos, recognized that there were several major problems with its existing bras. First, many bras contained metal objects that made them difficult to wash. Second, they provided inadequate support for larger women, which is a problem, as in the UK the average size of bra has increased from 34B in the 1950s to 36C today. Third, some bra designs pinched the skin around the armpit, the so-called 'ouch factor'. A study by Nottingham Trent University showed that almost 70 per cent of women were wearing a bra that did not fit them either because of their inability to find the right size or the fact that bra size alters with wear and washing.

Two potential design solutions to these problems involved either using stronger support material, which was often wire and did not solve the problem, or to provide less support for the bra, which was also unsatisfactory. Charnos decided in 1998 to produce a new kind of bra. Designing a better bra was a major engineering challenge, and Charnos engaged UK-based design firm Seymour Powell with the brief to go back to engineering fundamentals.

In order to better understand the design of bras, Seymour Powell conducted a range of user experience workshops with women using the current generation of products. It also explored the experiences of companies like Adidas and Nike in their development of new forms of wearable plastic in athletic footwear.

To find the solution to the problem it worked with a range of IvT. Seymour Powell designers began searching for a solution by scanning initial sketches into a CAD model using Alias Wavefront for form generation. Then, after early assessment of 3D elements produced by stereolithography, Seymour Powell tried them out on rigid dressmaker's busts. However, these rigid busts were a poor guide to actual behaviour.

At this stage Seymour Powell brought in Product Design and Development (PDD), a London-based product innovation consultancy, and it went back to scientific fundamentals to gain a better understanding of shape and movement of breasts. As many as 180 volunteers were laser-scanned with the help of Nottingham University and Coventry-based 3D scanners. The images of each bust were averaged to create a unique database of bust shapes. This database allowed Seymour Powell and PDD to better understand cup sizes and shapes and some generic structural shapes began to evolve. Whilst the scanning provided accurate data it could only be used to generate digital forms for either the unsupported bust or one held in a conventionally underwired bra. The scanned data, however, did provide a basis for scale and proportion for a 3D form, and allowed the project team to get closer to the final design much more quickly than by using traditional measuring techniques.

Phil Shade, senior designer at PDD (*Smart Technology* 2001), says: 'It was clear that the variety of shapes meant the geometry had to be far more than a mean average.' Based on rapid prototyping, PDD made silicon rubber moulds from the Alias Wavefront surfaces and produced foam castings. These wired-foam armatures were used in comfort trials. One of the early challenges facing PDD was to select the thickness of the armature: the structural element of the new bra. From the wearer's point of view, this needed to be thin enough to make it invisible and comfortable, but also needed to provide improved support and be robust enough to withstand repeated washing.

Another company, Arrk Formation, was sent a range of 3D models and used rapid prototyping to help produce moulds. These moulds, however, were still preliminary and incomplete. Through an iterative process of design and drawing from the experience of Adidas' running shoe design, the project team developed a mould that had a hard central cast surrounded by a soft rubber surround.

This new design, mixing a hard case with soft rubber, was then sewn into existing soft fabrics at Charnos and consumer-tested. The process still did not lead to a fully satisfactory design and the team realized that it still did not know enough about the movement of the human body and how these movements relate to the design of the mould. In early 1999 the team approached Arup Advanced Technology Group to conduct an FEA of the breast. Within Arup, the project was led by Louise Waddingham, and her team drew from a wide range of skills developed from working with designers, engineers, and manufacturers and from specializing in using 'advanced engineering methods in the vehicle, nuclear and seismic engineering industries'. The idea of this simulation was to see how the new design would perform under stress and loads:

Arup used dynamic non-linear finite element techniques to analyse the bra's structural performance. A computational representation of the bra on a body was created by scanning the geometry of a model. The bra was then constructed using techniques usually associated with the modelling of airbags and seatbelts in cars. This enabled the non-linearity of the bra material, contact interaction with the body and large displacements to be represented. The performance of the bra was then analysed by applying vertical accelerations to simulate a person jogging lightly or walking briskly. The analysis displayed fluctuating stresses in the bra cups and straps, varying with the walking pattern, and a higher constant stress around the base band where the bra was pulled tight onto the body. (*Smart Technology* 2001)

The analysis revealed several interesting aspects of the design that could not be seen in the earlier design and testing exercises. It was found that the behaviour of the underwiring was essential to the proper functioning of the new design. The underwiring in a bra is a 2D form, and when it is being worn the wire bends in two directions, around the body as the bra is put on and down as it supports the weight of the breast. The axial forces along the length of the wire are significant in its tendency to pop out of its casing after repeated wear (*Smart Technology* 2001).

The lead designer, Dick Powell, realized at this point that bras are more complex than he first imagined and this had forced the project team to rethink several aspects of the new design. Breasts tend to want to go 'east–west, while bras want them to go north–south,' he explains. 'The resulting force causes a fairly considerable amount of rubbing and irritation' (*Smart Technology* 2001).

The solution to the problem was developed by using an aerobie involving a two-shot moulding process where the inner core or armature replicates the underwire, but is infused in a softer polymer that holds and shapes the breasts. The bra cup is made from a soft, body-forming polypropylene thermoplastic elastomer (TPE) supported by a high isotactic polypropylene homopolymer. Arup's FEA was also able to refine the structural performance capabilities of the bra sizes and the results of the simulation gave Charnos the confidence to commit to the seven sizes of production tooling. The final working product saw skilled seamstresses at Charnos making several minor adjustments to the position of the mould in the bra to further improve comfort.

The Bioform range was introduced to the UK and US markets in 2000. Tony Hodges, Managing Director of Charnos says: 'Sales of Bioform have exceeded the expectations of ourselves and our retailers. Bioform has become the number one selling bra in those outlets lucky enough to have it' (*Smart Technology* 2001). Some commentators called it 'the first miracle of the millennium' (Weston Thomas 2004/www.fashion-era.com). Despite the early success of Bioform, Charnos was bought by another company in 2003 and the Bioform bra has been losing some ground in the market. It seems that the bra design was undermined by unpopular fabrics (Weston Thomas 2004).

Playing with simulations

Ricardo Engineering

Ricardo is an engineering technology company conducting research, design, and development for major automobile manufacturers. Originally based in the UK, it has expanded into the USA, Czech Republic, and Germany. With 1,800 employees, it grew its sales from £91 million in 1999 to £137 million in 2003. It has highly specialized expertise in vehicle, engine, and transmission engineering and works closely with product development departments in leading automotive manufacturing firms. It also provides testing and calibration services and has developed a range of simulation tools in its own software division.

Software for engine design

The software engineering group in Ricardo grew in the late 1980s out of an in-house requirement for specialized software analysis tools. There were no third-party software products available at the time and it was necessary for Ricardo to develop its own analysis software to support engine design projects. The software evolved and enabled fundamental understanding of physical processes to make informed design changes. Ricardo's customers demanded to use the software and the company repackaged it for them as a product. As this business grew, it acquired software capabilities from outside sources. In 1995, the software group was established in its own right as Ricardo Software, designing, developing, selling, and supporting its own software. Its products are used by a wide range of industries, including motor sport, automotive, motorcycle, truck, agriculture, locomotive, marine, and power generation. Most of the customers are large automobile manufacturers and their suppliers. There are two main simulation software areas: fluid systems and mechanical systems.[75]

One of the drivers of the need for simulations was the increased complexity of the product to be designed. In the early 1980s, engines were largely mechanical and there were only a few elements that controlled their performance. Throughout the 1980s and 1990s, however, interactions between the engine and the rest of the vehicle increased significantly, particularly through new electronic control systems. As the market for Ricardo Software expanded, the firm became more dependent on external users for feedback and ideas for future developments to manage this new complexity. In 2003, Ricardo Software employed fifty-five staff and had three technical centres in Chicago, Shoreham-by-Sea (West Sussex), and Prague.

Ricardo is developing products that integrate different software applications. Various simulation tools will allow designers and analysts to see how different systems within their vehicle interact with one another and to manage their complex integration, thereby allowing designers to see how decisions in one area affect other parts of a system. This is a considerable technological challenge, as in Ricardo's business different parts of the system may be designed by organizations in various locations around the world; for example, the engine might be designed in country X, the transmission in country Y, and the vehicle in country Z. In addition to the geographic barriers, each of the different partners involved in the design process may be using different simulation software, adding to the problems of systems integration and limiting opportunities for working collaboratively across organizational boundaries.

Within the industry it is observed, furthermore, that more automakers are collaborating on new engine projects, adding to the challenges of integration. Mistakes in transmission of data and information from one partner to another are common in engineering projects. Each organization and country has its own engineering approach and culture.[76] Ideas about how much and what type of information should be shared with partners often differ from partner to partner. The potential for miscommunication rises considerably as the number of partners increases. The idea of this new generation of integration software for collaborative engineering is to help remove these types of dangers.

Software for collaborative engineering requires the adoption of open systems. This allows organizations to 'mix and match' different software tools, including those developed internally. In-house software tools remain vitally important for many organizations as they usually contain embedded methods, knowledge, and experience that have evolved over many years. New integration tools, therefore, must allow organizations to exchange information effortlessly between these different software environments.

Similar to the model of Arup described in Chapter 3, many of Ricardo's simulation tools have been built up slowly over several years and emerge out of internal research projects or requirements to satisfy external consultancy requirements. Lead users have occasionally asked the firm to develop software for a particular task. In the case of most of the current simulation tools, their capabilities have been developed well beyond the original intention. Richard Johns, head of Ricardo Software, suggests that if the architecture of the software is well thought out, simulation tools can be highly flexible, malleable, and robust, allowing future developers to include a range of new features and design elements. An example of robustness of design can be seen in the development of WAVE, its gas dynamics simulation program. Originally designed as a simulation for engine performance, it has been extended into many areas such as the prediction of noise and integration with control, vehicle, and mechanical systems. Few of the initial designers of these simulations could have predicted the eventual uses for their programs when they were initially written, but given their flexibility and robustness, they have made such a transformation possible.

The movement to IvT has allowed designers and analysts to change the way they solve problems. With the earliest generation of simulation tools individual components and elements would need to be analysed on a step-by-step basis, building up understanding of one system with relatively simple, often inexact, connections to other systems with which they would interact. Models would run independently of each other. This was a slow and laborious process involving considerable effort in translating the impact of outputs from one part of the system into inputs for the next part of the system. According to Johns, it made the process of managing system interactions a time-consuming, error-prone, and approximate process requiring skilled operators and great care. The new generation of simulation tools helps resolve this problem by allowing designers and analysts to connect interacting processes and to co-simulate across different simulation tools.

Simulation tools are used across all stages of engine design. There is no point, however, in conducting large-scale detailed simulation of the system until the design begins to take shape. Instead, the designers start by focusing on key features of the engine, such as the bore, stroke, number of cylinders, and their configuration. In doing so, they use a range of conceptual tools and draw on past knowledge and experience. During this concept design phase, the configuration is established with basic geometric information about the engine and how different parts of the design relate to one another. At this point, the designers conduct 'low-cost' and 'fast-concept' analysis, exploring how the system might function and how its elements might interact. Elements of the design become more and more established over time, and more detailed simulation allows the design process to refine the concept design.

Designers in the early stages think about, and explore, different options and assess the performance of each alternative compared to design targets, then in later stages seek to optimize the design. The use of the tools is also reducing the time and effort expended in physical prototyping and testing. Once the design moves from digital to physical testing, the costs of changing the design increase exponentially.

Ricardo would like to have confidence that the design will satisfy functional requirements before moving on to physical prototyping and testing. This requires designers to have greater and greater faith in the simulation tools and their ability to predict the actual performance of the system.

The use of the simulation tools alters both the speed and cost of the design process for engine design. Building physical prototypes and testing the design of a combustion system, such as the use of different pistons or cylinder heads, is both time-consuming and expensive. Analysing them on a computer is relatively inexpensive with two advantages accruing, namely the tangible cost savings in product development and a reduction in the time-to-market, which potentially provides a major commercial advantage. It is estimated that the number of physical models has declined dramatically in Ricardo over the past years. Regardless of the power of the simulation tools, however, the company appreciates that there will still be a need to physically test model performance.

The increasing use of new and more powerful simulations in auto-engine design has major implications for skills and roles of designers and analysts. Simulation work in engine design was traditionally undertaken by analysts, while designers focused on the conceptual, detailed dimensioning and manufacturing. In this case, designers are generalists with knowledge about materials, engines features, and manufacturing processes. Analysts, in contrast, are highly specialized users of simulations able to correctly set up inputs and interpret outputs. Despite the increased complexity of the products, performing simulation has become easier as user interfaces have advanced. Thus, designers can become increasingly involved in analysis. Many designers, however, still lack the depth of knowledge in a particular area to be able to conduct analysis competently. According to Johns:

It is now possible for designers to undertake quite sophisticated analysis and 9 times out of 10 they will do this without a problem. However, more dangerously, 1 time out of 10 they will analyse a design and get it wrong because they do not have the specialist knowledge and experience to be able to recognise mistakes in either input or output or limitations of the modelling that render the analysis plausible but wrong.

There is still plenty of room for mistakes in analysis and even experienced analysts can make mistakes from time to time, especially when the analysis is not routine. In theory, designers could work from design templates embedded in the tools and using these design templates they could quickly create functioning engines. By using such templates, however, the designers would limit the scope for innovation in the design of the engine. As Johns says: 'Templates are straightjackets. They are fine if you want to do repetitive analysis but not if you want innovation.' Once it becomes necessary to go beyond the template embedded in the program, the skills and the experience of specialist analysts come to the fore. It is only these skilled operators and interpreters of the inputs and outputs from the simulation who can deal with new features and elements in the design.

In this way the use of the new tools creates a greater need for skilled analysts and designers. For Ricardo, today's research becomes tomorrow's commodity. Deep knowledge of the simulations and systems is required to ensure that mistakes are avoided and new opportunities for innovation achieved.

The relationship between designers and analysts in engine design has become more intertwined as a result of the use of new simulation tools.

Decisions by designers can have implications for a wide range of interacting systems. Analysts working with designers can explore and interpret these interactions, seeing how one change may spill over across the system. The tools force designers and analysts to see the engine as a system rather than a number of components. They force them to collaborate with more people and to open up to new connections across the design process.

Using IvT, Ricardo has changed the innovation process for engine design. IvT has created the potential for new forms of integration across organizations and across countries. New simulation suites allow firms to co-simulate across different simulation packages, enabling them to adopt a 'best-in-class' approach to simulation.

Playing with users

Collaboration with customers and end-users results in improved product development processes in many industries (von Hippel 1988). When product and service suppliers forge deep relations with particular customers, they are sometimes able to create 'robust' or 'dominant' design (Gardiner and Rothwell 1985; Utterback 1994). The design integrity of these products is such that the function and overall architecture creates a norm upon which subsequent generations are based and which competitors attempt to emulate. The Sony Walkman is a good example.

Feedback from customers enhances knowledge about the performance of products in use and this can be used in next generation product development, giving rise to iterations in design, and what Gardiner and Rothwell describe as product families: improved generations of Sony Walkmans, digital cameras, and PCs.

IvT provides a medium through which producers and users can communicate about innovation. The simulation of the use of products and facilities, for example, sometimes enables firms to work closely with users to evaluate options as part of the 'design conversation'. This is becoming an important part of the design and engineering process. In the case of P&G, user reference groups test virtual products. These groups are given videos or simulations of products on websites to review, with questions about positioning of products on supermarket shelves provided through virtual fly-through simulations. In the 1990s, companies like Sekisui Housing and Toyota and Mazda automobiles opened 'customer experience centres' in Japan to enable them to get closer to their customers in new product design (Barlow and Ozaki 1999). In their studies of Japanese housing production, Gann et al. (Gann 1996; Gann and Salter 1998) have shown how several large producers use technology to assist in customer choices. Sekisui manufactures around 70,000 houses a year, each one customized from a large choice of pattern-book designs. After the overall size, shape, layout, and appearance has been decided there are almost endless possibilities in choices of fixtures and fittings, including the position and height of handrails. The company uses an artificial intelligence selection system to coordinate design into production from a stock of over 2 million possible parts. Customers make choices, guided by designers in the experience centre where they can touch and feel different components. If they take their swimming costumes, they can even test the quality of particular shower heads. Designers input these choices into a CAD package during a lengthy consultation process. Once initial design decisions have been completed (often after two days in the centre), customers are given a CD-ROM with the digital designs of their houses, including a virtual reality fly-through. They are able to explore options and modify them later, they can consult their family, friends, and neighbours as to whether the design is suitable. Sekisui uses feedback from their customer experience centres and customer design consultations to inform next-generation product development. Toyota, Mazda, and other motor vehicle manufacturers use their experience centres in much the same way. Some of these tools link with marketing groups. For example, in 1999, Ford established a new business group called ConsumerConnect to attract new customers and maintain sales through the development of a specific Internet portal that could also provide feedback to product development (Vandermerwe and Taishoff 2000).

Users have become a central resource for innovation in the development of new services, particularly for firms in the IT and computer games sectors. For example, Meg Whitman, Chief Executive of Ebay says: 'The R&D lab is our community of users and it's an undirected R&D lab; they figure out how best to use this platform. The organic nature of this business is really quite stunning.'[77] Computer games companies are increasingly relying upon what they call their 'hardcore enthusiasts' to test prototype versions of new games. These users are highly discerning about the ways games should work: if they are too easy, people will not buy them, and if they are too difficult, they will only sell to a small market. But if there are inconsistencies in the ways in which games play out, hardcore enthusiasts quickly tell the rest of their friends and the rest of the world through critical reviews on the Internet and in magazines, ruining sales figures. This problem occurred in previous versions of the Star Wars Galaxies: Jump to Lightspeed game developed by Lucas Arts.[78] In the previous version, there was a lack of fidelity in the speech of the bearlike characters called Wookiees that would have been enough to put off many of the game's audience. Now, games producers often beta test with user groups, sometimes working with a small hardcore group of games fanatics, sometimes with a larger, more diverse group of users. The question of whom to solicit test results from has become important and producers use message boards on the

Internet to attract beta testers.[79] Companies like Atari are finding a correlation between reviews at beta-test stages and longer-term success in the market. They are increasing their development budgets to ensure that users 'play' with their games in order to prove the games' functionality.

The ability to engage with users has led to the development of what von Hippel (2002) calls 'user tool kits'. These create real, social, and virtual environments that allow users to play with different designs, often resulting in their own highly customized products made from existing modules. Sekisui provides a good example where the product is customized to the extent that each house is different, the so-called 'market of one'. User tool kits can provide benefits on their own but they often result in incrementalist approaches to innovation, focusing on the needs of current generations of users. The real power of these tools is when they are used as part of the wider 'think, play, do' approach connected to the 'search' capabilities of 'thinking' and the operational options and procedures of 'doing'. If firms do not use this capacity, they could run the risk of being driven so closely by listening to their customer requirements that they might miss the opportunities and threats of larger, more discontinuous change in markets and technologies.

5.4 Benefits and challenges of playing with IvT

Failure in innovative projects is relatively common and can be highly expensive, damaging, and embarrassing. The ways in which choices are made about which ideas and solutions to pursue during design and engineering and the selection of the right components and systems has a strong bearing on ultimate success and failure. This is particularly so in the case of high-profile public projects. Failure to rectify the wobble in the Millennium Bridge (described in Chapter 3) would have severely damaged the reputation of the major companies involved. Miscalculation leading to the collapse of the Leaning Tower of Pisa would have destroyed an iconic historical monument. The inability to realize the ambitious design objectives of the Bilbao Guggenheim Museum would have adversely affected a massive programme of regional regeneration in the Basque Region of Spain, in which the building played an important symbolic role. Inaccurate projections on the consequences of traffic congestion charges (described in Chapter 4) would have had significant consequences for London's authorities and may have adversely affected the whole economic and environmental agenda of dealing with congestion on the roads. Choosing the right layout for the motherboard in the new Polaroid camera in a timely and cost-effective way was a critical success factor. In all of these projects, designers and engineers have played with options and made decisions supported by IvT.

5.5 Combining craft and code

Engineers in firms like Arup used to simulate *ex post* to verify the results of physical tests. Now they simulate first and carry out physical tests to verify simulation results, 'exploring digitally, confirming physically'. This has a big impact on the sequences and speed of design. But IvT and codified knowledge embodied in software programs on its own is not enough to guarantee success. Rigorous discipline-based skills, together with experience and ingenuity and the ability to understand and use the contribution of other disciplines, is a hallmark of success. These attributes can be described as 'craft' skills and they are evident in all the successful case studies observed in this book. The designers and engineers involved in serious play need both craft and code. In the case of the congestion charge model described in Chapter 4, Professor Glaister refers to the way he relied on past experience of economic modelling to guide him on what the essential economic features were and to judge what compromises and simplification had to be made in order to get the model to work in a way that would be helpful.

The work of geotechnical engineers illustrates this well. They are sometimes described as 'wizards' because it is not possible to make boreholes and trial pit tests everywhere, and they have to make inspired choices of where to search (Hough 1996: 22). Geotechnical engineers have to rely upon experience and judgement of evidence such as historical data, surveys, samples, and test results. Intuition and judgement remain very important and for this reason the engineering practice of soil mechanics and geotechnics can be described as a craft. As Hough points out, in most areas of engineering design an intuitive feel for materials helps engineers make choices earlier than would otherwise be the case. Knowledge based on experience of strength, stiffness, durability, and so on is useful to engineers because it enables them to choose which questions need to be tested. Citing the example of forging, pressing, casting, and extruding, Hough (1996: 20) argues that an intuitive sense of a material's formability is still the first source of guidance in designing new product shapes in spite of the growth of large deformation non-linear stress analysis. He explains that there may not be the time or resource available to build analytical models or carry out detailed tests, and sometimes properties are very difficult to model because of the number of variables that would be needed to express a wide range of conditions. Engineers rely upon their intuition in these instances to decide on a combination of computer modelling, simulation, materials quality, and workmanship tests to use.

An appreciation of the importance of analytical skills and judgement based on craft and experience underpins Burland's concern about the dangers of ill-informed use of models, which can produce inaccurate results and lead to catastrophic failure in civil engineering and construction projects.

It is very easy to dress this work-up using inappropriate terminology to describe the concepts and tools we are using and this could give it a respectability that it doesn't deserve. Modelling says what you are doing. It doesn't hide behind jargon. We have hugely powerful numerical techniques available to us. Any undergraduate can get hold of these. But unless they understand that these are used as a means of modelling reality the results can convey a sense of magic that doesn't exist. The value depends upon the user understanding the reliability of data put in, the assumptions and simplifications involved in the model and the results coming out.

He pays great attention to validation:

Validation is extremely important. It's all very well to have your all-singing-all-dancing model. But how reliable is it? Do you have to calibrate it? A huge amount of my work involves being sceptical about the particular programmes we are using. We test the model against known cases. We test it against physics. It is staggering how often really sophisticated models turn out to be garbage. Quite frightening. There are terrifying differences between well-known numerical models that can give differences in response in orders of magnitude.

Burland says that 'in your bones you begin to understand the ways things broadly behave'. He continues by arguing that the model sometimes comes out with surprising answers and these need to be questioned through expert interpretation of physical properties. An expert engineer can judge whether the results coming from a model are rubbish, because before modelling it is important to estimate what you think the model will show. The model has to be placed into the context of the whole problem. Burland always teaches students about how the models evolved. In doing so, students begin to understand their limitations. There are many debates and arguments over appropriate ways to model physical properties. People put their personality into their models and defend them vigorously.

Many software programs are sensitive to the kind of boundary conditions that are assumed in their use. If these limitations are not recognized, it is difficult for designers and engineers to know whether the results are usable or nonsensical. The danger is that people become seduced by the 'magic of the simulation' and suspend their judgement and critical faculties (Groak 1998). Sometimes small divergence in inputs can cause huge differences in outputs, and sensitivity studies are needed to calibrate the tools. Well-planned reliability tests and parametric studies can be used to test solutions when inputs are varied. Unless this is done it is difficult for engineers and designers to make judgements about the reliability or the brittleness of the overall model.

5.6 Reflections

New design and engineering processes are evolving centred on the use of IvT. In this emergent model, the balance of power is shifting away from traditional, narrowly demarcated design disciplines towards those who are able to manipulate digital data. In some cases, computer programmers are becoming the dominant 'players'. Programmers 'knowledge engineer' design programs, sometimes from evidence and information gathered from practising designers. In some cases the programmers who write these design packages do so with little or no knowledge of design; it is just another area of knowledge for them to engineer and code. Quality is guaranteed in this system by the programs that check designs against sets of criteria, rather than through the use of professional guidelines. Several of the software tools developed by Arup (described in Chapter 3) illustrate this trend, and these can be used to complement the expertise of traditionally trained designers.

Case studies reveal the ways that some uncertainties in innovative projects can be ameliorated by the use of IvT. In the case of the Millennium Bridge, IvT provided the basis for a distributed, international team of engineers and designers to solve a particularly visible problem. Numerous technical solutions had been proffered to prevent the Leaning Tower of Pisa from falling down and modelling showed that had any of these been applied, the tower would have collapsed. Very careful iteration between historical architectural knowledge, computerized modelling, and physical changes led to a high degree of confidence in establishing a correct diagnosis and rectification of the problem. Gehry's Guggenheim Museum could not have been built without IvT. The technology extended the boundaries of what was technically feasible in building design and construction and was instrumental in bringing together very diverse communities of practice—architects, planners, project managers, contractors, suppliers—around a complex project. A combination of software packages enabled planners of London's Congestion Charge to assess, in an easily comprehensible form, a very complicated project of considerable social, economic, and political consequence.

Added value in design and development processes also comes from creative and schematic work, where designers produce radical solutions that are beyond the calculations embedded in routinized software programs for modular designs. Designers can use IvT to produce 'visual cues' to increasingly interact with one another about new virtual product and process models in specific social and political contexts. This schematic work is about understanding the interfaces in the design process and obtaining commitment from different specialists and interested parties. It is also about new forms of systems integration, effectively designing the process as well as the product.

IvT is a relatively novel technology and its consequences for the skills of engineers and designers are still being enacted. It is possible to envisage a deskilling trajectory similar to that predicted by the application of computers to advanced manufacturing technology (Braverman 1974). Whilst some firms may embark down that road, the result will be similar to that found in firms that unsuccessfully tried to use OMT to deskill. Productivity depends upon the merger of the new technological possibilities with the appreciation and understanding of the old principles and 'ways of doing things', the established rules of thumb and norms. The most effective users of IvT may well be those who would find solutions to their problems without IvT, albeit much more slowly and painfully.

The case studies show that IvT is being combined with more traditional forms of design and problem-solving in novel ways. It is possible to draw upon skilled professionals working in dispersed locations. At the same time, techniques for problem-solving, particularly around modular components, are being routinized in computer models. These are changing the ways in which problems can be solved. But evidence from the case studies suggests that this is not leading to a simple process of automation and deskilling. Instead, quite the reverse, deep craft knowledge is often required and this expertise can provide innovative solutions when aided by the new digital tools. The case studies illustrate the importance of craft knowledge and the limits of attempts to routinize many aspects of engineering knowledge.

The underlying principles of design as a process and practice endure in the emerging world of 'play'. Imagination, experience, analytical capabilities, and judgement—theory and practice—are all necessary, and choices are made under pressure of resource constraints, particularly in time and budget. IvT can enable these principles to be brought into productive use by helping designers select potential solutions for analysis and adding value to the innovation process. IvT can aid both concurrent and sequential processes, freeing engineers from the need to slog through routine calculations where errors can creep in. This provides more time for them to focus on engineering boundaries and interfaces. IvT can provide the means for shorter and more frequent feedback loops allowing designers to play with more options.

As well as breaking down some of the traditional demarcations between scientists and technologists and professional and organizational boundaries, IvT has the potential to provide added dynamism to the design business. Barriers to entry are being reduced with new IvT products and services providing opportunities to create new businesses.

5.7 Conclusions

The emerging process of 'play' improves design. It can enhance the ability to capture and learn from feedback and can enable new tests to be carried out, therefore assisting in refinement of design earlier, at less expense than before. The use of IvT brings together different facets of design and problem-solving and enhances the craft of designers and engineers. More significantly, the concept of 'play' enables the link between ideas and action. 'Play' is the medium between 'thinking' and 'doing'. It is the primary activity for unlocking value in the fifth generation innovation process by providing opportunities for thinkers to explore the possible outcomes of their ideas and to make choices over which ideas might bear more fruit than others. It enables those responsible for making new products and services to become an integral part of the selection process, helping to engage with users at an earlier stage in new product and service development. 'Play' is the linchpin between the generation of new ideas and their articulation in practice. It enables thought to be put into action virtually, harnessing IvT for speed, efficiency, focus, and accuracy. 'Play' gives shape to ideas, enabling selection, manipulation, and learning about possibilities and focusing the mind of doers on action. IvT provides new forms of representation that become tools for thought, exploration, and interrogation. But like all design tools, they only reach their full potential in the hands of good designers (Groak 1998).

Engineering design and problem-solving involves more than simply choosing among a variety of technological options. Technological choices are shaped by the social and economic context in which they are made, such that engineering principles usually form only part of the solution. These have to be integrated within a set of ideas from a range of diverse disciplines including economics, management, sociology, and political science. Conversely, engineering has become so ubiquitous that engineers are involved in producing and maintaining artefacts in almost every facet of society and the economy. Engineering is becoming more specialized on one hand, with many new subdisciplines emerging (such as fire engineering, acoustics engineering, lighting), and on the other, it is becoming more generalized. In consequence, the role of engineers is changing with a shift towards what Williams (2002) describes as the 'expansive disintegration of engineering knowledge'. In the world of play, designers and engineers will increasingly need to work either in highly creative ways or as systems integrators drawing together the work of multidisciplinary teams. IvT can enable both, but in each case craft will need to guide the use of code: analytical and predictive software has to be coupled with shrewd and experienced judgement, recognizing the limitations of IvT. But judgement is fallible and to engineer, after all, is human (Petroski 1985).

6 'Do'

6.1 Introduction

In 2003, Professor Andrew Amis was asked to assist in a delicate operation to extend the jawbone on one side of eleven-year-old Rosemary's face. She was suffering from an unusual genetic defect causing one part of her jaw to grow more slowly than the rest of her face. Amis, Professor of Biomechanics in the Department of Mechanical Engineering at Imperial College, London, works with surgeons at Guy's Hospital and heads the biomechanics research team. In the past, this type of operation was not possible until the child had stopped growing, and then entailed an extensive operation that included taking a section of a rib as a graft that would be fitted using plates and screws. The surgeon would have had to rely upon his or her experience and ingenuity to adapt and fit the graft and plates during the operation. As part of the research team, Amis is able to take a new approach to preoperational planning that provides far more information with the aim of increasing accuracy, reducing risk, and speeding up the process. Taking computed tomography (CT) scans, he creates digital images of the skull enabling him to think about the problem and play with potential solutions. Data from medical imaging has become far more accurate, allowing non-invasive exploration prior to surgery. Before doing the operation he sends the digital data to a rapid prototyping machine in the Engineering Faculty Design and Engineering Workshop at Imperial College. A 3D jet-printed prototype Z-Core injection machine creates an accurate, full-size replica of Rosemary's skull. Using this model the surgeon can choose the optimum place to cut the bone and then decide how to move the cut ends apart. With that knowledge Amis has a precisely fitting facial plate made for insertion in the operation. The advantages are that the plate is far more accurate than would have previously been the case, requiring smaller incision and less adjustment during the operation, which is carried out faster, with fewer risks.

In another example, a cancer survivor was able to eat his first solid meal in nine years after receiving a custom-made bio-engineered jaw transplant. Professor Patrick Warnke and his team from the University of Kiel, Germany, took a 3D CT scan of the patient's jaw, and using CAD techniques was able to produce an 'ideal virtual jawbone replacement'. The data were used to create a scaled Teflon model over which a titanium mesh cage was constructed. The Teflon was removed and the titanium shell filled with bone mineral blocks and recombinant human bone protein taken from the patient's bone marrow. The new jaw was grafted beneath the patient's right shoulder with its own blood supply so that the bone could grow. Seven weeks later, the new jaw was removed and fitted into the skull. It produced a perfect 3D fit (Warnke et al. 2004).

The ability to produce accurate 3D physical models quickly and cheaply has many advantages in putting ideas into action. Biomedical engineering is just one of many applications, which also include more traditional manufacturing processes. It illustrates the ability to produce bespoke artefacts that are carefully designed and chosen to meet individual requirements, often involving the end-user directly in the process. In biomedicine, integration takes place across the activities of think, play, and do, with links between medical imaging, CAD, FEA, rapid prototyping, and production of bespoke body parts. This enables medical practitioners and researchers to explore ideas, experiment with different approaches, and play with solutions to a wide range of anatomical problems, resulting in the design of devices and new treatments, such as customized implants and prosthesis. The use of rapid prototyping illustrates the links between choice of solution and implementation. This form of IvT is being used in an increasingly wide range of applications from computer-aided tissue engineering through to reconstructions for forensic purposes. In the latter case, rather than exploring what might be done, IvT is used to explain how and what has been done.

In this chapter we explore how IvT can be used to connect the option-creating activities of 'thinking' and selection activities of 'playing' with those of putting chosen ideas into practice through 'doing' in the development of new or improved products and services. Examples from different industries illustrate how IvT enables firms to propagate and develop solutions, putting ideas into action more swiftly and cost-effectively than before. The ability to use IvT to rapidly explore implementation and exploitation pathways provides a link to production coordination and control, where a range of other advanced manufacturing and operations technologies are used. This connectivity can also provide feedback from production, furnishing data to assess lessons from previous operations in order to create greater predictability, refine future processes, and test different functional, build quality, and aesthetic aspects for commercial viability. IvT—principally in the form of rapid prototyping and simulation—provides a new physical and virtual interface between the design of new products and services and their production.

We approach the analysis of these tools and techniques from both an innovation and a production perspective. This allows an exploration of the two-way, increasingly concurrent relationship between innovating and making. From a technology point of view, the interplay between IvT and OMT links new product development processes with production. Data, and in some cases the instrumentation and tools used in OMT, are being 'pulled' into the innovation process. Whereas previously OMT was primarily developed to enhance performance in manufacturing, it is beginning to be used to support an integrated innovation process.

The chapter begins with a description of advances in operations and production brought about by the transition from mass to lean production, from Fordism to Toyotaism. It highlights their specific implications for the development of standardization and modularity of products, and the organization and integration of workflow. This is followed by a discussion of 'innovation technologies for doing', including a description of rapid prototyping technology. The ways in which IvT assists in planning production and affects how operations are conducted are then examined through a number of case studies. These illustrate different aspects of the use of IvT in a range of sectors, including rapid prototyping in the motor sport and automotive sectors, fashion industry, and in welding and fixing technologies. The chapter concludes with a discussion of the limitations of IvT, together with its implications for the development phase in the emerging innovation process that links design with production.

6.2 Fordism: standardization and modularity

The possibilities for product innovation depend upon an understanding of the relationship between design options and the process and economics of production. This relationship is best understood through the concepts and practices of standardization and modularity in components that have developed over the past 150 years. Traditional mass production provides three main advantages over other systems of manufacturing: it affords producers the benefits of economies of scale, when cost per unit falls more quickly than production costs rise as the volume of production increases; it offers technical possibilities to develop and deploy automated capital equipment; and it provides opportunities for tighter management control over operations with increased predictability of the quality of outputs.

These benefits were exploited in the mid nineteenth century by companies like the Colt Armoury and, fifty years later, famously by Henry Ford, whose adoption of scientific management and invention of the mass-production line facilitated the manufacture of high volumes of standardized products made from interchangeable parts. Womack et al. (1990) summarize the main attributes of this system with the key being complete and consistent interchangeability of parts and the simplicity of attaching them to one another. The same gauging system was used through the entire manufacturing process, driven by the search for savings on assembly costs. It was these innovations that made the assembly line successful. They allowed further subdivision of labour, employing unskilled or semi-skilled workers to use high-cost, dedicated machinery. Design and management were carried out as specialist functions. Moreover, because machinery was expensive, firms could not afford to allow production lines to stop. Buffers such as extra supplies of materials and labour were added to the system to assure smooth production. Producers kept standard designs in production for as long as possible because changing machinery to produce new products was expensive. This resulted in consumers benefiting from lower costs but at the expense of variety and choice.

In the USA, General Motors quickly showed Ford the marketing benefits of differentiating products to suit customer preferences, even if this initially only meant producing vehicles of a different colour. Alfred Sloan's approach to new product development at General Motors aimed to produce 'a car for every purse and purpose'. This opened the possibility of 'economies of scope', the ability to produce a variety of products with the same production equipment at no additional cost, when previously different production lines would have been required (Chandler 1990).

Standardization and modularity remains an important feature of competitive success in many industries, particularly those for whom high-volume sales are important. Firms' abilities to develop standard modules and universally required components or platforms sometimes result in de facto standards. This is seen, for example, where such products provide the basic technological architecture on which other products and systems are built, like Intel's microprocessor chips, or Microsoft's Windows Operating System (Gawer and Cusumano 2002). Using IvT in think, play, do processes to develop next-generation platform technologies in these markets can provide firms with distinct advantages in components that integrate in a wider range of systems and faster times to market.

6.3 Toyotaism: integrating workflow and innovation processes

The breakthrough in meeting wider customer choices whilst improving efficiency in production came from Japan. The revolution in Japanese manufacturing began with experiments in Toyota in the late 1940s. It resulted in new approaches to the organization of production, the use of plant and equipment, management of resources, quality control, and relationships between producers, customers, and suppliers. After the Second World War, Toyota, Japan's largest car producer needed to match American mass-production techniques if it were to become a volume producer and compete in international markets. The local Japanese automobile market at the time was small but demanded a wide range of vehicles; its production techniques were primitive in comparison to those in the USA and investment capital and land for large factories was scarce. Japanese factory workers were also unwilling to be treated as variable costs like the interchangeable parts in Ford's factory system.

In 1950, Toyota's President, Eiji Toyoda, spent three months at Ford's Rouge Plant in the USA. He celebrated the total output of the plant, which in one year produced over 2.5 times the number of cars made by Toyota in the previous thirteen years. But while output was impressive, Toyoda thought the system wasted labour, materials, and time. He could not afford to produce cars with specialized managers overseeing unskilled workers tending expensive, single-purpose machines with buffers of extra stocks, and rework areas needed to ensure smooth production and final quality. Toyoda's objective was to create a production system that combined the advantages of craft production with those of mass production whilst avoiding the high costs of craft and the rigidities of factory systems. The result was the evolution of Toyota's lean production system, which employed teams of multi-skilled workers at all levels of the organization and flexible, automated machines to produce both volume and variety of products.

By the 1980s, the Fordist mass-production system had been transformed into a more efficient and responsive system that came to be known as Toyotaism, or 'lean production' (Womack and Jones 1997). The system used less of everything compared with US mass production: less labour, manufacturing space, and storage; lower investment in tools; and, importantly from our point of view, fewer engineering hours to develop new products. Products had fewer defects and there was greater and ever-growing variety to meet differentiated customer preferences. The success of lean production depended on many improvements across the whole system through a tightly coupled set of product and process innovations and a regime of continuous improvement. To achieve this, Toyota had to gain better information about production and the use of its products; it also needed to develop new product and process technologies such as simple dies that could be changed quickly, and the just-in-time supply of parts. This required closer links with consumers to identify and understand customer needs, investing in R&D in both product and process engineering, and establishing joint technology development activities with suppliers. These techniques made Toyota a world-class car producer against whom other manufacturing firms are often benchmarked. By the mid-1980s when Japanese manufacturing—not just Toyota—became the subject of study by many management researchers, such examples illustrated the emergence of the fourth

---

Box 6.1 Predictive technology assisting supply-chain management at Wal-Mart

Wal-Mart[80] is the world's largest retailer. It has over 4,000 stores across the world and it had $256.3 billion sales in 2004. Each week more than 100 million people visit its stores in the USA. Since 2000, it has added $100 billion in turnover to its accounts. Wal-Mart's success has been based on its ubiquity, high value and often low prices, and a powerful and lean supply chain. It is also a skilled user of new technology, being one of the first retailers to adopt bar codes and to use electronic data interchange. It also works closely with its suppliers, sharing sales data, to streamline and automate its supply chain. In 2004, it was planning to use radio frequency identification (RFID) transmitters to tag shipments to assist in tracking every item it sells.

Wal-Mart has become increasingly conscious of the creative potential of using IvT to help better understand its customers and its supply chain. It has 460 terabytes of data about its customers' purchasing decisions and supply-chain interactions. When combined with powerful data mining tools, this information tells it what goods are sold where and when. According to Linda Dillman, Chief Information Officer of Wal-Mart, this information allows the firm to develop 'predictive technology'. It can 'start predicting what is going to happen, instead of waiting for it to happen' (quoted in Hays 2004). One example of how the technology can work in practice was when a hurricane was approaching the south coast of the USA. Wal-Mart noticed a spike in sales of not only traditional goods associated with hurricanes, such as flashlights, but also Kellogg's strawberry Pop-Tarts, and beer. Using this information, Wal-Mart was able to pre-stock its stores to ensure that there were enough Pop-Tarts to go around in forthcoming hurricanes.

IvT also shapes Wal-Mart real estate decisions, determining where a new store will maximize potential new business. It also enables the company to decide how many staff and cashiers to locate at a particular store at different times of the day.

Technology is central to its distribution system. Wal-Mart uses its information to study the flow of goods into its stores, keeping track of delivery times of its suppliers. It also uses the information to restock, sending just-in-time information to its suppliers to make sure that stock levels are optimized. The data are used to help monitor and map the performance of the organization. Wal-Mart jealously protects its data.

The data mining tools at Wal-Mart act as the central nervous system of the organization, providing the opportunity to reshape practices, better understand performance, and create new product offerings. Its ability to mine its internal data has become a key element of its overall competitive strategy, helping the firm achieve its ambitious growth targets.

---

generation innovation process with its close coupled networks of activity involving technologists working with customers, suppliers, and other research establishments (see Chapter 2 and Graves 1994).

The need to meet increasing levels of customer choice for different model options means that factories have to cope with millions of possible build permutations. Toyota managed this by minimizing the number of parts in new models and by pushing some of the build complexity out of the assembly plant into the retail network where customer options are installed as bundled packages (Brooke 1994). This led to an extension in the use of 'platform' designs and standardized subassemblies, with closer supplier involvement in research, design, and engineering. Toyota has continued to develop and integrate workflow and innovation processes by deploying new technologies in areas such as advanced materials and process techniques, including computer-integrated manufacturing (CIM) and flexible manufacturing systems on medium-variation, medium-volume, production lines. This combination of technical and organizational innovation has resulted in benefits in economies of scale and scope, such that Toyota in 2004 was the most profitable motor vehicle manufacturer.

There is no relief from the pressures to innovate that result from fiercely competitive markets for motor vehicles and the need to respond to new challenges such as reducing environmental impact and creating safer means of transport (see Chapter 3). Toyota's ability to link next-generation product development with knowledge about current products and production systems illustrates the benefits of integration between product and process innovation. It has a reputation for rapid prototyping, tooling and manufacture, and integrating the technologies of design and engineering with those of production. In response to pressures to improve environmental sustainability, Toyota has become a world leader in the development of fuel cells and hybrid cars, such as the Prius. It also invests heavily in the development of product recycling and component reuse systems, such that only 3 per cent of a Toyota need be wasted at the end of the product's life.[81]

These capabilities are indicative of a fifth generation innovator, demonstrating the strategic use of technologies, seen in the ability to merge two different types of technology in the hybrid car, and the use of IvT to integrate innovation processes associated with production. Other leading car manufacturers exhibit similar capabilities. Daimler Chrysler, for example, opened in 2001 what was at the time the most advanced virtual reality centre in the automotive industry. The facility enables production engineers to simulate the integration of assembly processes for new component parts before physically reengineering expensive production systems for the Mercedes E-Class. It can do this using data gloves in what is known as a virtual reality 'cave' environment.[82] In this application of IvT the engineer becomes part of the virtual environment and the hand movement representing a robot arm positioning a part can be viewed and assessed in the virtual model. The possibility of using a range of IvT such as this allows better links between product and process innovation, contributing to the activities we describe as 'do'.

To summarize, the world of production is changing in a way that directly bears on the relationship between product and process innovation. Box 6.2 lists some of the major technological trends found in contemporary manufacturing technologies. The old scale- and energy-intensive technology paradigm is being challenged by requirements to produce differentiated, customized products and services offering individual choices in niche markets. Pressures for change are being driven by the need to conserve resources, reducing waste, emissions, energy, and materials consumption. There has been a shift towards the

---

Box 6.2   Trends in advanced manufacturing[83]

- Use of reconfigurable production systems and flexible, integrated micro-assembly, utilizing intelligent, self-learning systems, resulting in some sectors in the production of bespoke products
- Development and use of advanced robotics, particularly for precision engineering or in dangerous or dirty environments
- Process intensification, including very small-scale plants such as 'factory on a chip', particularly in biochemistry and other process industries
- Exploration and experimentation with nanotechnology and nano-engineered materials and components, including the use of new biomaterials, giving rise to (a) the possibility of process-based approach to developing materials and parts rather than traditional cutting and machining; and (b) the opportunity to design performance characteristics into materials and components in what has come to be known as 'made to measure' (Ball 1997)
- Development and use of 'smart materials', which have capabilities to adapt to different conditions in use, including shape-memory materials
- Development of ubiquitous computing, including use of microsensors in production processes and embedded in component parts (e.g. use of RFID chips)
- Adoption of new supply-chain management approaches and logistics management, including better linkages up and down supply networks for new product and service development
- Wider use of renewable resources, and recycling, reuse, and waste reduction, in response to environmental concerns
- Better knowledge and management of whole-life attributes of products and their component parts

---

integration of products and services, particularly where value is generated through the provision of facilities and services delivered through complex systems (Davies et al. 2003).[84] The tools and techniques of production are increasingly overlapping with the tools and techniques of product development to enable producers to meet these challenges.

6.4 New technologies for doing

The previous discussion describes a close relationship between operations, production, and process technologies, and there is also a close link with the scientific knowledge that underpins them. The development of advanced manufacturing is closely linked to progress in science and a number of core technologies such as instrumentation for sensing and monitoring process performance. In the production of Activ, for example, a new form of self-cleaning glass made by Pilkington, a film of titanium dioxide 15 nm thick is bonded to the glass surface during the production process. New instrumentation in the form of an electron-tunnelling microscope—to observe atoms and molecules—is required to monitor production. Engineering the glass surface using nanotechnology provides two improvements in performance: it gains photocatalytic and hydrophillic properties, reducing adhesion of city dirt and stopping water droplets forming so that rainwater spreads and washes down the glass. Closer integration between science, technology, engineering, and production can stimulate new opportunities for product and process innovation such as in the development of Activ glass. IvT provides an infrastructure and set of tools to enable this link between 'playing' and 'doing'.

The ability to share information about design and production is most commonly seen in the links between computer-aided design and computer-aided manufacture: CAD/CAM. The ability to capture and share information about the design of products and services, their production, and their use has been enhanced by the integration of OMT, ICT, and IvT. In some cases, sensors and instrumentation are introduced into products to enable automated testing and diagnostics. This provides feedback from products in use enabling more efficient maintenance cycles and a better understanding of performance, which feeds into next-generation product development. Examples can be found in a wide range of products from jet engines, where a number of key indicators are monitored in real time, such as oil viscosity, to washing machines. In both these cases the shift is towards understanding performance of the facility or service delivery over time, rather than a traditional description of product performance at the point it leaves the factory.

One principal IvT used for production is rapid prototyping, which fabricates physical objects directly from CAD data sources. These methods are unique in that they add and bond materials in layers to form objects. Such systems are also known by the general names of solid free-form fabrication or layered manufacturing. Pham and Dimov (2003) argue that these technologies offer advantages in many applications compared to traditional subtractive fabrication methods such as milling or turning, which cut and remove material around the desired shape:

- Objects can be formed with any geometric complexity or intricacy without the need for elaborate machine setup or final assembly.
- Objects can be made from multiple materials, or as composites, or materials can even be varied in a controlled fashion at any location in an object.
- Solid free-form fabrication systems reduce the construction of complex objects to a manageable, straightforward, and relatively fast process.[85]

These properties have resulted in their wide use as a way to reduce time-to-market in manufacturing (Pham and Dimov 2003). Today's systems are used extensively by engineers to better understand and communicate their product designs as well as to make rapid tooling to manufacture those products. Surgeons, architects, artists, and individuals from many other disciplines also routinely use the technology. Rapid prototyping quickly fabricates physical models, functional prototypes, and small batches of parts, including moving parts. It provides physical representations quickly and cheaply, enabling design

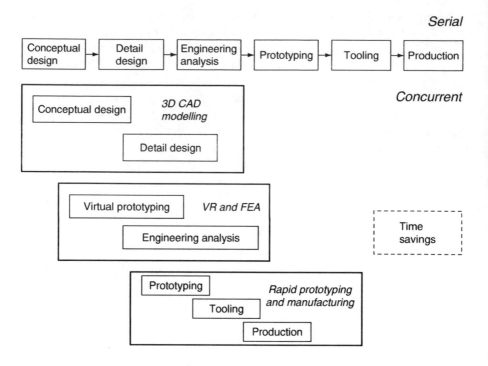

Fig. 6.1 Time compression through rapid prototyping
Source: Pham and Dinov 2003

and problem exploration and verification. Rapid prototypes make excellent visual aids for communicating ideas with co-workers or customers. In addition, prototypes can be used for design testing in aerospace, for example, where an engineer might mount a model airfoil in a wind tunnel to measure lift and drag forces. One of the main aims and benefits of rapid prototyping is time compression (see Fig. 6.1). In manufacturing environments the goal is to reduce time-to-market by supporting concurrent design and engineering activities. In some cases, this can enhance creative selection processes in 'play' by providing more time for exploring design options. Although designers have always utilized prototypes, rapid prototyping allows them to be made faster and less expensively. Figure 6.1 illustrates the speed advantages of concurrency in the new mode of development compared with traditional sequential approaches.

The technology connects the world of manufacture with that of choosing what designs to make. It provides a direct link between innovation and production. Design and engineering data are managed in some cases in a single product/project model, which can be worked on concurrently by everyone involved in the project. The aim is to eliminate duplication and reduce the

---

Box 6.3   Three types of rapid prototyping machines

1. *Stereolithography* (SL) relies on a photosensitive liquid resin that forms a solid polymer when exposed to UV light. Stereolithographic systems consist of a build platform (substrate), which is mounted in a vat of resin and a UV helium-cadmium or argon ion laser. The first layer of the part is imaged on the resin surface by the laser using information obtained from a 3D solid CAD model. Once the contour of the layer has been scanned and the interior hatched, the platform is lowered and a new layer of resin applied. The next layer may then be scanned. Once the part is complete, it is removed from the vat and the excess resin drained. The 'green' part is placed in a UV oven to be postcured.

2. *Selective laser sintering* (SLS) uses a fine powder, which is heated with a carbon dioxide laser so that the surface tension of the particles is overcome and they fuse together. Before the powder is sintered, the entire bed is heated to just below the melting point of the material in order to minimize thermal distortion and facilitate fusion to the previous layer. The laser is modulated such that only those grains that are in direct contact with the beam are affected. A layer is drawn on the powder bed using the laser to sinter the material. The bed is lowered and the powder-feed cartridge raised so that a covering of powder can be spread evenly over the build area by a counter-rotating roller. The sintered material forms the part whilst the unsintered powder remains in place to support the structure and may be cleaned away and recycled once the build is complete. Another process, laser sintering technology (LST), employs the same physical principles. Currently dual-laser systems are available for processing thermoplastics and sand.

3. *Fused deposition modelling* (FDM) systems consist of two movable heads (one for building the part and the other for the supports), which deposit threads of molten material onto a substrate. The material is heated to just above its melting point so that it solidifies immediately after extrusion and cold welds to the previous layers.

---

likelihood of errors in analysis, design revision, production planning, and later, in the manufacturing processes. This can result in the intensification of engineering and production, saving time, improving predictability, and reducing costs.

Pham and Dimov (2003) describe three generic types of rapid prototyping machines used commercially in 2003 (see Box 6.3). The cost of these machines ranged between $7,000 and $1 million.

6.5 The impact of IvT on manufacturing processes

The practice of producing customized products using standardized parts through modular design protocols has become widespread. It is used throughout manufacturing as well as in many project-based industries, such as the production of fixed capital goods and buildings (Gann 2000). As the examples below show, these practices are increasingly supported and integrated through the use of IvT, which assists in simplification and concurrency in design and production even in complex systems and products.

But the reliance on modularity may be changing because of more flexible opportunities offered through the combination of IvT and OMT, with the development of rapid prototyping systems that link directly to manufacturing, making it possible to produce components in very small volumes, sometimes of single units. For example, cost reduction and quality improvement have been driven by standardization and modular design in the construction sector but the sector often needs to produce unique, one-off products.

Our industry is geared towards using standard forms and components in order to minimise waste, pollution and cost.... This stifles creativity. Soon we will be able to look at building and component design in a different way. Rapid prototyping will lift the current restrictions and allow us to develop unique buildings and their individual components to really enhance our environment. (Alvise Simondetti[86])

Other industries are in a similar position, such as the biomedical transplants discussed at the beginning of this chapter or the need for a mix of modularity and tailored parts in orthodontics, fashion, or ski boot design. The challenge is to individualize where it matters, tailoring the parts that have a bearing on the customer whilst providing the desired quality at the right price. These requirements are leading to changes in markets where there is much more distributed intelligence of what and how to produce when collocated closer to end-users. In markets of one, the product is sometimes finished at the point of consumption, such as in buildings or dentistry or in services of all kinds. In these cases every product is innovative and requires particular thinking, playing, and doing processes. Production and innovation processes overlap. Project-based modes of organizing delivery become the norm, and success increasingly depends upon the ability to use IvT. A number of examples illustrate this.

3D blueprinting in Formula One car design[87]

One of the key factors in designing racing cars is understanding how aerodynamics affects performance and the trade-offs between drag and down forces. Mike Gascoyne, technical director of Renault Formula One (formerly Benetton Formula One), is an aerodynamicist by training and his team deployed IvT with the aim of revolutionizing its aerodynamic development programme. In spite of advances in CFD, extensive wind tunnel testing on scale model cars forms the bedrock of a Formula One team's development programme. Leading teams own and operate wind tunnels, and for design solutions to progress quickly, a team's development programme must have the resources to operate the tunnel with a continual supply of models for testing. Results have to be analysed quickly and efficiently. Historically, Renault, like other teams, employed highly skilled model makers to handbuild parts for its wind tunnel programme.

Whilst the cost of skilled modelling staff was not crippling in the rich world of Formula One engineering, they could not build models fast enough to cope with the rest of the team's requirements for wind tunnel test data. The tolerances required were a challenge for even the most skilled model maker. To get the best out of a test, Renault's engineers take a wind tunnel model apart and put it back together to within an accuracy of 0.1 per cent. In 2004, Renault radically altered its wind tunnel test programme in partnership with rapid prototyping equipment manufacturer, 3D Systems.[88] Parts are produced rapidly and accurately on the 3D Systems SLA 7000 machines, significantly increasing performance in aerodynamic testing and design.

Commenting on the use of SL rapid prototyping, Jim Wall, Engineering Group Manager of Hendricks Motorsport, says:

[R]acing is a process of continual change and it can be very difficult to manage that change. Technology has allowed us to do things faster, be more creative in what we develop and use our creative abilities at a higher level rather than just our skills at reproducing components. . . . Everybody makes mistakes but stereolithography allows you to make your mistakes on the front end of manufacturing. It is a time-saving procedure. If you can eliminate that wasted time on the front end it allows you to move quicker—beat the competition to market. That is the bottom line for us. . . . Things that we could not do before, such as CAD header designs, are being done in a revolutionary way. Complex 3D tubes are difficult to reproduce as accurate prototypes, but with the SLA system we are able to design, print, and manufacture new headers for testing and production. For example, there can be design interference issues in the chassis. Rather than designing the tubes in the computer and then going straight to production before we have verified it will fit, we can take a 3D CAD design of the header and print it on the SLA system. This gives us a beautiful 3D part made out of an extremely accurate plastic material that can be used for mock-up in the actual race vehicle. . . . Essentially what you have is a 3D blueprint.

But one technical manager said that 'model making used to be the bottleneck. Now the large amount of data available, in such a short time, is the bottleneck.'

Another example of the ways prototyping increases speed is seen in the PalmV handheld computer, one of the most successful personal digital assistants (PDAs) ever produced.[89] Its design involved many iterations through a large number of prototypes. The device was half as thin as, and four ounces lighter than, the previous generation. But what appeared to be a leap in engineering was in fact a series of incremental steps. Each prototype produced demonstrated a few ideas, for example, in methods of attaching the stylus to the case with one prototype using a magnet and another slotting the stylus into a groove, as in the final product. By producing many rapid but rough prototypes, mistakes were flushed out early in the design process. 'Fail early, fail often' is the creed at the IDEO design firm that worked with Palm on the product. Dennis Boyle of IDEO says:

Once you have ideas, or more likely a set of competing ideas for solving a problem, you have to render them in a way that people can experience. Prototyping is ultimately about getting the people who are going to use the product, who will pay for it, to experience it—even in a crude way—so that they can articulate what they like and don't, or at least so you can infer such by their actions. CAD combined with rapid prototyping has put design iterations on fast forward.

Doing it with style in the fashion industry

Similar technologies are playing a major role in changing the way the fashion and clothing industry operate. Both the business-to-business (B2B) and business-to-consumer (B2C) markets are benefiting from IvT. Companies like Benetton have successfully speeded up the design, production, and distribution of garments using integrated CAD/CAM technologies that connect design and manufacturing, with automated warehousing and distribution linked to sales trends data collected from the point of sale (Dodgson 2000). A number of other new technologies are being used to assist designers and manufacturers and to bring customers into the design and manufacturing process.

A wide variety of virtual and digital technologies have been developed to enable speed to the marketplace. Some of these technologies allow product to be designed and communicated in a digital format up to the point of product prototype, reducing the product development cycle by months and the man-hours by thousands. Other digital technologies enable faster product design by reducing the amount of effort required to visualize the new product. Other digital technologies allow quick customization of products that will better meet the needs of consumers.[90]

Rapid prototyping is being used by designers as a tool to 'sculpt' the shape of a garment. Traditionally the process of creating a garment would take around six weeks and require design and cut of the pattern, making the garment, and trying it on a mannequin. Using rapid prototyping technology, data from a flat pattern cutting is inputted into a CAD/CAM file and a virtual prototype is produced. A 3D mannequin, with real-time simulation of cloth parameters and fabric animation, provides designers with an accurate virtual prototype. It is now possible to produce a prototype of a dress in just 3 hours, instead of six weeks.[91] An example of rapid prototyping technologies being used in the industry is MIRADreams Fashionizer, a virtual Try-On 3D with animation prototyping program.[92]

Sue Jenkyn Jones, a digital fashion consultant with The School of Fashion, Central St Martins College of Art & Design, London, says that rapid prototyping has shown great benefit in design but also in helping to eliminate items from collections. The result is that fashion designers no longer have to make a whole collection in different locations around the world; they can now visualize and remove garments from the collection without actually having to make them. Decisions can be made simultaneously by videoconference, and nearer to the time of production, which speeds up the whole process significantly.

IvT is enabling the customer to be engaged in the design of clothing and shoes through

- body measurement software, which translates body measurements into production instructions at the factory for batches of as little as one garment;
- 3D software[93] and visualization tools;
- Smart Cards, where body scanned data is held in a portable digital format;
- Modems and Kiosks, used for information and communication between retail shop/customer and manufacturer.

These technologies link customers with the manufacturer. The customer plays with style, colour, and fabric choices (although the manufacturer will have played in the original design choices available to the customer) and the manufacturer 'does'. This initiates a more intimate dialogue and relationship between the customers, designers, and the manufacturer and can act as a differentiator in a highly competitive market.

The following examples illustrate the way suppliers, users, and researchers are using IvT. Bodymetrics is a supplier of the technology and Levi Strauss is a user. The Engineering Design Centre at the University of Cambridge researches how designers and technicians interact in the production of garments.

Bodymetrics

Bodymetrics, a spin-off from University College London, is a body scanning and visualization system provider. It sees the future of shopping for clothes in the following way:[94]

You step into a body-scanning cubicle and your 3D image is encrypted onto your personalised credit card or smart card. You sit in an armchair with a personal shopper and choose a few items from the shop's range—a jacket, a shirt and trousers. Using virtual-reality software, you can see yourself—your digital twin—in those clothes. You can add accessories, change your hair colour, parade up and down a virtual catwalk and give yourself a twirl. If you like the results, the assistant presses a button and your digital body map is transferred to the factory where a laser-cutting machine reads the software and alters the pattern to fit you. In a few days, your jacket, shirt and trousers are couriered to you. They fit. Welcome to the world of e-couture.[95]

Bodymetrics clients include Selfridges, Marks and Spencer, and Boden and Wallis. Selfridges uses a Bodymetrics body scanner to help match customers to their ideal pair of jeans.

Levi Strauss

Levi Strauss has a 'personal pair' custom-made jeans campaign. A trained sales person takes the customer's measurements, which are then entered into Levi's computer system. The computer suggests a possible prototype jeans fit that is closest to what the customer wants. This is a real garment that Levi already has, for example, the 501 jeans. The customer tries on the suggested jeans; adjustments are detected (e.g. tighter, shorter) and fed into the computer. An order is transmitted to the factory electronically and the jeans are made by a flexible manufacturing system. The customer receives the jeans two to three weeks later. The cost to the customer is around $10–15 more than an off-the-shelf pair.

Cambridge Engineering Design Centre

University of Cambridge has a research project on creating visual representations and computer tools to facilitate better interaction between designers and producers of knitwear. It poses the problems faced:

Knitwear design has many features of engineering design. It involves a complex interaction between technical and aesthetic design, to meet tight deadlines and fixed price points. Knitwear designers design the visual and tactile appearance of a garment: technicians have to interpret their specifications to create a program for a knitting machine, while solving many detailed design problems. Due to a lack of technical feedback only 30% of designs are technically viable; and suboptimal products reach the market.[96]

The research project examines the problems of effective representation in design, and how this is essential for communications between designers and makers.

Problem-solving using finite element analysis

IvT can be used for problem-solving in production processes as well as assisting in the design of new products and processes. Furthermore, some of the technologies used at the interface between innovation and production are becoming mature. Evidence of this can be found in the confidence with which a customer in a high-risk environment accepted decisions made by a specialist consultant, based on a computer model of potential outcomes. The example is taken from a maintenance regime, where unscheduled repairs can be costly because they involve unplanned shutdowns of expensive plant, with additional loss of output to the owner. The case shows that through technical examination using FEA the consultant engineers were able to save a customer from an unplanned shutdown in a chemical reactor which would have proven extremely costly. The quality of investigation and technical modelling were such that the customer had confidence that predictions made in the FEA model were correct, in spite of being in a safety-critical environment and where the cost of a mistake may have caused extreme financial stress. This confidence in the technology was borne out in practice.

The Welding Institute (TWI) is a UK-based, world-renowned research and technology organization specializing in material joining technology. It has an industrial membership to which it offers a range of advisory and problem-solving services.

One of TWI's clients had experienced damage in a column of a chemical reactor in the Netherlands. It was anxious to quickly prove to safety inspectors that the damage was not problematic and the reactor was 'fit for purpose'. To close the reactor in order to affect repairs would have significant consequences for the company. It would fail to meet customer contracts and the delay would have financial implications potentially reaching billions of dollars, adversely affecting its overall financial stability.

National regulations require regular service inspections of the reactor column. In preparation for inspection the company was repainting the column when a 10-mm-thick piece broke off. This was seemingly significant damage as the width of the chemical reactor column was only 16.3 mm. The company engineers, however, suspected from previous experience and well-documented stress analysis studies that this damage would not present any problems and that the reactor could still be used. The problem was that they needed to prove it to the inspectors and so they turned to TWI.

TWI engineers decided to use a standard commercial simulation package ABAQUS Standard 6.3[97] for an FEA[98] of the flaw in the pressure vessel. The output of the FEA demonstrated that local yielding of the material occurred at the base of the flaw but that the stresses in the remaining section of the column rapidly diminished to 'normal' values. By using the simulation package for analysis of the reactor column the TWI team was able to provide evidence that the reactor remained fit for purpose. The client presented this evidence to inspectors who agreed the reactor was safe.

One of the main benefits of using the simulation technology was speed; the simulation of the defect took only two days to complete. If the company had had to shut down the column for a physical welding repair, this would have taken considerably longer because of the permits needed and health and safety regulations to be complied with when a physical repair is required. The company will still need to undertake a physical repair at some stage but it will be a scheduled shutdown that fits in with the commercial demands of the reactor column.

6.6 IvT for production planning

The ability to prototype products and simultaneously simulate manufacturing processes presents new possibilities for firms to plan and optimize production. It offers the potential to provide information for logistics and operations earlier in the production cycle. Information can sometimes be provided concurrently with detailed product design, enabling firms to reduce time-to-market because production facilities can be developed or adapted whilst product development continues. This brings production planning and logistics into the 'doing' activity of the innovation process.

In some cases, the relationship is reversed. By working on a better understanding of a process, production engineers and researchers are able to explore opportunities to design and create new products. Examples can be found in chemical processes and the fabrication of silicon wafers. Here, the product and the process share a common basis during production. In the fabrication of silicon wafers, for example, three variables govern the type of product and also regulate the production process: temperature, pressure, and time. In the late 1990s, a process flow representation was produced by researchers at MIT to improve knowledge about semiconductor design and manufacture.[99] In many ways, semiconductor fabrication is analogous with biological processes, where organisms are 'grown' rather than manufactured from discrete parts. In the MIT project, chip designers wanted to know if by making small changes to the process, they could manufacture new types of chip. The design space in semiconductors is the manufacturing space. In other words, the fabrication processes determines design choices such that each particular production process results in a unique product. The researchers were able to use the newly developed process simulator to design new products.

There are other connections between 'doing' and operations in the innovation process. The use of sensors in production, for example, can capture new data, which are fed back to models of the process. These can subsequently be refined in tandem with incremental improvements and modifications to products. Quality control regimes are also linked to the ability to use IvT in the final stages of product and process development. For example, production engineers can test for accuracy in processes using better product and process models, exploring more about what they are going to make before production starts, thereby reducing the risk of error.

From an institutional perspective, the ability to connect innovation processes with production has resulted in new business opportunities. The organization in the previous case, TWI, has been able to diversify its research on materials into work on production processes. It has developed new knowledge about processes and how they can be managed more effectively in its project NOMAD.

Simulating production environments: Project NOMAD

NOMAD (Autonomous Manufacturing of Large-Scale Steel Fabrications) is a European research project aiming to create a manufacturing system using autonomous mobile robots to fabricate customized large steel products. It is part-funded by the European Commission and involves two robotics companies, a manufacturing software solutions company, a welding equipment manufacturer, a structural steel fabrications company, a multinational large equipment and engine manufacturer, and two industrial research and technology organizations. The project is a response to increased competition in the European steel fabrication industry resulting from the market entry by low-cost overseas manufacturers, labour shortages, and increasing demand from customers for rapid production of bespoke products. The project has developed an integrated automated planning system for welding, robot programming, and robot transport vehicle positioning. Several technological developments have resulted including simulation software enabling feedback on the position of robots and components in the actual work environment that help optimize positioning for the robot arm. To support this, NOMAD has developed a vision system for accurate navigation of the mobile robots and a part-recognition system to relate CAD data in the simulation model with actual components being welded.

The process begins by entering design data in a CAD system. When the CAD model is completed, it is loaded into the simulation system. At this point the simulation system can use a 3D virtual model of the component and the welding cell.[100] By using this in conjunction with the images from the vision system it is able to match the virtual component position and orientation to that of the real component in the welding cell. The next stage is for the simulation system to develop a path for the robot transport vehicle (RTV) and the motion of the robot arm. This can be demonstrated by simulation. The simulation system generates a program for the robot, which is then used to control the real-life equipment. The real RTV and robot motion is activated by the simulation system. By using feedback from the vision system the position of the RTV and the robot can be adjusted on an iterative basis and changes are based on the final destination of the RTV once the previous command set has been executed. Work only progresses if the simulation system recognizes the component.

According to Nick Spong, an engineer at TWI, the integration of technologies is only made possible by the use of advanced simulation technology software. Without the simulation technology the robot would have to be physically programmed for each new product. The NOMAD project's two-way feedback process means that instead of having to take the robot off-line and physically program it for each new product, NOMAD has a closed loop process and the system has all the information it needs to do the job.

This project engages with the interfaces of IvT, OMT, and ICT. The end objective is implementation: the efficient manufacture of one-off products using OMT. The process involves ICT: the infrastructure enabling the transfer of information between design, planning, and operations. It also involves IvT: the use of simulations to facilitate the economies of effort and definiteness of aim in the system.

Spong points to some of the advantages and potential dangers of using simulations:

I think the NOMAD project will become the norm. As software becomes more sophisticated and leads to greater integration of systems, greater predictability of outcomes and profits, simulation technology will be used more and more. Simulation technologies will increase innovation, but we do have to be careful that we don't only rely on simulations to tell us about our world, if we take out the human element totally we risk all sorts of mistakes. At the moment simulations are tested against real world examples, in the future we may become so secure about our simulation technology that we stop testing against the real world, this would be a mistake.

The uses of IvT described in this chapter have so far been seen to support later stages of product and process development. In Chapter 3 we showed how Arup used a suite of Internet tools to create a communications and data exchange system enabling the company to develop innovative solutions across its projects. IvT is being used to assist designers, engineers, and managers to make choices that simultaneously improve product development and production processes. Many examples of integration between ICT, IvT, and production technologies can be found even in traditional industries like housing construction.

Willmott Dixon Housing Ltd, for example, a privately owned UK housing contractor working in the social housing market, devised a database of components, products, processes, and previous case histories of projects that are linked together through an interactive website called Matrix 1 available on the firm's intranet. The Matrix is a searchable relational database that provides an integrated source of information on many aspects of housing design and construction associated with technology, suppliers, production schedules, costs, standard elements, detailed designs, environmental assessment, and production data about time, quality, waste, and defects. Development of the tool began in the late 1990s and was built over a five-year period as more component, project, and process information became available during its use.

It was originally used as an in-house tool for specifying parts that helped link potential housing designs with process issues that the contractor needed to deal with including issues about regulatory compliance. Through time the tool proved a reliable and useful source of guidance for design and production management, so much so that Willmott Dixon gave access to the intranet site to a number of its clients with whom it had partnership arrangements. It also provided access to key external design consultants and first-tier suppliers. These external collaborators found the tool useful in helping them make decisions about housing production, with the unintended consequence of stimulating deeper interaction with Willmott Dixon, which was viewed as an innovative industry leader because of the way it had introduced technology to link product design with production processes.

In 2003, the company won a UK-wide industry award in recognition of its innovativeness and use of Matrix 1. This also helped secure a stream of new orders such that the company enjoyed a full-order book.

A further use of IvT in relation to prototyping processes and improving operational performance can be found in the use of models to analyse why accidents occur and to demonstrate how these can be ameliorated through innovative changes to these processes. The Australian mining industry shows how IvT models and simulations can be used for thinking, playing, and doing. It illustrates how these tools can be used for a wide range of purposes including the improvement of safety performance.

6.7 Improving processes in the mining industry

The mining industry has traditionally been seen primarily as a developer and user of relatively unsophisticated technology. In this view, simple technologies are used by prospectors to find minerals deposits; rocks are blasted or cut on a massive scale, transported in vast bulk, and then smashed and processed to get at ores or highly valuable substances, such as gold and diamonds. To add to this image the mining industry is notorious for damaging the environment, and for being a dangerous place to work in.

In reality the mining industry is capable of being highly innovative, and some of the new technologies being developed and used in it are not only improving the economics and efficiencies of the industry but also reducing environmental damage and improving safety. The industrial processes in the industry include exploration, mine planning, extraction, and processing. All are affected by IvT.

In the field of minerals exploration, satellite and aerial remote sensing provides substantial new data sources on minerals deposits. Research being conducted at Commonwealth Scientific and Industrial Research Organization (CSIRO), Australia in the so-called 'Glass Earth' project aims to make the first kilometre of the Australian continent 'transparent' to enable the discovery of new ore deposits, as well as assist in future land management. The project entails the development of geo-informatics, which enables and enhances management, integration and interpretation of spatial data, and research collaboration based on next-generation airborne gravity gradiometry, a tensor magnetic gradiometer and associated software platforms for data integration and interpretation.[101]

Traditional geophysical and geochemical exploration is being combined with the new data processing, modelling, and visualization techniques, to improve the design of mines. 3D mapping of ore bodies determine precise geological structures, enabling better targeted and more efficient extraction. Greater accuracy in extraction efforts reduces collateral damage to areas surrounding deposits, improves energy consumption, and reduces the time miners need to spend underground. These techniques not only provide information on new deposits but can also extend the useful life of existing mines.

Start-up companies, such as Fractal Graphics, are being created to use the new data sources and are producing integrated and accessible visualization environments to assist decision-making. Fractal's software aims to produce efficient data modelling and representation of geoscientific information that can be used intuitively. The company conducts collaborative research in a number of areas, including the development of a spatial information system in which data from different sources, visualized in a 3D environment, may be handled, integrated, and queried (Vandermark 2003). The use of these tools around the new data sources enables better mine design, and reduces the number of on-site geologists required (and hence reduces costs and risks).

As well as being applied to solve many of the complex problems of mine design, virtual reality is being used in experimental modelling, accident reconstruction, education and training, and in environmental monitoring. Many of the processes involved in mining are either unobservable or simply too dangerous to observe. Virtual reality tools are used to overcome these problems and are being applied in examining, for example, the processes of spontaneous combustion in coal, and gas leakage and flow.

All fatal mine accidents are subject to extensive reviews. The causes of accidents are often complex, difficult to comprehend, and their examination is very lengthy. Virtual reality facilitates quick representation and understanding of the causes of accidents, allowing fast remedies. With safety being of paramount concern, and the high cost of equipment damage (particularly underground), the use of virtual reality to train staff about safe and productive practices, and hazard identification and response, can produce significant economies. Mining engineering academics argue that graduate education of mining engineers has improved substantially as a result of the development of interactive 3D models of mine development, operations, and equipment.[102]

Accurate virtual maps of mine sites, produced through the combination of aerial photography and topographical maps, enable the visualization of the environmental impact of mines. Mining companies can use this for operational purposes, and can demonstrate in detail the visual consequences of developments to local residents and concerned environmentalists. Virtual reality can identify particular features of a site, such as a storage pond, and can model its changing chemical constitution and toxicity over time.

IvT is being applied to minerals extraction in a number of areas. The world-famous Julius Kruttschnitt Mineral Research Centre has developed a modelling approach with accompanying software to help engineers design and run their operations better. A typical application is in designing a comminution circuit (that is, one in which the ore is crushed and ground prior to treatment to extract the valuable components). Comminution is capital-intensive and one of the most energy-intensive processes in the world, so there are strong incentives to make the process as efficient as possible. The software allows steady-state simulation of the process so that the engineer can size the equipment and lay out the circuit optimally to achieve the right product size of the ore at the right feed rate (tonnes per hour) and at minimum capital and operating cost. An example is provided by the Cadia Gold Mine in New South Wales, which uses the world's largest mill of its type. The design of its comminution circuit followed two years of study and evaluation, predominantly using simulation techniques.

A wide range of new technologies are being developed and applied in the processing of minerals. New tools are being used that enable experimental development work to proceed without the production of physical prototypes (which in the minerals industry can be large in scale and expense). For example, the development of CFD based on mathematical models for multiphase fluid processing systems has enabled better predictive modelling in the design of new smelting technologies, such as Rio Tinto's HIsmelt technology (Vandermark 2003).

Whilst many of these new technologies have significant potential consequences for the efficiency and profitability of the minerals industry, mining companies are notoriously conservative in their use of technological advances. Many of the technologies are still emergent, and their wide diffusion may take some years. The industry is renowned, however, for being relatively quick at adopting proven technologies, and once a technology is utilized effectively by lead companies, it is likely that diffusion will occur rapidly throughout the industry.

6.8 Conclusions

In this chapter we have explored the development of new ways of putting ideas into practice supported by IvT. The process of propagating ideas once selected has been illustrated in a variety of sectors from solving problems in biomechanics to innovation in motor vehicles. The use of rapid prototyping technology has been shown to be an essential component of the IvT tool kit in the 'doing' phase of the innovation process. 3D models highlight issues about how parts fit together earlier in the product development process. The use of rapid prototyping machines is becoming ubiquitous with examples in engineering analysis, product modelling, architecture, manufacturing, construction, and surgery. New and old sectors alike have been able to use rapid prototyping to create a form of dialogue between designers, their creations, and their makers. The development and use of simulation software has been of particular importance in the integration of production process models with real-life production activities.

The availability of better instrumentation in production processes provides fine-grained data and rich feedback, which can be used in subsequent design iterations. In areas where new materials or advanced processes are used, such as in the application of nanotechnology, or in environments used to fabricate silicon chips, we have found that instrumentation used in production provides data that feeds directly into next-generation product and process innovation. In other sectors such as biomedicine, it is possible to explore the likelihood of disease occurring in particular segments of the population and then develop finely tuned treatments such as those described at the beginning of the chapter, coupling macro data analysis with bespoke solutions.

Tightly coupled feedback from production processes to technical development activities is creating scope for more scientific approaches to 'doing'. In some industries, manufacturing and production is becoming closer to science. Production processes are becoming closer to think and play. Looking at the innovation process from the point of view of manufacturing and OMT, it appears that manufacturing requires more knowledge of the sciences than ever before. In some sectors, science is limited by the ability of manufacturing practice to put the outcomes into application. There is therefore a need for closer integration between science, technology, engineering, and design. IvT can help in this regard and *Think, Play, Do* provides a schema for organizing this knowledge.

Integration of what have traditionally been separate activities is an important outcome of the ability to prototype. This is occurring within the innovation process through the links between 'play and do' and between 'think and do'. In some instances they can be integrated with product development and design activities through the use of IvT. But in some industries it is not clear how the scale of operations relates to these development processes. In nano-engineering issues relate to scaling production down to the nano-level. In other areas, such as the development of fine chemicals, the scale-up of operations from laboratory test tubes to commercial production facilities is notoriously difficult to simulate or prototype. These attributes of 'do' and IvT are creating new opportunities for concurrent engineering in which the 3D model becomes a central data-set for thinking, playing, and doing.

The use of IvT linked to ICT and OMT has consequences for the organization of processes and relationships between different participants in research, design, engineering, production, operations, and maintenance. In order to benefit from the collection and use of performance data in innovation processes firms are beginning to coordinate information up and down supply networks. This often leads to new forms of partnerships and coordination in supply chains to exploit opportunities for accessing and using specialist knowledge from different parts of the supply network. In manufacturing in the past, linkages between suppliers and assemblers have helped manufacturers to make products more efficiently and effectively. With the advent of IvT, such linkages can be exploited to enable supply networks to innovate. The digital tool kit for design, manufacture, and coordination is increasingly being used for multiple purposes; for example, in Chapter 3 we illustrated how P & G uses simulation tools to enable better supply-chain management. The 'doing' phase in innovation processes connects information from design with that of production and use, enabling engineers and technologists to prototype, test commercial viability, predict likely market and production requirements, and thereby implement new ideas.

The 'doing' part of the innovation process is evolving rapidly as IvT and new ways of organizing processes emerge. It is possible to envisage a closer coupling of the system in many industries as firms seek to differentiate products and services by designing for niche markets or in a bespoke manner for individual customers. In future it may be possible to 'grow' objects, particularly through the evolution of bioengineering, or to print products at the point of consumption following a pick-and-mix, design-your-own process. Designer Ron Arad foresees a time when

you won't go to the shop to buy a toy for your child. You'll go online, pay by credit card and simply download the toy at home. Or, when you call the plumber to mend a fault he'll check out the problem, find the product required from a database in a palm-top computer, then manufacture it on his mobile rapid manufacturing outfit in the back of his van. It will be that simple.[103]

7 The Strategic Management of Innovation

7.1 Introduction

The changes in the innovation process associated with the use of IvT in thinking, playing, and doing have considerable consequences for managers. Innovation is a core business process and its outcomes are of critical importance for competitiveness. Managing innovation cannot be left to chance; it is too important, expensive, and risky. Managers need to use every means available to produce results quickly and efficiently.

IvT assists the management of innovation, but only when an appropriate strategy is developed and deployed, with related organizational and skills issues being addressed. Developing a strategy and organizing effectively requires a deep understanding of the potential uses and limitations of IvT and how this technology relates to ICT and OMT, as well as the new processes of think, play, and do in specific worksettings. Preceding chapters have shown how IvT can increase variety and options through thinking, improve selection choices through playing, and enhance efficiency in turning ideas into action through doing. With the right organizational structures and skills profiles the technology can reduce the cost, increase the speed, and ameliorate some of the uncertainty of innovation. These are all important contributors to the overall objectives for managers of creating and delivering value, and constructing sustainable competitive advantage through innovation.

Previous chapters have described some approaches firms have adopted to manage thinking, playing, and doing. Chapter 8 considers some of the future management challenges in the new innovation process. This chapter is concerned with the ways managers can gain *strategic* benefits from using IvT to unite thinking, playing, and doing.

There are many different theories of, and approaches to, strategic management and our intent is not to criticize, test, or develop them. Our purpose is to consider how IvT can and may affect some of the major components of strategy formulation and implementation. Hence we propose a relatively simple and highly stylized characterization of strategy. In our formulation, strategic advantage derives from the ways firms establish a 'base' or 'core' set of resources or competencies that enable them to create value and compete on the basis of cost or differentiation. Hereafter, we refer to these simply as 'competencies'.[104] These competencies are adapted and changed over time by what are called 'dynamic capabilities' by some researchers; those elements of firms that facilitate the reconfiguration of existing, and creation of new, competencies to meet new opportunities. Hereafter, we refer to these simply as 'capabilities'.[105] The chapter examines the way IvT can assist in establishing the competencies of the firm and the capabilities that help them recombine to face new competitive challenges.

The chapter concentrates primarily on capabilities, or those factors that provide the potential for change. Three groups of capabilities are considered: integrating across boundaries; organizing internal structures and processes; and learning, creativity, and knowledge. Some of the most important management issues related to the implementation and development of these strategic capabilities are discussed. The focus is on the relationships between IvT and these capabilities. Based on the case studies and other research, the chapter presents observations both on the ways IvT is currently managed strategically in the emerging innovation process, and also some speculations on the way it could be managed in the future. The key elements of the chapter are shown in Fig. 7.1.

Before examining the impact of IvT on competencies and capabilities a number of the major features of strategy are described in Box 7.1 on strategic management theory. This briefly describes some of the rich literature from which our simple conception of strategic management is derived.

7.2 The impact of IvT on competencies

IvT may help firms with strategic focus and direction because it can provide the confidence to specialize in activities grouped around a 'base', and then to diversify from that base. When used effectively, IvT can enable the creation of highly specific and difficult-to-replicate competencies, whilst also providing the ability to relatively simply communicate and integrate those competencies with those of others. It is the way that the innovation process, assisted by high levels of integration and the application of learning, knowledge, and creativity, allows competencies to be exploited and developed that is the essence of an innovation strategy.

Enhanced industrial specialization and disaggregation may result from the capacity of IvT to better involve and integrate users and consumers and to manage and represent knowledge more effectively. IvT enables firms to concentrate upon their areas of comparative expertise and position themselves in the stream of activities that create value safe in the knowledge that the capacity exists to search for, and effectively access, complementary technologies and

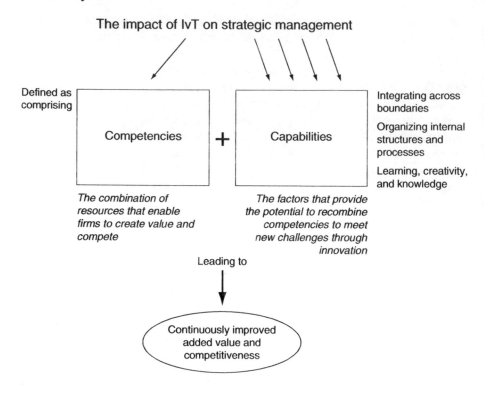

Fig. 7.1 The impact of IvT on strategic management

services.[106] In this sense a technology that is capable of integrating a range of activities is also capable of supporting a disintegrated industry structure.

Some firms are making the transition from being product-based to becoming solutions providers. As the traditional distinction between manufacturing and services blurs, many managers have had to give greater attention to how they will position their firm's products and services in relation to the streams of activities in their industry. The use of IvT provides opportunities for firms to realign themselves in their value stream and has enabled some firms to position themselves as systems integrators. We have described the way IBM has repositioned itself as a solutions provider combining service provision with in-house and external equipment.[107]

Knowledge of 'think' and 'play' is leading some organizations upstream to become product development and software houses. Firms, such as Ricardo and Arup, are developing software business capabilities. They are transferring their in-house technological competencies in IvT into a new range of products and services aimed at a variety of sectors. In other cases, firms are moving

Box 7.1   Strategic management theory

Strategy is especially important in circumstances where products, services, markets, and technologies change quickly, in unpredictable directions, and with the potential of hugely disruptive consequences. Here it is strategy that helps forge a path through the mass of options and choices and the fog of uncertainty surrounding firms. Strategy guides decisions about what firms should do, and what they should not. It directs the selection of business activities and technologies that firms need to attract customers and to remain competitive.

There are advantages in possessing a relatively specialized 'core' or 'base'—those activities, or 'bundles of resources', that provide focus to a firm's operations and identity—around which a strategy is developed and implemented. This base provides the reference point to which competing developments and projects are referred for legitimation and resourcing. This element of strategy is a matter of knowing what you do best, sticking to it, whilst also allowing for related development, and outsourcing all else that is needed to satisfy customers. The essence of the importance and nature of strategy was nicely summarized by Edith Penrose (1959: 137) over forty years ago:

'In the long run the profitability, survival, and growth of a firm does not depend so much on the efficiency with which it is able to organise the production of even a widely diversified range of products as it does on the ability of the firm to establish one or more wide and relatively impregnable "bases" from which it can adapt and extend its operations in an uncertain, changing and competitive world.'

For Penrose, it is the firm's capacity to dynamically adjust its resource base that sustains competitiveness.[108] Dynamic changes are also a feature of evolutionary theory (Nelson and Winter 1982), which identifies the significance of routines as the economic analogues of genes in biology. Routines are the organizational memory for an organization, its base repository of knowledge and skills. These theories resonate with contemporary 'resource-based theories' of strategy (Barney 1986; Grant and MacNamara 1995) and notions of 'core competencies' (Prahalad and Hamel 1990) that identify the importance of focus and diversification around a base. Case studies of large companies, such as IBM and Ericsson show how important this base is, and how it is possible to reconfigure it even in quite profound ways. So IBM has made a major transition from being a product-based company to being an e-business-based service company (Gerstner 2002) and Ericsson has changed from being product-based to being an integrated solutions company (Davies et al. 2003). Both these companies have made this transition around their core technological base.

The concept of having a focused base in strategy does not apply only to large firms. Roberts (1991: 283) argues, based on his studies of high-technology companies spun-off from MIT:

'The best opportunities for rapid growth of a young firm come from building an internal critical mass of engineering talent in a focused technological area, yielding a distinctive core technology that might evolve over time, to provide a foundation for the company's product development.'

A firm's core or base of resources is supported, exploited, developed, and diversified by means of 'dynamic capabilities' through which new knowledge, learning, and creativity can be orchestrated for competitive advantage. Dynamic capabilities are particularly valuable in rapidly changing and uncertain environments, where the ownership and reconfiguration of knowledge resources are the primary means of creating competitive advantage (Teece and Pisano 1994; Grant 1996; Kogut 1996). They are most useful in 'high-velocity markets', typified by 'ambiguous industry structure, blurred boundaries, fluid business models, ambiguous and shifting players, nonlinear and unpredictable change' (Eisenhardt and Martin 2000: 1115). Dynamic capabilities provide a mechanism for preventing core competencies ►

becoming 'core rigidities' (Leonard-Barton 1995). A dynamic capabilities approach has been used to analyse strategic management in, amongst others, the international biotechnology industry (Madhok and Osegowitsch 2000), small UK manufacturing firms (Bessant et al. 2001), the disk-drive industry (King and Tucci 2002), and the growth of the search engine companies, Yahoo! and Excite (Rindova and Kotha 2001).

Dynamic capabilities are most simply conceptualized as tools that manipulate resource reconfigurations (Eisenhardt and Martin 2000: 1118). They are not an end in themselves: they are a means to an end; the combinations of resources that create value and competitiveness.[109]

downstream to focus on operational services. The use of IvT in itself does not necessarily lead firms to choose to move downstream or upstream in the value chain but does sharpen the decision environment by forcing them to rethink their competencies, skills, and expertise on an almost continuous basis.

By facilitating the opportunities for firms to both integrate across boundaries and focus on core activities, IvT extends the strategic choices open to firms. As shown in Box 7.1, however, the strategic management challenge extends beyond the definition of competencies and includes the development of those capabilities that enable their recombination. Key amongst these capabilities are the ways in which firms integrate across boundaries, organize themselves, and manage knowledge, creativity, and learning, and it is to these issues and their relationships with IvT that we now turn. Some specific organizational and skills matters related to IvT are discussed to illustrate how innovation strategy can be implemented in practice.

7.3 Integrating across boundaries

Integrating across boundaries—what Rothwell calls 'strategic integration' in the fifth generation innovation process—is important both within and outside the firm and necessary for thinking, playing, and doing in the innovation process. Whilst such integration is often an essential management requirement of particular projects, more importantly, as in the case of P&G in Chapter 3, it is a continuing feature of the strategic management of firms. The effective management of contributions to an integrated innovation process is a key to continuing competitiveness.

Thinking, playing, and doing can be better interwoven and unified as a result of the use of IvT. It can have an impact on both managers' attitudes to, and relationships with, their firm's internal and external environments. It can assist with forming effective new partnerships and business relationships, bringing the science base, customers, suppliers, and partners closer to the innovative organization, and facilitating internal integration of different domains of activity, such as research, engineering, manufacturing, design, operations, and marketing.

There is substantial evidence showing the value of technological collaboration across company boundaries and how it allows firms to learn not only about new technologies but also about new organizational practices and strategies (Dodgson 1993a; Powell et al. 1996; Sakakibara 1997, 2001; Child and Faulkner 1998).

Whilst networks of relationships between firms and their external environments can play an important role in shaping strategic performance, managers need to ensure that both their organizational structures and technology are supportive in building those links (Dodgson 1993b). In the following sections we describe the role IvT can play in breaking down boundaries and supporting collaboration between organizations involved in innovation.

Integrating with customers

One of the most important aspects of successfully managing across boundaries is the quality of linkages with customers in innovation. Since Project SAPPHO in the 1970s (Rothwell et al. 1974), numerous research projects have shown that successful innovation in a wide range of industries requires the integration of different productive domains—research, production, marketing—and the involvement of customers. This is still the case. The UK government's innovation survey of 2,634 manufacturing firms in 2000 found that 66 per cent of firms source knowledge and information for innovation from customers (DTI 2003).

Engagement with sophisticated end-users enhances innovative product development (von Hippel 1988) and can lead to the development of 'robust' design iterations and families of products (Gardiner and Rothwell 1985). Various kinds of IvT are being used to support this engagement. As seen in Chapter 5, 'innovation tool kits' are being used to involve the customer in the development of new products and services. This is part of the process of the strategic shift in some sectors from customer-involved innovation to customer-driven innovation, and is associated with the ways in which ease of customer input is facilitated by the creation and development of IvT such as virtual prototyping.

Simulation of the use of products and working with users to evaluate options as part of the 'design conversation' is also a new and important part of the design and engineering process. We have seen the way Sekisui in housing, Toyota, Mazda, and Ford in automobiles, and companies in the computer games and fashion industries systematically use customer feedback based on virtual products and simulations to improve their new product development processes. The virtual product testing approach by P&G sees users and customers as central actors in the refinement and selection of concepts for further product development.

Integrating with suppliers

IvT also enables more effective management of the integration of suppliers into the innovation process. The UK's innovation survey shows 68 per cent of firms source knowledge and information for innovation from suppliers of equipment, materials, components, and software (DTI 2003). A classic case in this regard is the use of CATIA in the design of the Boeing 777.[110] The concurrent involvement of design and engineering was a critical element of the 'working together' philosophy of the 777 team. Substantial elements of the design and manufacture of the aircraft were subcontracted, notably the engines and large elements of the airframe and rudders, and combining these various contributors was extremely important for the success of the whole process. IvT played a central role in this integration. Boeing distributed 2,200 computer terminals amongst the 777 design team, all of them connected to the world's largest grouping of IBM mainframes. Key suppliers, such as manufacturers of airframes in Japan, of engines in the UK and USA, and of rudders in Australia, were linked to this system enabling immediate communication of design changes. The massive machine tool used to assemble the aircraft, the Automated Spar Assembly Tool, was designed by a team that involved the manufacturer of the tool, Boeing engineers, and production staff. In all, Boeing created 250 'design-build' teams to produce the 777, many of them relying on the use of CATIA to assist their task. In essence, IvT helped enable the decision by Boeing to move away from being totally internally integrated in its design and manufacturing towards being a systems integrator that partners with, and purchases from, a range of suppliers. It helped the company realize its new strategy.

P&G relies on specialized suppliers to help it develop its own IvT capability. It works closely with technology brokers such as IDEO in the early stages of concept design and with suppliers of rapid prototyping equipment to develop highly refined models of its products. The construction of Gehry's complex buildings depend upon the capacities of IvT to manage the supply and delivery of their various components. Relationships of firms with intermediaries such as TWI and Internet-based brokers such as InnoCentive are assisted by the use of IvT.

Integrating with the science base

Innovation is not always market-driven and integration with the science base facilitated by technologies such as the Grid can, as we have seen in the case of Rolls Royce, be very important in certain circumstances. Innovative firms can draw on knowledge by collaborating with universities to help them develop

170

and commercialize new technologies. There is a large body of literature exploring the links between universities and industry in the innovation process (Hicks and Katz 1997; Meyer-Krahmer and Schmoch 1998; Mowery et al. 2001; Cohen et al. 2002; Lambert 2003) showing that industry–university links differ across industries and that there is rarely a direct transfer of ideas from universities into commercial products.

Indeed, there are a variety of mechanisms used by firms to manage their access to, and interaction with, the university system. Those firms that do collaborate with universities do so in different and highly interactive ways. Cohen et al. (2002), for example, found that universities help not only to generate new ideas but also to complete existing R&D projects. Recent research in the UK suggests that only a modest percentage of firms use universities as a source of knowledge for innovation, and that these firms tend to be those who adopt open-search strategies, combining collaboration and knowledge from universities with other sources of ideas (Laursen and Salter 2004). The UK innovation survey shows 27 per cent of firms source knowledge and information for innovation from universities, and 18 per cent do so from government research laboratories.

Our case studies have shown how firms and public policy-makers turn to research providers in universities and research institutes to help solve problems. Whether it is to analyse and then fix a wobbly bridge, plan a traffic congestion charge, save a historic building, check the safety of a chemical reactor, or design a new bra, universities have the instruments and the brainpower to assist the thinking necessary to solve complex technical problems. As we saw in Chapter 4, the enormous expansion of the university and research sector with the increased capacity for thinking about potentially useful new options provides an additional incentive for firms to collaborate with it.

Integrating with competitors

The case of the engineering services firm, Arup, shows how IvT has created new relationships between competitors. Arup works with its competitor, Mott MacDonald, to refine the STEPS model. In this case, improving the software benefits both organizations, and the benefits of cooperation outweigh the advantages of competition. By working together, the firms can continuously develop and refine software, allowing both firms to develop evermore sophisticated understanding of the movement of people in a building during extreme events. The UK's innovation survey shows that 54 per cent of firms source knowledge and information for innovation from competitors. The management of such relationships when firms collaborate and compete at the same time is a continuing challenge.

Systems integration

In Chapter 6, the importance of modularity in production was discussed. Systems integration has become more important as production is increasingly modularized. Systems integration can be defined as the capability to design and integrate internally or externally developed components into a finished product (Brusoni et al. 2001; Davies et al. 2003; Prencipe et al. 2003). Systems integrators are responsible for coordinating a network of upstream component suppliers and subcontractors, designing and integrating systems and providing services that add value to the product. Firms that are system integrators often need to retain deep technological knowledge about components and systems in order to be able to integrate them.

IvT offers the potential for much more collaborative working across organizations and countries to help produce integrated systems. It allows firms to more easily transfer technical information and knowledge across different technological platforms. For example, Ricardo's new simulation suite allows organizations to use 'best-in-class' software and to combine and mix tools from different service providers. By using these integration suites, engineers are better able to see how changes in one part of the system may affect other parts. In doing so, they support systems integration, enabling managers to better understand how to combine and integrate different systems, modules, and components for business advantage. When combined with sophisticated use of ICTs, IvT creates new opportunities for communication and integration across organizations. For example, Arup's project extranets allow organizations to share knowledge and drawings without an independent capability in CAD. In the case of P&G, virtual models are emailed to lay users around the world where they can see, manipulate, and play with different technological options.

The greater use of modular components in design and development could also shape the use of IvT. In theory, by allowing individual producers to concentrate on the design and development of their components, modularization could support greater efficiencies in design and greater specialization in the production system. In such circumstances the capacities of IvT to assist systems integration are extremely valuable.[111]

All these different types of interactions—with customers, suppliers, science base—are an important part of the movement towards more distributed and networked models of the innovation process, and require more open and collaborative management practices and approaches with complementary and integrated investments in IvT. The strategic management challenge is to use IvT to its fullest extent in building relationships so that innovation becomes a collaborative activity whilst at the same time managing issues like pricing and ownership of intellectual property. The challenge is to use all the connections, opportunities, and learning from linking with external parties to develop and use the competencies in the firm.

7.4 Organizing internal structures and processes

Questions about the way firms can be structured in order to benefit from IvT revisit one of the perennial issues of management and technological innovation: how do firms organize themselves to both exploit their existing ways of doing things and explore new ones (March 1991).

In many routine operations and production activities, creating, refining, and optimizing the performance of formal and consistent processes remain central to productivity improvements. Efforts to make processes leaner and to compress the time required to deliver products and services are well advanced and an essential part of the benefits that accrue to firms and society from the use of OMT (see Chapter 6). Innovation and creativity, however, require a very different organizational approach. Innovation tends not to prosper in organizations reliant on highly formal processes and procedures. In some ways, these processes are anathema to creative people in manufacturing, service, or creative industries. These people may find that such processes and rules constrict their freedom of movement and flexibility to move from task to task and output to output.

From our observations of workers in the companies we studied, the innovative people who use IvT—the thinkers, players, and doers—respond to enthusiasm, opportunity, and newness as well as to achievement through delivery. In this environment, managers' attempts to formally plan, direct, and coordinate sometimes fail. The use of IvT creates the need for managers who can find ways to utilize the energy and dynamism of their workforce around IvT to stimulate opportunities for innovation, often by encouraging working across internal and external boundaries.

We can speculate that the kinds of organizational structures, skills profile, and management styles that are more effective at using IvT are similar whether they are applied to disruptive or incremental innovation. This is because investment in IvT provides an infrastructure for the continuing cost-effective search for, and selection of, new options, which may involve exploiting existing capabilities in novel ways or combinations, or exploring new ones. Once the IvT-enabled work environment has been constructed, with the capacity to think, play, and do quickly and relatively cheaply, all possibilities can be considered for improving existing or developing new products, processes, and services. New opportunities to use IvT may produce unforeseen step-change improvements in products, processes, or services that previously improved only incrementally, and may provide an early-warning system on potentially disruptive innovations, which can then draw on the IvT-enabled networks and capabilities to rapidly assess their potential. IvT brings both market and science closer to the innovator, rapidly providing knowledge about how things might be done better or differently. As seen in Chapter 1, despite many firms' best efforts, innovation remains uncertain. It remains difficult to predict when incremental innovations may be superseded by disruptive changes and when disruptive innovations begin to become incremental. It is therefore useful to be able to use IvT for both, and the technology may assist in delivering the 'ambidexterity' necessary to organize for incremental and disruptive circumstances.

In the following sections we analyse some practices that support the implementation of this organizational element of an innovation strategy.

Project-based structures

Some firms using IvT appear to have adopted an organizational form that is similar to Mintzberg and McHugh's 'adhocracy' (1985). In ad hoc organizations, there is no formal separation between those planning and designing work and those executing it. Most of the work is done in projects, either in-house or for external clients. In Mintzberg and McHugh's formulation, these organizations are separated administratively from the rest of the organization, reflecting a division of labour between projects and routine operations.

The characteristics and advantages of such project-based organizations are that they offer a new model for coordinating loose networks of highly skilled individuals performing specific tasks (DeFillippi and Arthur 1998) and for coordinating complex innovations involving a variety of contributors (Hobday 1998). Like Burns and Stalker's 'organic' form of organization (1961), this environment is useful for promoting innovation. Ad hoc project-based organizations allow managers to combine and recombine skills and capabilities in different and sometimes new and serendipitous ways. They provide an organizational environment that enables staff to work in collaboration internally and with a range of external sources of knowledge on technological or market opportunities. The project-based nature of work means that staff are able to shift from task to task, avoiding the boredom that may be associated with carrying out routine operations. Adhocracies help keep things lively for easily bored employees and they directly appeal to the work styles of creative, skilled professionals.[112]

In some of the professional design and engineering firms described in this book, an ad hoc, project-based structure is the preferred form of organization, not only for part of the company but for the whole firm. The size of the company is not the issue here but the nature of the market: Arup, for example, is a large, project-based firm. Depending upon the extent of the routine activities of the firm, project-based organization can be used in a part or in the whole of a company. One of the future challenges for managers is establishing the extent to which project-based organization may exist alongside other divisional, functional, or matrix organizational structures to assist in helping firms realize Tushman and O'Reilly's strategy (1997) of creating two different, ambidextrous, organizational structures: one for formal processes and delivery, and one for innovation.

Teamworking

New approaches to teamworking can be assisted by IvT. In these approaches, a premium is placed on the ability of the team to create and nurture innovation, and IvT can play a role in the construction and operation of these teams.

In more traditional organizational structures, teams are often coherent, durable, and consistent. Numerous research projects have shown the need to have balanced representation and involvement of different domains in the project team and how there is value in building up organizational routines and memory in teams (Iansiti 1993). Such teams may involve people from different disciplines and backgrounds and members can work together for long periods, building up strong routines, memories, and habits. These teams are highly effective at conducting a series of related projects in a particular technological or market area. Many of these teams are concentrated in a particular location to take advantage of close physical proximity to share knowledge. If it becomes necessary to promote or change innovation practices, however, these long-lasting teams can become a constraint as they have a tendency to suffer from considerable inertia, often resulting from a propensity towards autarky and internal dependence for information. In order to avoid these problems of organizational introspection, management scholars have argued for team structures to be made more permeable and flexible (Wheelwright and Clark 1995). To deal with the challenges, many organizations have created new team management strategies that involve high rotation between team members, high diversity amongst staff in discipline and nationality, and the use of teams from a variety of different geographical locations.

Firms locate teams in key places to benefit from the innovative opportunities that may be present in a particular region (Gerybadze and Reger 1999). Their teams act as a local node in a global network of innovation, creating opportunities for the firm to benefit from the variety of different knowledge-intensive communities around the world allowing home-based activities to be augmented as well as exploited (Kuemmerle 1997). P&G teams in the UK, for example, work with partners in the USA, Belgium, India, and China on new product development. Such global networks can effectuate a valuable nexus for creating and sharing ideas across space and time.[113]

The use of IvT enables distributed and diverse teams to become even more effective. Its use produces greater confidence in the teams' ability to integrate different components or elements of a product, service, or project, and through their ability to represent complex designs in more readily comprehensible ways, they facilitate more effective knowledge flow. Through easily accessible and intuitive search tools, thinkers, players, and doers may come to rely less on existing repositories of knowledge which could be codified in ways that may be limiting. They can search for, and shape, the information they require in the ways most useful to them. If the cost of experimentation and failure is reduced, there is also less concern with precedents and being locked into past practices and behaviours.

Whilst IvT can enable knowledge to be created, represented, and transferred across fluid and changing boundaries, managers in the case studies recognize that electronic media exist alongside and never replace face-to-face communications. Sharing information in a cost-effective and prompt manner by means of technology is relatively simple: sharing knowledge is considerably more complex. Lester and Piore (2004) highlight two important strategic management activities that are necessary in creating new products and services through the process of turning information and shared understanding into useful knowledge. The first is the ability to analyse, using rational, problem-solving skills, resulting in clearly articulated decisions. The second is the ability to interpret, gaining new insights and ways of seeing opportunities and problems that do not fit a rational model of decision-making. Harnessing both, they argue, can significantly improve innovation outcomes.

Observers of electronically mediated knowledge sharing emphasize the manner in which effective knowledge exchange occurs amongst groups with some sense of shared identity or trust, whether they are 'epistemic communities' (Steinmueller 2000), 'communities of practice' (Brown and Duguid 2000), or communities of 'shared space' (Schrage 2000). Salter and Gann (2003) show that, although designers are keen users of electronic tools, they nonetheless rely heavily on close, personal interaction to solve problems, to develop ideas, and to assess the quality of their work, making the building of effective 'communities' critical to their success.

Physical work environment

The work environment around IvT shapes the innovativeness of its use, and IvT together with the think, play, do innovation process, presents new demands for particular types of physical space. Since the Hawthorne studies at the Western Electric Company from the mid-1920s to the early 1940s, it has been widely recognized that the physical layout of workspaces shapes the productivity, innovativeness, and effectiveness of teams. Allen (1977) showed in the early 1970s that patterns of communication amongst people on workplace were strongly shaped by their physical location. After 30 m, for example, the propensity of people to talk to their co-workers declines dramatically.

If IvT coupled with processes of thinking, playing, and doing is to result in more intensive innovation processes, it is likely that they will need to be conducted in appropriate spatial settings within buildings designed to accommodate the new innovation practices and technologies. There are multicausal relationships between the use of IvT, thinking, playing, and doing, and physical spaces that innovative people inhabit. Understanding how these issues relate to one another in particular business processes and providing the right quality of physical environment has become a strategic issue for management. New working patterns associated with think, play, do may require different spatial configurations, particularly if IvT is to be used to its maximum effect. For example, interdisciplinary, team-based project work requires space for informal meetings, brainstorming, and working in small groups with visual display tools. In other cases it is beneficial to bring customers and users into the process, working alongside designers, in the types of 'experience centres' developed by companies like Sekisui.

Since the early 1980s, some firms have begun to respond to the recognition that the type, quantity, and quality of physical space relates to the ways in which staff perform in particular functions. For some firms, appropriate space that accommodates new forms of interaction associated with the use of IvT, ICT, and OMT in offices, design studios, workshops, and production facilities has itself become an instrument of change, and a core part of the innovation process. Firms such as SAS, British Airways, Boots, Capital One, and the BBC have reconfigured their use of space to maximize the benefits of communication using digital media. This has had profound consequences for the types of buildings and their location in central business districts during the expansion and liberalization of financial services and telecommunications in the late 1980s (Gann 2000). The work of Duffy (1997) and Hillier (1996) has helped establish both a taxonomy of space and an analysis of space utilization.

Duffy identifies four types of space:

1. *Cells* are important for individual, specialized, contemplative, and reflective work. Cellular space is the traditional style of space used by thinkers with deep historical links, for example, to monks in their monastic cells.
2. *Hives* provide the opposite types of space in which multiple and similar tasks can be carried out independently by specialists working on dedicated equipment; examples include data processing in call-centre environments, or specialized and routinized scientific testing in pharmacology. In some environments these spaces resemble 'Fordist' production-line

spaces and they can be useful in the 'do' phases of the new innovation process.

3. *Dens* provide an environment for small, often multi-disciplinary teams to brainstorm, use whiteboards, prototype, and play with ideas. Dens are clearly the space for 'play'.

4. *Clubs* provide an environment for casual and informal interaction, for browsing, meeting people, and rubbing shoulders with colleagues. These are analogous to the debating chambers and 'smoking clubs' of the nineteenth century, where business is transacted and ideas exchanged in pleasant and relaxed environments. The modern-day equivalent may be found in some airport business lounges, hotels, conferences, and sports venues such as golf clubs. These types of space enable people from different businesses to trade ideas in informal settings.

Studies of university research centres show that better flows of information can result in increased information consumption, which in turn may aid innovation processes. For example, the two most significant determinants of productivity of scientists relating to their use of space are their ability to support concentrated work (cells) and to conduct impromptu interactions in their own workspaces and elsewhere (dens and clubs) (Brill 2001) Toker (2005) shows that amongst scientists face-to-face consultations predominate over electronic media as an information resource and form of communication. He shows that a number of features of space utilization can enhance the all-important face-to-face consultations amongst scientists that improve the opportunity to share and develop new ideas during thinking and playing. These include spatial configuration, visibility, walking distance, perceived environmental quality, and space-use attractors such as amenities (Toker 2005). In summary, proximity remains important to scientists and researchers, particularly in connectivity to other scientists, their tools and materials, local amenities, and space for casual, unprogrammed, coincidental encounters.

But the design and utilization of appropriate space presents considerable problems for strategic management of investment decisions, the provision of flexibility to meet unforeseen future requirements, the need to manage status associated with office size, or to deal with sporadic usage because people no longer only work at the laboratory or studio. Greater flexibility is required, because sometimes thinkers prefer to think in the quiet and privacy of their homes. IvT and the need to collaborate and interact in play and do can produce a creative buzz. Whilst in some instances, creative employees are attracted to workspaces that resemble clubs and cafés—places that are informal, loose, and friendly—this may not be desirable all the time. Dens and open-plan offices can be too noisy and chaotic for some activities and for certain types of people who need the contemplative space to think and work with rigour.

The challenge is to create workplaces that are flexible enough to accommodate the quiet required for contemplation with the energy and buzz needed to create and share new ideas in groups. With WiFi and portable, powerful computers, the workplace for some activities within the innovation process can be accommodated wherever people want to be. For example, the beach at Brighton in England has a wireless network, and there are around 400 small start-up multimedia companies working in the vicinity. People enjoy the local amenities and sometimes work on the beach.

There are downsides to the extensive openness of communication enabled by technology. Too much interaction can create a 'time famine' and cycles of overwork and related stress (Perlow et al. 2002). Many of the IvT environments studied for this book are work-intensive, involving long hours and high effort. Substantial interaction is necessary to create ideas, to play with and solve problems, and to consult on solutions. Thus, despite the time-saving benefits of IvT and its ability to assist interaction, work around it is often highly time-intensive and people still need time for solitary work and contemplation. The management challenge is to find a balance between solitary work and interaction. The balance chosen will change according to the type of work task that a person is involved in at any particular time. Multiple physical spaces may be required throughout the day. Essentially, IvT is one of the technologies that is breaking down the boundaries between work and play.[114] This brings benefits and problems, both of which require sensitive management.

Merging media

The use of technology like ICT and IvT is often seen to be the harbinger of the paperless office. But as Seely Brown and Duguid (2000) have argued, the paperless office appears to be a long way off. Information, they contend, has a social life. Visual representations both on paper and in digital form remain central within the innovation process. As seen in the case of P&G they help engineers tell stories, think, and play. Using IvT is often a visual activity, requiring extensive paper and digital drawings. Engineers working with IvT often switch between the two media continuously and effortlessly. They use sketching on paper because it is quicker and more immediate. Sketching is also a social activity where different problem-solvers gather together in groups and work through a problem, building one sketch upon another to communicate, direct, and stimulate thought (see McGown et al. 1998; Bilda and Demirkan 2003; Tovey et al. 2003; and Chapter 5). As Henderson (1999) argues, engineers use mixed practices, drawing from a wide range of tools and technologies as they go about solving problems.

From observations of designers and engineers in companies such as Arup it can be seen how IvT enhances the importance of sketching as a mechanism for creating conversations between team members who may come from very different technical disciplines. Sketching allows designers to play more quickly on paper and then take these ideas and input them into a digital model. The digital model is made into a prototype, which is further refined by more sketching and modelling. Offices using IvT are often strewn with paper, prototypes, tools, toys, components, artefacts, and digital images. In these environments, engineers 'dance' across different media in search of ideas and solutions to problems. Providing an increasing number of such working spaces, where play with mixed media is encouraged, will be an issue for managers as IvT becomes more widely diffused.

Skills and skills mix

IvT changes the skills composition of the firms, using it as they have to diversify their pool of staff to include a wide range of new skills and disciplines. Product development organizations employ sketch artists, designers, ethnographers, sociologists, and economists alongside their traditional staff of scientists and engineers. Engineering has become diffuse and less concerned with the physical manipulation of matter: it now has to focus on the social and economic consequences and impact of technological solutions. In order to understand how the technologies shape and interact with the external environment, managers have sought to bring in new skills and practices into their organizations, drawing from social science and other disciplines to better realize the opportunities that new technologies might provide.

The value of 'boundary-spanners', 'technological gatekeepers', or 'technology brokers' has long been appreciated in the innovation literature (Allen 1977; MacDonald and Williams 1994, Dodgson and Bessant 1996; Hargadon 2003). Such people and organizations search across organizational and disciplinary boundaries to find potential solutions to problems, and are expert at transmitting knowledge to where it is needed. IvT enables thinkers, players, and doers to boundary-span more easily and effectively and provides improved tools to enhance the performance of those given that specific task in innovative organizations.

Lester and Piore (2004) highlighted the need for analytical and interpretive skills for innovation. These relate to a range of major new skills that appear to be required in many sectors that use IvT for modelling and simulation. These skills include *pattern recognition*. The ability to recognize patterns in turbulent systems has become particularly important in work as diverse as combinatorial chemistry for drug discovery to weather forecasting and assessing climate change. Economists are also using similar approaches to study stock market prices. Skills in mathematics often lie at the heart of these forms of analyses and interpretation. Similar forms of mathematical modelling using differential equations can be found, for example, in techniques used in weather forecasting and analysis of economic trends. Decision-support tools, such as expert systems, are also used to assist in making decisions actions from complex sets of data in an increasing number of professional activities, including medical practice (Berg 1997).

Creating new value through innovation by interpreting and acting upon the data produced by IvT in thinking, playing, and doing requires other new skills. Evidence suggests that new ideas can often be developed when analysing data by *applying analogies*; this can assist in developing a wider range of insights (Schwartz 2004). Schwartz argues that *multiple insights* assist innovators in creating options. These skills would appear to be particularly useful during thinking and playing phases of the innovation process. He also argues that the ability to *think systematically* is of critical importance to the integration of a new idea during implementation within larger social and technological systems. In most cases, new products and services are introduced and implemented in the context of existing technologies and processes, and in many industries a number of vintages exist. The capability to apply systems thinking, sometimes envisioning systems of systems, is an important strategic management skill across thinking, playing, and doing and is particularly important during the playing and doing activities.

Other skills requirements have emerged alongside the specific strategic management skills associated with IvT and think, play, do, because of the new ways businesses can relate to their customers. These include:

- *Key account management*: knowledge of customers' markets, business processes, and their own customers in particular market segments (e.g. airline industry, education, health, rail transport). This might include staff willing to become embedded within the customers' businesses over a long period of time.
- *Risk analysis and management*: deployment of new skills in identifying, evaluating, and managing risk, including valuing options in innovation, the management of risk registers, and the ability to understand long-term risks in supply streams.
- *Legal skills*: new capabilities in contracting long-term framework agreements, concession-building, joint-venturing, risk mitigation, and intellectual property ownership.
- *Information management*: skills needed to manage information over very long timescales and across different vintages of technology.
- *Portfolio management*: skills in building teams and consortia, and assembling and managing concession partners.

Leadership

Leading a think, play, do innovation process may involve the amplification of many existing trends in the practice of leadership. Like the managers of many professional services firms, IvT leaders may need to adopt a 'first-amongst-equals' approach, facing as they do the challenge of being responsible for providing direction and encouragement to peers, and for performance, whilst at the same time being unable to exercise traditional authority. As the senior manager in Arup, quoted in Chapter 3, says, 'you can't tell people what to do'. The requirement of leaders is to blend organizational objectives with the idiosyncratic motivations of creative professional staff.

Leaders also need to manage across organizational boundaries. Excellent advocacy and diplomacy skills are required to ask people in other organizations to comply with requirements over issues such as timing, investments, and priorities when there is a lack of direct organizational sanction or discipline.

Although united more than ever before through the use of IvT, leaders still need to combine the talents and contributions of the different types of people who might primarily identify themselves as thinkers, players, or doers. And whilst leaders may identify themselves primarily as thinkers, players, or doers, they need to be able to lead people, teams, and organizations that identify themselves differently. They need to appreciate the synergies and iterations behind all three activities to truly become innovation leaders by mastering an understanding of the whole innovation process. All these organizational issues affect the ways capabilities are created. They all facilitate and encourage change and are, therefore, in combination, important strategic management concerns.

7.5 Learning, creativity, and knowledge

Learning and the creation and use of knowledge are central elements of the strategies of firms in the knowledge economy (see Box 7.2). Knowledge, learning, and creativity are key capabilities that allow firms to change their competencies, and their management is therefore a crucial strategic concern. Each is affected by IvT.

IvT, learning, and knowledge

A range of theories and analyses (Argyris and Schon 1978; Senge 1990; Dodgson 1993c; Brown and Duguid 2000) consider learning and the creation and

---

Box 7.2   IvT, tacit, and codified knowledge

Discussion on the possibilities and limitations of the use of technology in the management and economics of knowledge has been restricted in its analysis of the way knowledge is constructed. A key issue in the debate about the creation and use of knowledge is the relationship between its tacit and manifest forms, and much discussion on these technologies has focused upon the single and limiting issue of the codification of tacit knowledge.[115]

'Codified' knowledge is knowledge explicitly represented in papers, drawings, plans, patents, or any form which makes manifest knowledge that was previously unwritten and unarticulated, or 'tacit'. Codified knowledge is easier to transfer and share.

The value of technology to manage existing, codified knowledge is widely acknowledged. As Nonaka et al. (2001) contend, technology is now mostly used as a set of tools with which to improve efficiency in combining and disseminating existing information and explicit knowledge. They argue, however, that 'these tools do not offer an integrated and holistic way of dealing with tacit and explicit knowledge in the context of the knowledge economy' (Nonaka et al. 2001: 827). In contrast, Antonelli and Geuna (2000) argue that the new technologies enable firms to accumulate tacit knowledge more systematically.

In practice, there are important reflexive and iterative relationships between tacit and explicit knowledge (Nonaka and Takeuchi 1995). Neither form is mutually exclusive nor exists purely by itself. There are additional complications: research mapping and measuring technical excellence in twelve international engineering design firms found it difficult to establish an agreement over the definition of what constituted 'good' design (Gann and Salter 1999). This was because the types of design activities involved a lot of craft knowledge that was difficult to articulate and codify. The group of firms was nonetheless able to develop a shared understanding of what types of working environments led to better design results.

These issues have significant consequences for managers. Although IvT has some potential to codify, represent, or make more explicit actions and behaviours that were previously tacit, no matter how automated or codified the technology, there will remain a tacit element to the use of these technologies that may ultimately provide the defining element of competitive advantage.[116]

---

application of knowledge at various levels, its centrality to organizational performance, its construction at an individual and group level, and the ways in which individual learning becomes an organizational property.[117] Dynamic capabilities theory (Teece and Pisano 1994) is built around the ability of firms to learn to sense the need to change and then reconfigure internal and external competencies to seize opportunities created by rapidly changing environments. In this theory, the essence of the firm is its ability to create, transfer, assemble, integrate, and exploit difficult-to-imitate assets, of which knowledge assets are key (Teece 2002). In this regard IvT is the technological complement to dynamic capabilities in the ways it links thinking, playing, and doing. Another valuable approach is the concept of absorptive capacities (Cohen and Levinthal 1990; Zahra and George 2002), which indicates that the conduct of a firm's own R&D improves its ability to learn from others. This is essentially a theory of the importance of internal R&D in the integration of external knowledge. IvT can help in building the digital infrastructure and supportive organizational structures that facilitate the addition of externally derived knowledge to internal competencies.

The connection between technology and knowledge creation is complex and poses many challenges for managers. Technology can be assessed according to its capacities to store, search for, connect, represent, and create knowledge—all of which are important for integrating the thinking, playing, and doing in the innovation process and constructing capabilities.

The value of ICT and IvT in producing digital stores or repositories to assist both individual and organizational memory is obvious and relatively uncontroversial:[118] both are useful in searching for, connecting, and disseminating sources of knowledge. Connections through ICT such as email and intranets increase the efficiency and speed of sharing documents, diagrams, formulae, symbols, and images. Data mining using IvT helps the search process and assists in the automatic connection of diverse materials in ways that can support the innovation process. Internet-based networked innovation markets used by companies such as P&G are important mechanisms for technology brokering. Grid-based computing and visualization technologies are used to search for and connect different sources of information and knowledge in, for example, skin science and cell biology.

The fact that these technologies have significant consequences for representation and creation of knowledge is beginning to be appreciated within the innovation studies literature (Antonelli and Geuna 2000; Pavitt 2002). But this discussion has focused on ICT. Knowledge creation and innovation has become more complex and it is here that IvT helps managers through its capacities to model and represent complexity and to create virtual research communities that bring many minds to bear on the creation and diffusion of useful knowledge. IvT can provide the technological bridge between knowledge residing in the science base and that found in the market. It can help create the absorptive capacities of firms to enable them to use these external sources of knowledge.

IvT and creativity

Perhaps one of the most intriguing questions about IvT is the extent of its influence on the creativity of individuals and groups. These technologies can enable the automation of more mundane, repetitive tasks, allowing better utilization of creative people's time for developing and sharing ideas. By facilitating better and more comprehensive communications and representations, they again reduce the time spent on less productive activities. But do they actually enhance the amount of creativity occurring?

More than ever before, we are living in an age where notions of creativity are ubiquitous and 'creativity' is widely recognized, realized, and rewarded. We talk of 'creative industries' (Caves 2000), a 'creative class' of workers

(Florida 2002), are entranced by the creativity of individual minds (Boden 1990), and concerned for the impact of technology on creativity (Greenfield 2003).

For Florida (2002: 56), creativity is now the decisive source of competitive advantage in the economy: 'We are embarking on an age of pervasive creativity that permeates all sectors of the economy and society.'

Florida takes a broad definition of creative workers. He argues that as a result of the combination of many factors, a new class of workers has emerged in the USA. These factors include the rise of spending on R&D, high-tech start-up companies and the formal venture capital system, the systems of the creative factory that involve new technologies, forms of work organization and subcontract manufacturing, and a new creative social milieu. Florida contends that in the USA the traditional working class has 33 million workers, or 25 per cent of the US workforce, and the largest group in the USA is the service class, which includes 55.2 million workers or 43 per cent of the US workforce. The fastest growing group in the USA, however, is what he calls the creative class, which now includes 38.3 million Americans, roughly 30 per cent of the entire US workforce. At the heart of the creative class is the 'super-creative core', comprising 15 million workers, or 12 per cent of the workforce. It is made up of people who work in science and engineering, computers and mathematics, education, and the arts, design, and entertainment (Florida 2002: 74).

The implications of the emergence of this creative class are enormous for the ways in which work is conducted, for the location of that work, and for its impact on open, distributed innovation. More creative people provide greater opportunities for creative collaboration.

Margaret Boden, one of the leading researchers in the field of creativity, argues in her book, *The Creative Mind*, that the ability to be creative resides in us all: 'Creativity draws crucially on our ordinary abilities. Noticing, remembering, seeing, speaking, hearing, understanding language and recognizing analogies: all these talents of Everyman are important.' She continues that creativity can be 'based in ordinary abilities that we all share, and in practiced expertise to which we can all aspire'. With more opportunities to collaborate creatively through the use of IvT, there may be greater advantages for managers to develop these abilities that reside in us all. IvT provides ubiquitous and accessible tools to a broader franchise of thinkers, players, and doers. The Grid enables an amateur astronomer to discover a new star from his own home. Virtual reality enables a local theatre group to plan stage productions quickly and cheaply. Home renovators can clearly envisage their planned constructions before a brick is laid. Remote researchers in Asia, Eastern Europe, and Latin America are brought into the development programmes of major US and European multinationals through networked innovation brokers. By moving industrial creativity into the virtual world, where experiments and prototypes are conducted cheaply, quickly, and effectively, far greater numbers of people can participate in creative endeavours.

As a means of supporting creativity, IvT can provide useful digital connections, built intuitively. The value of imagination and intuition based on experience is shown by the following quotation by one of the Directors of Arup (Hough 1996: 27).

Whatever the state of the technology, intuition will always be our guide in applying it: in first framing the question, in finding the shape of the answer, and then in the technical details of its resolution. That will remain true as long as our engineering supports a human end and as long as we remain interested in seeking the human face of technology.

Two examples from the life sciences show the continuing importance of intuition and judgement: 'bioinformatics'—the use of computer databases and algorithms to facilitate and expedite biological research, particularly in genomics; and 'bioprospecting'—the use of new technologies, such as high-through-put devices to search for naturally occurring molecules with potential as drugs. As seen in the case of data mining in cell biology in Chapter 4, the value of bioinformatics lies in the way connections are built using the creative intuition of informed researchers. The term 'bioprospecting' is itself revealing. The traditional mining prospector does not dig just anywhere: he searches on the basis of data and understanding of geological principles but also uses experience and the ability to 'read' terrain. Similarly, the bioprospector needs these craftlike skills: he or she needs to search the enormous wealth of data on genes and DNA sequences with clear understanding of the nature of scientific investigation, of the role new technological tools can play in assisting this, and of the capacity to read complex and ambiguous signals from the data.

The combination of IvT and knowledgeable, creative people stimulates learning by increasing the porosity of organizational, disciplinary, and professional boundaries. It facilitates an innovation process that is collaborative, networked, and distributed, and a creative process that borrows and embellishes by using scientific method and intuition. It integrates a business process that involves all elements of the firm—from research to operations to marketing—giving organizational boundaries an 'incredible lightness of being'.

7.6 Conclusions

IvT provides new mechanisms for the management and integration of thinking, playing, and doing in innovation processes, and the construction, organization, and evolution of those competencies that are the basis of competitiveness. Gaining competitive advantages from innovation depends on aligning many factors: the ability to strategically focus and change competencies; the integration of innovative activities across organizational boundaries; effective organizational practices and structures; and the management of creativity, learning, and knowledge. It is through the management of these issues that some of the uncertainty around innovation reduces (see Chapter 8).

By understanding the use of IvT as part of the innovation process—the creative motor in the firm—one can then start to see how and where technology can be used for strategic management. Technologies that support the management of knowledge, learning, and creativity, notably scientific instruments in research, simulation and modelling in design, and rapid prototyping in production, are increasingly integrated in innovation processes. IvT is not only improving the performance and technological integration of these activities but is also enabling a more strategic approach to be adopted towards the integration of the whole innovation process. Companies like P&G, Arup, GSK and Ricardo are successfully using IvT to manage in this new environment. IvT has helped integrate internal processes and external relationships, assisting the thinking, playing, and doing necessary to develop new markets through innovation. The customer has been brought centrally into the innovation process and technologies such as user tool kits and virtual product testing have been instrumental in changing customer relationships. Firms are better able to develop options for, and make choices about, innovation as a result of IvT. Built on new forms of infrastructure, such as the Grid, it helps create virtual research communities. It assists in managing knowledge, through data mining and through the range of simulation and modelling technologies that contribute to experimentation and prototyping.

The effective use of IvT often depends upon flexible forms of organization. Formal, hierarchical structures are ill-suited to the loose, fluid, and interdisciplinary nature of the skills and teams that work with IvT. New forms of projects, teams, skills mixes, working environments, and leadership are required to create the capabilities necessary to adapt to rapidly changing environments and to implement innovation strategies.

IvT may also enable firms to focus their activities around a core or base. It provides a core technology that, like Arup's use of simulation technology, allows firms to specialize in and then diversify from.

Yet IvT remains a tool. It is an adjunct to the intuition and imagination of thinkers, players, and doers. When it is used effectively, in the hands of skilled, well-organized, and focused creative and knowledgeable people, and is working productively across organizational boundaries, IvT becomes the most important technological tool for the strategic management of innovation ever to have emerged. If used to its full potential, it can help managers build firms' competencies and capabilities and, as we shall see in Chapter 8, deliver those most welcome of advances in an uncertain environment: economies of effort and definiteness of aim in the innovation process.

8   A New Innovation Process

8.1 Introduction

Schumpeter's stark reminder that innovation offers the carrot of spectacular reward or the stick of destitution remains topical today. In the knowledge-based economy, firms become bankrupt unless they innovate. Without the income generated and taxes paid by companies and wage-earners in innovative firms, economies stagnate. Innovative new products and services have quickly created incredible industries in mobile telephony, financial securitization, and Internet-based auctions and bookstores. But innovation is not only about products, profits, and wealth creation; it is also about producing better homes, cleaner environments, and healthier lives. Innovation preserves the beauty of ancient monuments, and creates breathtaking new opera houses, museums, and bridges. It produces safer industries, mines, and transportation systems. Innovation helps researchers cure psychiatric disorders and surgeons conduct better operations. Innovation is what helps make work a positive, creative experience; in Marx's terms, by emphasizing social relationships with others, and changing the worker's own 'particular relationship towards the object that he is making, and towards his own talents for work'.[119]

Innovation is so important for so many in so many ways, it is essential that we understand its contributions and the ways in which it is changing. We have focused on the emergence of a new innovation process using IvT in activities described as thinking, playing, and doing. Our most fundamental assertion about these changes is simply stated. Manufacturing technology underpins industrial sectors in the economy based on the technology of production: automated machines linked to the flow of operations. Information and communications technology underpins service sectors in the economy based on technologies that enable the flow of information in generating, diffusing, and delivering services. IvT, we contend, is underpinning the emerging knowledge economy based on technologies that encourage and facilitate creativity and the application of knowledge to thinking, playing, and doing in the flow of the innovation process. IvT is the capital good of the new economy.

History teaches us to be cautious of predicting technological futures. Lord Kelvin, one of the most brilliant scientists of all time, claimed that heavier-than-air flying machines are impossible and extraordinary claims for the potential of new technologies such as cold fusion are made regularly. Evidence in this book provides substantial support for our arguments but, as Metcalfe pointed out in Chapter 1, there are always uncertainties about technological futures, and IvT may not continue to provide its present contributions and deliver its potential. History teaches us to be circumspect about claims for new technologies. It also reminds us of the complex interrelationships of factors behind technological change that we have been careful to respect in our analysis. There are lengthy timescales involved in innovation with high levels of interdependency between various vintages of technology, indicating that infrastructure is of great importance and technological change requires associated social, organizational, and managerial changes. This perspective poses major challenges for those wishing to examine and test our assertion about the importance of IvT and the new innovation process. Nonetheless, this chapter outlines what we have found to be the main features of the new innovation process and some of the new issues and challenges confronting innovators related to IvT and intensification, skills, management, public policy, and research. First, we summarize some of the key arguments developed throughout the book.

8.2 Summary of the key arguments

1. The innovation process involves various interactions between 'thinking', 'playing', and 'doing'. Existing categories of 'research' and 'development' are unable to capture the breadth of innovative activities of companies and these new terms more accurately capture the contemporary reality and idiom around the innovation process. Think, play, do moves discussion away from the traditional terms—'research', 'development', 'engineering'—that bind the study of innovation to functional activities.[120] A distributed, open innovation process often involves a range of organizations that do not necessarily conduct formal R&D. Large companies like P&G are becoming less reliant upon their R&D departments. Think, play, do better captures the importance of design and prototyping in innovation and highlights the scope of the innovation process ranging from scientific thinking on the one hand to the practical delivery of products and services on the other.

2. A whole new category of technology is being applied to thinking, playing, and doing—including Grid-based computing, modelling and simulation, visualization, data searching and mining, virtual and rapid prototyping—and we call this 'innovation technology' (IvT). This category of technology is ubiquitous; it is found in a wide diversity of firms and sectors. IvT exists alongside, and

builds upon, the existing categories of information and communications technology (ICT) and operations and manufacturing technology (OMT). Along with new technologies, such as Grid computing, IvT includes existing technologies, such as simulation and modelling, that have migrated and developed from their previous use in particular functions towards their present capacities to support the innovation process more widely. By means of IvT, information and knowledge about innovation is more accurate, produced faster and more cheaply, better represented, and more easily communicated and integrated across boundaries. IvT breaks down the barriers between functions, professions, disciplines, and organizations and is the enabling technology for distributed innovation. It brings both science and the market closer to the innovator and helps merge thinking, playing, and doing into concurrent activities. The complex relationships and iterations in the innovation process are assisted by IvT but the technology and its use are socially embedded. Technology does not generate and share knowledge; people do, using technology, and the motives, capacities, and incentives of individuals and organizations determine its future contribution.

3. The effective use of these technologies involves combining the new digital 'code' in IvT with existing and developing 'craft' skills and flexible, often project- and team-based, organization. The future utility of IvT depends upon the emergence of a new generation of innovation players—designers, engineers, researchers—capable of using IvT for exploring new combinations of ideas, built upon training, experience, and intuition and then successfully choosing, exploiting, and delivering them within different local, idiosyncratic contexts. These new innovation players are supported by the construction of new working environments or knowledge spaces. There are considerable dangers in over-reliance on IvT-based technological solutions without these new skills and an absence of understanding of the principles that underlie their use. The most effective use of IvT could well occasionally derive from people skilled in the art who would eventually find solutions without the technology, albeit more slowly and expensively.

4. All these changes are combining to lead to the intensification of innovation by producing more economical and definite outcomes from investments and ameliorating some of the many uncertainties in innovation, thereby lowering the risk of failure. Successful scientific breakthroughs, radical innovation, and creative design solutions always have depended, and likely always will depend, upon a degree of serendipity. As Louis Pasteur said in 1854, 'chance favours the prepared mind'. IvT and think, play, do, provide the technical infrastructure and organizational processes to assist smart firms in exploiting their chances more often than not.

8.3 IvT and the intensification of innovation

The new innovation process will be quicker and more deliberate. Our evidence shows how IvT has shortened development times in a diverse range of technologies, industries, and sectors such as household products, crash testing, drug development, chemistry and chemical engineering, buildings, cameras, engine designs, Formula One racing models, Palm Pilots, dresses in the fashion industry, and safety testing in a reactor. We have seen how IvT has reduced the cost of innovating by reducing the amount of coated steel used in buildings, by simulating crash testing and consumer goods, and by experimenting with high-performance liquid chromatography (HPLC) and the 'robot scientist'. Cases have shown how IvT produced better quality data from experiments in the laboratory with the Grid and data search tools, by using simulations of the performance of buildings during fires to establish more accurate insurance assessments and by improving the quality of data on customer requirements in the design of cars, clothes, and homes.

Such improvements are welcome because although innovation is necessary, it has become increasingly costly and risky. A faster, better, and cheaper innovation process will enhance efficiencies and provide the potential for saved resources to be reinvested to increase the amount of innovation occurring. IvT helps ameliorate some of the many uncertainties surrounding innovation as we shall see by reference to the different types of uncertainty described in Chapter 1. IvT's greatest contribution is through the way it ameliorates *technical* uncertainty:

- It helps better integrate disparate technologies involved in the innovation process and used in thinking, playing, and doing, including ICT and OMT, and other technologies of different vintage. It builds upon existing, proven technologies, notably CAD, CAM, and ICTs in general.
- It allows more accurate and speedy experimentation, producing more technological options with better and new accompanying data.
- It enables playing with technological options cheaply and quickly, in order to select the best.
- It provides an understanding of the requirements of new production and operations systems and processes prior to their implementation. It allows exploration of what is going to be made before production starts, thus providing the confidence that what is designed can be made. Simulations can help overcome the problems of scale-up in production and can create efficiencies in supply-chain operations planning.
- It represents technical knowledge in a manner that assists more effective communications across technical boundaries between basic and applied

research, public and private sectors, product and process innovation, scientists and researchers, engineers and designers, and across disciplines and national borders.

- It assists in the fusion and combination of different technologies. It allows you to see if technologies and components will fit together, for example in drug design.

IvT helps ameliorate *market* uncertainty in a number of ways. It brings the customer or user into the innovation process ensuring that what is produced is more likely to be what is required. Customers can experience outcomes before expensive decisions are made, thereby reducing risk of disappointment and failure. It helps overcome some of the *social* uncertainties in innovation by bringing groups and teams together and facilitating intense interaction through 'conversations' about solutions to problems. As with the development of Linux described in Chapter 2, the use of IvT depends upon the development of practice-related communities sharing experience and knowledge. *Political* and *cultural* uncertainties can be ameliorated by involving regulators, politicians, and interested parties in the innovation conversation by simply representing complex issues and thereby improving their understanding and confidence in the issues and proposals. Virtual reality is used by Australian mining companies to represent to concerned locals and environmentalists what mined land will look like during and after mining operations. As seen in the case of P& G, the effective use of IvT and its associated practices is accompanied by marked cultural changes: in this case increased receptivity to external inputs. International collaborations, where the potential for cultural miscommunications may conceivably be higher, are assisted by the common language of IvT.

Uncertainties in innovation related to *timing* and *speed* can be ameliorated by IvT. The high speed of development in experimentation through high-throughput chemistry or time compression by using rapid prototyping, for example, enables the production of outcomes quickly, which, if that is what the market demands, confers great benefits. In fast-moving and turbulent environments late design freezes enable innovators to take advantage of new technological improvements or market intelligence and delay the commitment of resources until circumstances become clearer.

Finally, IvT assists in overcoming some of the *complexities* in innovation by helping effective collaboration between organizations and the integration of systems. A distributed innovation process has many complex interdependencies—in innovation systems of various descriptions and between customers, suppliers, and collaborators—and IvT helps bring them together. If, as Simon (1996) suggests, the way to deal with complexity is to break elements down into smaller components, IvT helps in the analysis of these decomposed problems and then assists their reintegration. It can be used by Ricardo to integrate diverse sources of software and by Pilkington to bring science into everyday products, such as glass. It massively increases the sources of potential answers to problems: in an attempt to find solutions to sixty projects, P&G accessed 500,000 people through one of its innovation intermediaries.

8.4 New craft skills in innovation

The new innovation process requires the continuing development of the 'craft' skills of its contributors, ranging from data searching and mining to using simulation and modelling and rapid production technologies. Vast amounts of potentially useful new data are being produced by scientific and market research and new skills for finding, combining, and disseminating information are necessary to guide its use. Being able to use this data effectively and economically depends on the tools and instruments of IvT. In particular, visualization technologies, simulation, and virtual and rapid prototyping are providing the means for scientists, engineers, and users to see and feel data and designs in new ways. Skills in pattern recognition and interpretation are becoming more important along with the need to understand fundamental principles that underlie models.

The skills of data mining are essential in e-science environments where the interweaving of data, often constructed in a manner that is either personalized or based on the needs of real or virtual research communities, contributes valuably to thinking. This capacity to idiosyncratically weave disparate sources of information gives great autonomy to the individual and the team involved in innovation, in the sense that information is not structured or pre-packaged for use by others with different perspectives or backgrounds.

The Grid, data searching, and simulation technologies provide new instruments for scientific inquiry. The potential for these technologies was summarized by the young MIT researchers quoted in Williams (2002), one of whom referred to computer graphics as 'imagination amplifiers' and another described his computer as a 'laboratory'. Even when it has helpful and intuitive interfaces, the technology requires expertise to use it effectively. As Nobel Prize-winning physicist, Robert Townes, says: 'It takes time to get clever with instruments and experience counts.'

The cases of Arup and P&G have shown the importance of expert users of new data mining technology. Arup's experts in its R&D department and P&G's technology entrepreneurs are highly skilled at seeking and collating valuable information and disseminating it to where it is needed across projects and departments. These experts are sufficiently knowledgeable to appreciate the serendipitous find and are the modern incarnation of Allen's technological gatekeepers (1977) but, rather than operating solely as a conduit of information between parties, they are valuable contributors to the collective search for solutions.

Design and engineering are not solely about formal methods, nor are they deterministic in the sense that decisions are absolute and outcomes perfect. Engineering is both an art and an applied science and the 'craft' lies in finding a well-integrated solution to a problem. Engineers use their imagination and intuition to visualize solutions in the 'mind's eye' (Ferguson 1992) and prepare them for action and implementation. In very fast-moving environments there simply may not be enough time or money to carry out comprehensive prototyping or analytical modelling, and craft knowledge is needed to make judgements based on limited available data. Sometimes schedules require that modelling proceeds in parallel with production, which places greater reliance on the judgement of engineers. There may, nevertheless, be benefits in some circumstances in making decisions sequentially, allowing time for reflection and for ideas to mature through iteration and for unthought-through consequences to surface, which again requires great expertise and judgement.

The most important of all new craft skills are those that enable the crossing of previously existing boundaries. As we have seen, some users of IvT are the embodiment of 'practitioner-researchers': people capable of crossing thinking, playing, and doing activities.

Experts in simulation and modelling, John Burland and Nicole Hoffman, who have developed as well as used IvT, are highly conscious of the dangers of having it used by improperly trained hands. As seen in Chapter 4, IvT is best used by thinkers knowledgeable in theory and practice, aware of cognate disciplines, and capable of thinking laterally. The technology allows Ricardo's designers to successfully undertake the tasks of 'analysts' nine times out of ten. Serious problems emerge in the one in ten tasks that goes wrong. One of the possible outcomes of IvT in the future might therefore be fewer but more spectacular failures; when things go wrong, they may do so spectacularly.

Not everyone can do everything. Those creative, clever people, skilled at combining craft and code and playing with IvT to link with science, technology, design, and the market may not only capture greater shares of resources in firms but also establish themselves in privileged hierarchical positions. This would be counter to the more organic organizational structure that facilitates effective use of IvT and the new skills may therefore result in new organizational tensions. For example, internal competition for power and resources related to IvT within firms may result from tensions between different project leaders and their teams competing with one another. Successful project teams may be more likely to break away, establishing new ventures, to maximize their own rewards from thinking, playing, and doing using IvT. This, as we have seen, creates new business opportunities but it may leave significant capability gaps in the remaining group.

8.5 New management challenges of innovation

As we saw in Chapter 7, achieving the benefits of the new innovation process is highly demanding of managers who have to establish new working practices and strategies and master new forms of team working, work spaces, partnerships, and technology. Here our attention turns to the new challenges that managers may face in the future as a result of the new innovation process.

Strategic focus

We have argued that in the context of distributed innovation, relationships in the value stream are changing as a result of the use of IvT. As boundaries in the value stream become more permeable, firms, somewhat paradoxically, need to establish their position in the value creation process even more clearly. They need a base of specialist and distinctive resources in technology, organization, and people and the dynamic capabilities to reconfigure those resources. IvT can assist in the development of base competencies and the diversification that can valuably occur around them. In this way, IvT could contribute to an increased level of industrial disaggregation.

The management challenge in these circumstances is to continue to offer the specialist and not easily replicable competencies that are attractive to customers when the technology on which they are based is relatively cheap and easily accessible. The challenge lies not with the possession of resources but with the capabilities that surround them and particularly the incentives, work organization, and work environment that the company offers.

New business development opportunities

IvT provides opportunities for firms to diversify from their technological base and we have seen how firms have developed and then marketed their own IvT. In the cases of Arup, Ricardo, and Gehry, IvT has produced new business development opportunities. Similarly, TWI has successfully diversified from its research base into the control of operations processes by using IvT. Large companies like SGI and Dassault are developing IvT and so are smaller entrepreneurial start-ups.[121] The development of software or instruments for modelling congestion charges, soil mechanics, and body scanning from the university sector illustrates commercialization opportunities for emerging businesses. P&G is using a hybrid model of developing and sustaining its own capabilities with the support of a number of external specialist suppliers of services. If firms do not produce IvT themselves, they need to establish the best sources of supply, considering how they are to fit together and complement existing investments in other categories of technology.

It is possible that new markets will emerge based on exploration, learning, and exploitation offered by IvT and think, play, do. For example, third-party technology brokerage and design services are already becoming established. In some cases these new types of business are taking work away from long-established, internal providers. In other examples, firms like CREAX, Triz, and IDEO are creating completely new markets.

Whatever the source of IvT, using it to develop new business opportunities requires considerable absorptive capacity. This may count against firms that rely upon outsourcing technology: an approach that has been successfully exploited by some firms over the last two decades in markets as diverse as Dell computers to electrical utilities that offer a service but no longer have the capability to develop the sources of that service. Internal innovation efforts need to be positioned so as to fully realize the opportunities from networks and technological and systems integration. This is likely to require deeper technological capability, not less.

We have seen how technological development and bundled product/service delivery is becoming more closely linked to markets through IvT, helping customers to select the best fit to suit their individual requirements. The closer links between products and processes created by IvT enable smaller niches to be economically attractive with markets of one becoming more common in some industries. This poses particular challenges for those firms used to operating in mass markets where large-scale production or the 'blockbuster' product has been the norm. Nevertheless, many mass markets are likely to continue to exist, but even in these, the speed at which they change and diversify may increase.

Work organization and skills

Evidence from the case studies presented in this book suggest that IvT is not constraining. It can be used in different ways across sectors, in diverse ways within the same sector, and in a variety of ways in the same company.

As seen in the case of Arup, challenging work attracts creative people who contribute to winning more challenging work. A virtuous cycle can be created that both strengthens the firm's technical capabilities and its reputation for delivering innovative projects. IvT provides a means for exploring, experimenting, and engineering concurrently. A new mode of learning might be emerging in which people can simultaneously think, play, and do. Factories become laboratories, and robots undertake science. There is considerable blurring of roles in the workplace around think, play, do and new kinds of work environments supporting the creative users of IvT.

One consequence of IvT's ability to automate some elements of innovation is that the question of its deskilling potential may arise. Similar to the experience of advanced manufacturing technology in the 1980s, there may be attempts by some companies to deskill the workforce using IvT. As with advanced manufacturing technology, such attempts will prove eventually to be fruitless as productivity needs both code and craft.

As design, prototyping, and systems integration become even more important activities in the integration of the innovation process, there will be far greater iterations between real and virtual media and between the designer and their customers and suppliers. For example, a client procuring a new building in 2005 is able to enjoy more design content from Frank Gehry using IvT than was previously possible in 1995. Realizing the benefits from these interactions requires new and novel combinations of skills.

It is possible to envisage the emergence of a more flexible division of labour, enabling firms to play with solutions by locating designers and engineers in each other's businesses. IvT can enable skills to be deployed in new ways: there are already examples of engineers becoming facilities management specialists, architects becoming branded suppliers of particular types of buildings, non-architects designing buildings, watch companies like Swatch designing cars, and so on.

IvT is also enabling design teams to operate more effectively when members are remote from one another. Some of the information they require is becoming codified and less sticky and difficult to transfer. Traditional face-to-face contact and sketching may diminish in importance and a new generation of IvT-oriented designers may care little for old rules, procedures, and practices.

Partnerships

IvT has the potential to significantly affect the strategic nature of firms' relationships with customers, suppliers, and collaborative partners. IvT assists the building of relationships of firms within networks and it helps link firms more effectively with sources of innovation in the research base, supply networks, and market. When technology enables sharing of information and knowledge about innovation more easily, managers will need to assess its impact on partnerships. IvT could potentially lower the levels of commitment and trust normally required to share tacit and proprietary knowledge. When enormous amounts of information can be processed and utilized effectively for the purposes of innovation, the past necessity for high-quality relationships could be replaced by increased quantity of relationships, providing new challenges to managers.[122]

Competitiveness

Developing new quantifiable indicators that measure the intensification of innovation—that is, reduced costs and risks—will provide a challenge. There are many competitive benefits from the intensification of innovation: if more ideas are created and the right ones are selected, firms should have better and more efficient value-creating opportunities. If firms can exploit a distributed innovation approach and use richer information and knowledge for faster and cheaper responsiveness, they should gain distinct competitive advantage compared to those not using the technology. Similarly, greater recognition and reward may be given to highly successful individuals working within firms, and to those individuals offering expert inputs to innovation processes from outside.

New methods of assessment will need to be developed to measure these benefits.[123] Some of the activities to be measured will occur more quickly and concurrently making them difficult to assess separately. Verification in complex social and economic environments will remain problematic. The total cost of design and development may actually increase because more ideas are being created and assessed but the marginal costs per model/simulation/test will reduce. Once a model or simulation has been built it should be relatively easy to ask and test as many ideas as you can think of. This will, however, have implications for data collection and storage where requirements will be much greater (remembering that Rolls Royce generates 1 gigabyte of data for each jet engine in flight).

It is possible to envisage a 'hyperactive' firm, with employees driven by the desire for play rather than profit. Lost in a sea of play, they will lack the focus and drive to complete the innovation process to its commercial ends. The business could follow a path of diversification that lacks the focus, quality, and rigour of ideas needed to secure necessary sales and market share to maintain profitability.

Furthermore, in IvT environments, where knowledge is easier to copy, first-mover advantages may diminish. It is harder to maintain secrecy in open innovation systems. Overall the system may move faster and yet yield fewer returns to innovators. The management challenge is that of developing the dynamic capabilities necessary to thrive and stay ahead of the competition in such an environment.

8.6 Public policy challenges of the new innovation process

Innovation is immensely important in the public sector; it enhances the quality of our lives. IvT is already being used to help develop public policies for traffic congestion, social housing, and health, to find innovative solutions to waste, to improve response times for maintenance, and to mitigate environmental impact. Policy-makers would benefit from understanding how IvT might be diffused more deeply and broadly in the public sector, particularly in health care, transport, education, protection of the environment, the arts, and leisure. The public sector would benefit from learning to create new options for the future, playing with different solutions to problems, and implementing new ways of doing things, faster, cheaper, and more accurately than in the past.

Developing policies for IvT

Governments along with industry need to ensure that higher education and vocational training institutions recognize the importance of the new skills based on IvT and that the new skills being taught enable the productive use of the technology. These skills are theoretical as well as practical and students who may well be attracted to learning to play with the new technology may be less keen on the theoretical principles that underlie its use. New models of engineering and scientific education are required involving more than just adding a few social science courses to existing scientific and technical training and potentially using IvT itself to assist the thinking, playing, and doing in innovative educational programmes. IvT provides the means for new educational experiences, such that in some environments people can learn while they think, play, and do. To achieve this requires a new approach to skills development that places technical and scientific skills within the context of the entire innovation process and involves market, organizational, and strategic understanding. The vision of MIT in the 1950s, described in Chapter 4, of combining engineering education and social science is required along with the view that education and skills are not something developed in the past but something continually to develop.

As with previous generations of technology, such as OMT, governments can valuably play a role in improving awareness of IvT and encouraging its diffusion. Valuable policy lessons have been learned in the past about the efficacy of government innovation support schemes. The most successful policies have been those that link government support for technology investment through mechanisms such as tax and investment credits to skills, training, and organizational issues and to strategic decision-making about the competitive purpose of those investments. This approach can be used for IvT but for full effect the current generation of government policies needs to become much more integrated and less focused on individual types of technology. Policies need to focus on support for the collaborative nature of innovation and the integrated technology that supports it. There are serious and persistent market failures in collaboration, and government can help here by supporting research that cuts across boundaries and disciplines and that fits uneasily into traditional industry or sectoral policies or, indeed, disciplinary peer review and research assessment exercises.

As governments recognize the significance of IvT, this will create the policy challenge of constructing industrial support mechanisms for IvT producers. More strategically, governments may have to consider whether this technology lowers entry barriers to particular industries and what the resulting implications are for national competitiveness.

Government research funding for IvT infrastructure to enable virtual research communities connected by Grid technologies and data mining is 'public good' investment. But given the increasing interactions and blurred boundaries that we have described, it is also funding that supports innovation for private gain. IvT brings policies for science and research closer to innovation policy, thereby blurring policy objectives that need to be reconsidered and clarified.

Measuring diffusion

Governments make substantial investments in the measurement of R&D and also conduct periodic and increasingly sophisticated innovation surveys. Measuring think, play, do, however, poses significant challenges as it is attempting to measure a process, rather than particular inputs and outputs. New ways of measuring the new innovation process need to be devised (Dodgson and Hinze 2000).

Addressing the negative consequences of IvT

There are several potentially negative consequences of IvT and think, play, do that require further empirical research. These may exist for individuals, at the level of the firm, across sectors, and for society as a whole. Some people may never gain the craft and code skills necessary to practise rigorously and creatively based on a deep understanding of enquiry-based, problem-solving or design methods. Others may fail to appreciate underlying principles of science, engineering, and design, relying too heavily upon computer-generated results. Governments need to consider the costs of employment displacement and retraining related to IvT.

There are winners and losers in innovation and, for all the creative new opportunities provided by IvT, there are also failed firms and all they entail in job losses and lost investment. In some sectors incumbent players may lose to new entrants who are better able to identify and capitalize on market or technological opportunities because they have the skills to exploit IvT in think, play, do processes. Such losses have an immediate cost for those involved and assuming and offsetting some of these costs for them may be a concern for government.

Moreover, IvT has considerable potential for social exclusion. Not everyone can or wants to participate in the intensive world of IvT and innovation. There are also downsides of innovation intensity, people's working lives may be adversely affected through more people having less work and fewer people working harder to the point of breakdown. Governments will again be interested in the associated costs and perhaps in helping alleviate some of them.

8.7 Challenges of innovation research in the new innovation process

One of the major consequences of our approach for researchers is that future emphasis needs to be placed on the innovation *process* itself rather than its inputs, outputs, and outcomes. Think, play, do (TPD) is a much more fluid and holistic schema than sequential notions of research, development, and engineering: TPD not R&D. Previous vintages of technology such as CAD have contributed valuably *to* elements of the innovation process but IvT is the technology *for* the innovation process. IvT unites the different domains of research, design, production, marketing, and servicing such that it becomes an integrated process with activities in one part being consequential for others. There is increasingly tight coupling between thinking, playing, and doing using the same digital platforms. Data need only be entered once in the process. Its digital form allows it to be manipulated and for new data to be generated during the process, which could not have been developed before. This provides the potential for better and more sophisticated feedback that itself may be used for further exploration as well as learning in real time.

As a result, research needs to focus more on integrated technologies, organizations, and processes, which in turn requires a greater interdisciplinary approach examining how the flow of the innovation process is supported by science, technology, and engineering on the one hand and management and organizational issues on the other.

Although all the areas of the innovation process we have analysed are important, perhaps the one that is most deserving of attention is that of play. Play is the lubricant in the innovation engine, it is what keeps the parts working together to create movement. The roles of play, design, and prototyping are ripe for future research.

The changes we have described in the book have consequences for a number of theories and concepts in innovation studies described in Chapter 2. The concept of open innovation, for example, warrants further exploration in organizations other than large US firms. We have seen how open or distributed innovation creates opportunities for a wide range of organizations, and it would be valuable to appreciate the extent and consequences of this broader engagement. The speed of the changes occurring in innovation has consequences for our understanding of the formulation and dissolution of dominant designs. IvT might bring in users so quickly and effectively that dominant designs can change more rapidly than in the past and potentially be built around de facto standards, which may result in limiting potential innovation. If technologies and technological systems can be so quickly designed and assembled, what implications does this have for our understanding of technological trajectories, or the boundaries on the ways firms, technological developments are constrained? If intensification becomes ubiquitous, might we expect to see a shortening of timescales for long waves of technological advance?

IvT can help with both incremental and disruptive innovation. IvT provides richer information and knowledge about where opportunities for successful innovation might lie, as well as the means to exploit new ideas fruitfully. This means that IvT enables greater responsiveness to emerging requirements and the means to assess how to respond. At the same time it reduces the cost of both incremental and radical innovation, whilst making it possible to be more accurate in focusing on intended outcomes. This might also lead to a convergence of incremental and radical technological change, such that advances might flip between the two more quickly. There are research questions arising from this. From a knowledge and skills point of view, for example, does this mean that people will need to be more adept at both exploiting and exploring: a new ambidextrous skill set for innovation?

Many firms have a tendency towards locking-in past patterns of behaviour and attempting to do in the future what has been done successfully in the past. IvT can help overcome this through the continuing search for new ideas and combinations from research and the market. The issue, however, is the extent to which the tools being used are standardized and force modular solutions that may create new combinations, but are not innovative.

IvT enables the integration of information and knowledge up and down supply chains in close association and interaction with users. This creates opportunities to develop bundled products and services that may be more valuable to customers than separate, specialized solutions. It also offers possibilities to model and simulate processes concurrently with product and service development, thus enabling more accurate cost and delivery predictions. This has implications for product life cycle theory. We can posit the idea that what we have observed is the tip of the iceberg of what we might expect to see emerge in the next twenty years. For example, in future we might expect to witness a tighter coupling between product and process innovation. This might be achieved through development of more sophisticated tools for process representation and manipulation, simultaneously with product modelling and simulation. The future of research in this area is exciting. There are huge opportunities for thinking, playing, and doing around think, play, do.

Appendix
Research methods

The research underlying the book is based on a mixture of empirical methods. At the core of the research has been an interest in the use and development of IvT by public and private organizations as they go about attempting to innovate. We have drawn on many different sources in the course of the research, including in-depth interviews, workshops, observations of innovative companies, and previously published material. Given the wide range of applications of this technology, our approach has been somewhat eclectic. We have used a convenient sample of products, people, and organizations drawn from our experiences, contacts, and ideas. In the research, we have drawn inspiration from the work of others and have sought to expand their work and bring to the fore new questions and issues for debate and discussion.

Case studies are well suited to the study of how and why a particular technology is being used. They enable a deep understanding of an issue to develop through the use of several supportive research methods; in this instance, interviews, participant workshops, literature, and smaller case study searches and reviews. They enable the enrichment of knowledge about the essence and use of IvT by adding further information on its extent and nature and by describing mediating conditions and factors.

The emergence of our thinking on innovation technology and think, play, do

In developing the taxonomy of technology used in the study, we began with an interest in what Roy Rothwell called the 'electronic tool kit' for innovation. In Rothwell's work, this electronic tool kit included simulation and rapid proto-typing. More recent work by Thomke and Schrage has also focused on these technologies. We were also aware of the growing importance of virtual reality from the work of our Imperial College colleague, Jennifer Whyte. In the course of our research, we learned more about Grid technologies arising through the e-science programme of the Engineering and Physical Sciences Research

Council (EPSRC) in the UK. Our research brought to our attention other technologies, such as artificial intelligence and rapid prototyping, and their increasingly importance role in the innovation process. Whilst the early work of Rothwell pointed to the importance of these technologies as part of a 'tool kit', as the research developed, we became increasingly convinced that these technologies were more substantial and have common properties and unique attributes constituting a separate category of technology different from OMT, such as robotic systems, and ICT, such as the Internet. Although IvT builds upon both of these technological areas because of its capacity to integrate the innovation process, it requires very different managerial approaches and strategies for its use. In our discussion of the research, we developed the concept of *innovation technology* to refer to OMT and ICT.

This concept is not without controversy. Some of our colleagues found it tried to capture two very different things: 'innovation' and 'technology'. Some thought IvT was simply a subset of ICT. Others thought we were adding complexity where simplicity was required. Still others suggested that we were talking about 'innovation-enabling technology'. In the end, however, remembering the difficulties some had when the idea of 'information technology' emerged, we opted for brevity and chose 'innovation technology'. We respect all these comments and have used them to help refine and develop our understanding of this class of technologies. We felt strongly, however, that our research points to a technology that is much more than just an appendage of ICT or OMT. Giving a new name to something can lead to new understanding. It can also provoke response and debate, yielding new refinements in language and understanding.

Similarly, some colleagues have expressed reservations over the schema of innovation as 'think, play, do'. One very eminent friend described it as 'a bit Californian'. But we are convinced that this schema represents the new innovation process and have been heartened by the enthusiastic responses we received from a wide diversity of people who have said, 'yes, that is the way we work', in our respondent firms and from people including the chairman of one of the world's leading engineering companies, the leaders of top international business and engineering schools, and the most creative of thinkers, Philip Pullman.

Unit of analysis

We began the research for the book by developing a semi-structured interview template, exploring the key challenges that organizations may find when using IvT. The initial interview template was based on past research and experiences working with organizations in Europe, the USA, and East Asia. The idea of this initial template was to provide specific information on how different organizations approached the management and use of IvT. The template provided a tool for the collection of information and experiences of users of the technology, including the type of technology, the purpose of use, and the impact on the organization's activities (see Box A.1). In particular, we were interested to find out how the new technologies might be reshaping the process and skills required to innovate.

In the development of this template, we had several discussions amongst the research team about the intent and goals of the research. These discussions led us to adopt a multilevel perspective cutting across projects, organizations, and industries. We also decided to focus on public- as well as private-sector organizations. Given our previous experience, we realized that the single organization is often an unreliable unit of analysis for understanding the use of new technologies

---

Box A.1   Interview template

Background
- Type of firm—market, size, competence, products
- Organizational structure and context
- Innovation problems and challenges being faced

Use of IvT
- What technology is being used in the innovation process?
- What type of business is it being applied to (product, process, flow, mass, etc.)?
- What are the origins of the technology? (Where did it come from? Is it a bespoke or packaged system?)
- When is it used (experimentation, concept design, schematic design, detailed design, testing, and refinement or implementation)?
- How is it used? What is the character of the prototyping culture within the organization (playful/serious, closed/open)?
- Why was it used?
- What is required to enable its use (e.g. new skills in software)?
- How is the use of the tool managed? Are any management tools used?
- What type of output does it generate (3D visualization, data, prototypes, etc.)?

Impact of use
- What impact does it have on the problem at hand or the performance of the project or team?
- What impact does it have on the way the engineers or scientists solve problems? Does it change the way they work, and how?
- What impact does its use have on the way the engineers or scientists work with partners, clients or customers, suppliers, and across functions and other divisions?
- Does the use of the tool change the way the firm manages its innovation process?
- What lessons have been learned inside the organization from the use of the tool?
- What could have been done to ensure more effective use of the tools and to increase their impact on the innovation process?

Evidence of use
- Is there data that can be collected to provide evidence of the impact of use inside the organization (performance data, project data)?

---

on live projects. Often project teams combine knowledge and technologies from several different organizations in novel and unique ways, well beyond the capabilities of each separate one. Projects also provide episodes where traditional organizational routines may be unsuitable and require individuals to move well beyond the tried and tested tools of problem-solving. We were also conscious that previous research on IvT had tended to focus on the experiences of large, often US-based, manufacturing firms, which have extensive internal capabilities and often direct their innovation activities on incremental improvements in a continuous flow of products. Our idea was to look more broadly and to capture the experiences of project teams often working in 'low-technology' sectors, notably mining and construction. We were also keen to draw from the experiences of public organizations and how the use of the new tools might lead to new forms of public policy and interactions between universities and non-academic institutions.

We have tried to understand the organizational implications of the use of the new technology. The use of new technologies in thinking, playing, and doing in innovation activities in many organizations can be bounded within a single organization, albeit with significant external contributions. In some areas of the research we were able to combine organizational- and project-level studies to better understand experiences of the organization with specific time-limited tasks. In the case of Arup, in particular, we conducted both project- and organization-level studies in order to better understand how organizational routines are translated into solutions in individual projects. We were also keen to understand how lessons from individual projects were captured by the organization.

Given our awareness of the use of IvT across a wide range of industrial sectors, we chose to explore the use of the new technology across the public sector research environments. Working at two leading international universities we were well aware of the potential of the new technologies to reshape research activities. We also felt that previous studies of IvT had lacked emphasis on scientific research and that by adopting a wider perspective we would be able to gain insights into its ubiquity. In fact, it was only through our studies of public organizations and research processes that we became more fully aware of the diffusion and potential of the new technologies to reshape the way people were thinking in new ways. We became aware of the potential impact of the new tools on policy-making, helping governments play with different policy options.

Case studies

The main source of material for the book has been a number of inductive case studies. The selection of these case studies was based on a convenient sample.

In developing this sample, we were well positioned in that we were able to draw from our university and industrial colleagues who are working with these technologies on live projects and products. It was their experiences that drove the research and we have tried to remain faithful to their stories.

The approach followed in each case was based on a common method with slightly different procedures of implementation. In each case, we attempted to use our interview template and to conduct interviews with the people working directly with the new technologies. All of our interviews were transcribed and we wrote detailed summaries of our findings, which were examined by the interviewees. Interviewees were given the chance to correct statements of fact and to add information. Given the advanced nature of some of the technology we investigated, it was often necessary to have these sources 'hold our hands' through the description of the technologies and processes. Often our first description of a case was incomplete and our sources provided detailed and extensive revisions to our drafts, for which we are very grateful.

The bulk of the research for the book was conducted in 2003. We were also able to draw on some of our previous research from 1996 to 2002. We conducted a number of interviews and gathered new case material in 2004. In some cases our research relationships with industrial partners has been long-term and sustained. In the case of Arup, we have worked closely with them for more than sixteen years. Indeed, one of the key intellectual mentors for the project was Steven Groák, the former head of Arup R&D. Steven died before we completed this study, but we have continuously revisited his ideas and work for inspiration and to clear up some of our own muddled thinking. Steven was well ahead of us and the time he spent working with us on process representation and the use of new technologies in design remains a source of enduring insight.

Over the past four years as part of this study we have conducted a large number of interviews with Arup staff working on a diverse range of large and small projects, including the Swiss Re building, the Millennium Bridge, and the HSBC Tower among others. We have also benefited from continuing discussions with John Miles, Chris Luebkeman, Tony Sheehan, Richard Haryott, John Berry, Neil Noble, Turlough O'Brien, Bob Emmerson, Duncan Michael, and Andy Foster. We were able to draw on over thirty interviews with Arup staff and spent more than a month in their offices carrying out observational research inside Arup Fire and Building Group 4 in London in 2003. We would particularly like to thank Peter Bressington, Nicole Hoffman, and the rest of the Arup Fire team.

The observational portion of this research was spread over a three-month period and involved participant observation of work practices and projects. One of the authors attended design and client meetings, group discussions, informal debates, design critiques, and a range of other activities that make up the modern design process. We found these observations to be central to the development of our understanding of the use of innovation technology, and they made us more aware of the combination of 'craft' and 'code' that the successful use of IvT involves. This material provides the basis of a major part of the Arup case study in Chapter 3.

In the case of P&G, we were able to draw upon a mixture of public and private sources. A large organization such as P&G attracts a lot of research attention. Our case involved a deep engagement at a number of levels with the company over a two-year period from 2002 to 2004. P&G was one of the four companies invited to a daylong meeting of the Innovation Club (established by Imperial College London, with the universities of Sussex and Brighton), to discuss a paper by the authors on the 'intensification of innovation' (Dodgson et al. 2002). P&G's response to this paper included a presentation, which particularly related to the emerging connect and develop (C&D) strategy. This led to a continuing dialogue and to an invitation to conduct a daylong workshop at P&G's laboratories in Newcastle, UK, on 'Innovation and Connect and Develop'. At this workshop, the ways in which P&G engaged customers in product development was explored by around forty participants. The event was facilitated independently by a former director of research at ICI and the results were documented. During this process, a number of key interview respondents were identified, including Mike Addison (New Business Development), Larry Huston (Vice-President of Knowledge and Innovation P&G Worldwide R&D), and Neil McGlip (Head of the Corporate R&D, Packaging).

Before the workshop and interviews, background evidence was assembled by the authors into material from which detailed questions were generated relating specifically to the use of technology in distributed innovation. A semi-structured questionnaire was used in all interviews. This was slightly adjusted during the research process in order to ensure that questions better reflected the experience of the interviewees. The interviews provided an opportunity to explore different organizational environments, highlighting the particular features of P&G's history and managerial approach to using new technology in problem-solving and innovation. The interviews were conducted by two members of the research team, taped, transcribed, written up, and returned to interviewees for verification. The notes were also sent to knowledgeable members of project teams for checking and verification.

The C&D strategy at P&G has elicited considerable attention in the popular press, and there are numerous reports and interviews available on the Internet (see, e.g. the interview with the CEO of P&G in *Fortune* (Sellers 2004)). These added to the background knowledge of the research team, and in combination with the workshop material and interviews led to improved understanding of developments in the company. Furthermore, a number of cases of suppliers of particular IvTs to P&G are available, and two of these, from SGI and

Simulation Dynamics, are reported in Chapter 3. In addition, a member of the research team attended a one-day workshop on 'Managing Discontinuous Innovation' at Cranfield Business School, where a major case of P&G was presented by Roy Sandbach, P&G Research Fellow, and manager responsible for new product direction-setting and innovation in Europe.

P&G and Arup comprise the major case studies conducted for the book, and whilst the remainder of the case studies are shorter, they used similar research methods albeit with smaller numbers of respondents. The case studies based on secondary information are denoted by footnotes citing relevant sources.

We are grateful to our colleagues at Imperial College London and University of Queensland for providing us with their time. The case of the congestion charge is based on interviews with Steven Glaister and his team. The Leaning Tower of Pisa case is drawn from interviews with John Burland and previously published articles.

Finally, some of the management issues associated with IvT and think, play, do were developed and tested in workshops, symposia, and professional training activities with main board members and senior managers in a range of companies and organizations with whom we have been working. These include Arup, Ballast Needham, Broadway Malyan, Buro Happold, The Design Council, Constructing Excellence, DEGW, EPSRC, HBG, The Housing Forum, Institute for Manufacturing, The Innovation Club, PRP Ltd, Lemelson Foundation/LEAD, Mott MacDonald, P&G, Southern Housing Group, Sun Microsystems, TWI, W.S. Atkins, and Willmott Dixon Group. We are grateful to all those who participated in discussing these ideas and adding their own experiences and insights.

Analysis of the case material

In a large-scale project such as this one with a dispersed team, finding opportunities for case analysis was a challenge. The research benefited from frequent residential trips to London and Brisbane. These residential trips provided an opportunity to debate and discuss the ideas emerging from the case material. The concepts of *innovation technology, craft and code*, and *think, play, do* all emerged from our interactions during these periods of face-to-face (or shoulder-to-shoulder) interaction. We debated each of the case studies, what they meant, and how they fitted into the overall pattern of the book. Our framework emerged from discussions about the cases. We began by filling whiteboards with key lessons and ideas from each case and working through them in an iterative process of confusion, excitement, and eventually refinement. In this analysis, we tried to use simple diagrams as a guide to use and shape the analysis of the case material. We benefited in this process by working through a range of terms and language to describe the elements of the case studies. The overall framework emerged in late 2003 and after considerable revision was codified into the book in early 2004.

Some of the early ideas behind the book were published in a paper in *International Journal of Innovation Management* (Dodgson et al. 2002) and a book chapter in *Technology, Knowledge and the Firm: Implications for Strategy and Industrial Change* (Dodgson et al. 2005).

Future research

Although we felt that the research had reached the point of repetition in that many of our case studies were revealing common patterns, there is considerable research still to be done on IvT. We did not intend this book to be the simple reporting of research findings, passing all the often dry standards of academic rigour and convention. Instead, we see it as a call for greater managerial attention and scholarly research on the use of these new technologies. We still know little about the diffusion of these technologies and how their pattern of use varies across different sectors. We would like to know more about the use of the new technologies and how they may shape competitive strategies, how firms work with other organizations to innovate, and how the use of these new tools reshapes work processes and the knowledge required to innovate. A new language and set of concepts is required to allow us to better understand how innovation takes place in distributed, open, and networked environments. We need, as well, a new conceptual framework for understanding how innovations emerge from the use of new technologies in their production.

As Marx and Engels observed nearly 150 years ago, the engine of capitalism never rests, 'all that is solid melts into air'. IvT and think, play, do are the most modern version of the processes of change and refreshment that drive the economy and social relations onwards.

For managers, the challenges and opportunities of these technologies are exciting. This book is a call for greater attention to IvT and the new innovation process of think, play, do. We envisage that greater focus on harnessing the potential of IvT could have significant benefits for those organizations that are willing to change and adapt. We hope this book will bring greater attention to the exciting potential of these new technologies, the organization challenges associated with it, and the creative, analytical, and interpretive skills of individuals whose ideas transform the products we use and services we need and enjoy.

Endnotes

1 We use the term 'schema' in the sense of a pattern imposed on complex reality or experience to assist in explaining it, mediate perceptions, or guide responses (*The American Heritage*® *Dictionary of the English Language*, 4th edn, Houghton Mifflin, 2000).

2 The concepts of Research and Development were developed during the 1960s to assess the extent of formal, large, laboratory-based activities. The definition of R&D in the *Frascati Manual* includes all creative and experimental activities until the first working prototype is created. As we shall see, *Think, Play, Do* blurs these boundaries and makes the notion of the first working prototype largely inoperable, replacing it with a more realistic understanding of how ideas are developed and transformed into practice.

3 These models are described in detail in Chapter 3.

4 All typologies of technology are inevitably inexact: there are often blurred boundaries, and definitions are commonly transitory. What are often described as manufacturing technologies, for example, includes a number of concepts around quality control and supply chain management, which apply widely outside of the manufacturing sector. See note 5.

5 In this typology the high-level labels of 'production', 'communication', 'coordination', etc. are generic and robust, but the specific technologies we describe—'CIP', 'PMS', 'EDI', etc.—are somewhat transient in description as, although they fulfill the same technical role, they are analysed in various ways in different combinations at different times. This is seen in the current lack of concern for 'flexible manufacturing systems', once the focus of considerable attention, and in the evolution of developing frames of analysis, e.g. from 'lean' to 'agile' production (Womack and Jones 1996). See the glossary for descriptions of the various technologies. IvT builds upon existing ICT and OMT investments, and whilst the category is new it includes both new and existing technologies. Simulation and modelling tools used in CAD have migrated from supporting particular limited functions towards support for an integrated innovation process.

6 Thomke (2001) uses the example of a BMW side-impact crash simulation, where all ninety-one virtual crashes cost less than the $300,000 cost of a physical test.

7 Engineers at BMW dismantled a car into 60,000 pieces by means of computation. Using precisely defined accident data, the software calculates the mechanical forces that adjacent elements exert on each one of these finite elements. With knowledge of the material properties of the element, engineers can visualize the progress of the deformation process at the intervals of one millionth of a second (*Fraunhofer Magazine*, 1 (23), 2002).

Endnotes

8 CATIA is an integrated suite of computer-aided design (CAD), computer-aided engineering (CAE), and computer-aided manufacturing (CAM) applications for digital product definition and simulation. Developed by Dassault Systèmes, and marketed internationally by IBM, the software is commonly used for 3D product life cycle design, production, and maintenance.

9 A variety of databases on new production inductions show an increase in the number of new product introductions. For example, in food and packaging industries the number has almost doubled since the late 1980s. According to Productscan, there were 13,421 new products introduced in the worldwide food and packaging industry in 1988. By 1998, however, the number had increased to 25,181 and, in 2003, there were 33,678 new product introductions (Productscan.com).

10 Given the way that entrepreneurs commonly act for motives of personal expression, rather than economic rationality, and that often their success is determined more by the availability of opportunity or luck, the notions of heroic entrepreneurs shaping new economies are overblown. In combination, however, entrepreneurship is an important ingredient in the industrial development recipe adding to renewal and progress.

11 Changes that can occur very quickly: think of changing perceptions of airline safety—statistically one of the safest form of travel—post 11 September 2001.

12 The number of academic journals published has increased from around 4,000 in 1970 to around 11,000 in 1999 (Mabe and Amin 2001).

13 Amongst other technologies, biotechnology draws upon the diverse fields of biology, biochemistry, chemistry, physics, mathematics, pharmacology, and engineering.

14 Prencipe (1997), in his study of Rolls Royce aeroengines shows the substantial breadth of technologies necessary to manufacture this product.

15 E-science involves distributed global collaborations using very large data collections, massive computing resources, new analytical software, and high performance visualizations.

16 The diverse *motivations* for innovation are described in Chapter 1.

17 Developed in the early 1990s, the concept of the fifth Generation Innovation Process appears to be gaining increasing currency (ideas about innovation as well as innovations themselves can have long gestation periods). The exposition on the fifth Generation Innovation Process that follows is a development of Rothwell's thinking on this issue which was sadly curtailed due to his ill health in 1993.

18 Edgerton (2004) has questioned the simple representation of Bush's views, which have been widely interpreted to elevate a science-push model of innovation.

19 For a discussion of some of these projects, see Rothwell and Robertson (1973) and Mowery and Rosenberg (1979). Mowery and Rosenberg strongly criticize the methodology used in both these studies and the interpretation of some of the data which, they argue, point to multi- rather than unidimensional sources of innovation.

20 Examples include the Fifth Generation Computer Project in Japan, the Alvey Programme in the UK, the ESPRIT program in the European Community, and SEMATECH in the USA (Dodgson 1993*b*; Sakakibara 2001).

21 Rothwell's perspicacious thinking about these technologies was ahead of the actual development of many of the technologies we describe as IvT.

22 For example, in the fields of functional genomics and bioinformatics, following the Human Genome Project there are a variety of repositories of knowledge, ranging from basic gene sequences to complex, 3D protein structures. Researchers need high-level search and knowledge acquisition tools, including computationally intensive simulations, to enable them to study issues like protein folding or receptor docking mechanisms (www.rcuk.ac.uk/escience).

23 There is a substantial literature on the 'social construction of knowledge' (see Bijker et al. 1987). There are limits to this view: technological development has technological constraints upon it (see Pavitt 2003).

24 Part of the following section is based on discussions with Jennifer Whyte.

25 A leading design company, IDEO, has a collection of artefacts it draws upon as a design library to stimulate creative constructions across industry boundaries (Sutton and Hargadon 1996). Many design companies use this technique.

26 The research methods used for studying these companies is described in the Appendix (p. 205).

27 P&G website, company information: http://www.pg.com/main.jhtml

28 In 2002, twelve of P&G's 250-odd brands generated half of its sales and an even bigger share of net profits.

29 www.pg.com/science/mngmnt_commit.jhtml

30 www.innocentive.com

31 Its Web page includes details in Chinese, German, Russian, Spanish, Japanese, and Korean.

32 www.yet2.com

33 www.ninesigma.com

34 'Linking intellectual property buyers, sellers: Making R&D more lucrative', *Investor's Business Daily*, 9 November 2001. ChromaDex press release, 29 October 2001, www.chromadex.com.

35 www.yourencore.com

36 The business units were formed as part of the organizational restructuring at P&G to enable it to move from geographical representation to global business units based on product lines.

37 Silicon Graphics Inc. (SGI) is a world leader in high performance computing, storage, and visualization technology. Its hardware and software are used in many advanced complex applications from flight simulators to Disney games, by the defence industries and research scientists. Its facilities include group collaboration centres with immersive visualization capabilities. http://www.sgi.com/pdfs/3413.pdf.

38 The construction of the building was affected by parochial political concerns that distorted the architect's original vision; so much so that Utzon never visited the completed opera house. The acoustics in the auditoria have never been as good as

they should be. The use of contemporary IvT using the original computerized design models may help recreate or improve the original objectives for the auditoria's acoustics.

39 www.arup.com

40 Jones argues that often the introduction of new techniques can be as important to scientific discovery as the development of new theories or concepts. He uses the example of X-ray diffraction in the development of molecular biology, and the invention of scanning probe microscopes in the emergence of nanoscale science (2004).

41 Klystrons are microwave amplifiers. They are electron tubes used to generate and amplify a high-speed stream of electrons at the microwavelength.

42 Spotlight—Border-Crossing Science, EPSRC, Summer 2003.

43 www.skin-forum.org.uk

44 Efforts to use computational power in order to increase speed of experiments began after the Second World War in the work of scientists such as Feynman (1999). In the 1980s Feynman's team created a company called Thinking Machines.

45 It is rather difficult to predict how these numbers will change as a result of the homeland security measures in place in the USA since 2002. At the time of writing (2004), the numbers of overseas students allowed into the USA to study in universities is decreasing.

46 Business-funded research also allows industry to build on their own capabilities and to absorb and gain benefits from other research (cf. Cohen and Levinthal 1990).

47 In 1993 the computer program Mosaic Browser, together with the intellectual property protocol, transformed the use of what was an academic tool (the Internet) into a universal part of the ICT infrastructure.

48 'Rolls-Royce is confident grid technology will earn its wings', Glick, B, *Computing*, 30 April 2003.

49 The sales force must not be considered only as a cost in getting innovations to market. It provides informed feedback from users, which is invaluable in any innovation process.

50 *Investors Chronicle*, 5 December 2003 and *The Economist* (15 May 2004), suggest the loss associated with generics replacing Wellbutrin and Paxil could be $3–4 billion.

51 GSK R&D feature story 030613 http://science.gsk.com/news/features/030613-tres.htm

52 GSK R&D feature story 030613 http://science.gsk.com/news/features/030613-tres.htm

53 http://gsk.com/press_archive/press2003/press_10212003a.htm

54 We are very grateful to Ian Hughes at GSK Technology Development for his description of this process.

55 Part of a number or quantity that will divide it without a remainder.

56 GSK R&D feature story 030613 http://science.gsk.com/news/features/030613-tres.htm

57 *The Economist*, 15 May 2004.

58 *Investors Chronicle*, 5 December 2003.

59 'Beating Cancer: the new frontier of molecular biology', *The Economist*, 16 October 2004.

60 The information provided here was obtained from UQ News, 25 September 2003.

61 Our understanding of the term modelling is the establishment of the key parameters and relationships in a system, construct, or physical phenomena (how does this work?) and simulation involves the manipulation of some of those parameters (what happens if?).

62 The definition of artificial intelligence suffers the same terminological difficulties found in operations and manufacturing technology (OMT), described in Chapter 1. The term appears to have been coined at MIT and is discussed by Simon, who prefers 'complex information processing' or 'simulation of cognitive processes' (Simon 1996: 4). The same tools are described under different categories at different times. The kinds of technology described in this section are variously described as 'artificial intelligence', 'expert systems', 'scientific discovery', and 'computational discovery'. Simon argues that these tools differ from others found in operations research and OMT, because they allow for selective searching using rules of thumb, and find decisions that are 'good enough, that *satisfice*', rather than optimal. This is because the heuristic search capabilities are more complex and less well structured than those required in operations research. Thus satisficing in a nearly-realistic artificial intelligence model is traded off against optimizing in a greatly simplified operations research model (Simon 1996: 27–8).We describe them as IvT, as their purpose is the intensification of discovery and increase in variety—important components of 'thinking' in innovation processes.

63 As *The Economist* dryly noted, the Nobel Prize-winning ability of the robot remains uncertain.

64 Simon distinguishes between engineering, which he says is concerned with 'synthesis' (often synthesis of artificial objects) and science, which is concerned with 'analysis' (Simon 1996: 4).

65 Frank Gehry in S. Pacey, 2003, *RIBA Journal*, November: 78–9.

66 The developing use of graphic representation has played an important role in innovation since the fifteenth century, where improved technical drawings by Renaissance architects and engineers were essential in bridging the gap between theory and practice (Lefèvre 2004). Visualization still plays a central role, of course, in improving scientific understanding.

67 www-edc.eng.cam.ac.uk/materialsselection

68 Jose Antonio Vargas, 'Problems You Can Shake a Joystick At', *Washington Post*, 18 October 2004.

69 Vargas's article does not consider the awful potential for confusion between simulation and reality when the tools for engaging the destruction of bits of information and people are so similar.

70 A leading designer in the architectural industry has noted that during the 1990s, CATIA requires far greater computational power than most mainstream CAD modelling packages. It requires scientific workstations linked by high-bandwidth

Endnotes

communications. For this reason, only dedicated supply-chain partners—such as those found in the automobile or aerospace sectors—are likely to be able to afford the investment in machines, infrastructure, and skills needed to use it. Many smaller firms in project-based environments such as construction are likely to find these costs to be prohibitive barriers to the systems use (personal communication with Richard Saxon on 5 August 2004). There are, however, numerous other packages with less functionality and cheaper prices available to smaller firms.

71 http://archrecord.construction.com/innovation/1_techbriefs/0310Gehry.asp

72 As above and http://www.gehrytechnologies.com/

73 Sources: www.polaroid.com; Channel 4, Designing Series, 2003.

74 Sources: 'Bra Wars', *The Economist*, 30 November 2000; 'Better by Design', Channel 4 television programme; *Smart Technology*, Issue 164, January 2000; Pauline Weston Thomas at www.fashion-era.com; and Anne Harris at http://www.e4engineering.com.

75 Fluid simulation packages include *WAVE*—a gas dynamics simulation program enabling performance simulations to be carried out based on intake, combustion, and exhaust system design; and *VECTIS*—a 3D computational fluid dynamics program for solving flow equations governing conservation of mass, momentum, and energy. Ricardo has also developed a range of mechanical systems simulations, including *ENGDYN*—a simulation environment for analysing the dynamics of the engine and powertrain; *VALDYN*—for simulating the dynamics of the valvetrain; *PISDYN* and *RINGPAK*—simulation packages for design and analysis of piston/ringpack assemblies; and *ORBIT*—for detailed analysis of bearings.

76 See the case study of Ricardo's partnership with a Chinese company, DLW, in Dodgson (1993*b*).

77 Meg Whitman is quoted in *The Guardian* business interview, 12 April 2003. Prior to Ebay, she worked at P&G, gaining much experience working with user groups in new product development in household goods.

78 The information presented here is from Kamau High, 'Beta Testing: The Need to Probe the Virtual Waters', *Financial Times*, 10 November 2004.

79 Atari operates a special website for this purpose: www.betatests.net. It costs between $5 million and $10 million to bring a new game to the market.

80 Source: Wal-Mart Annual Report 2004 at www.walmart.com; Hays (2004), 'What Wal-Mart Knows About Customers' Habits', *New York Times*, 14 November 2004.

81 Visit to Toyota's Motomachi Factory and R&D Facilities, Nagoya, 25 November 2003.

82 Daimler Chrysler expects the virtual reality environment to enable cost reductions of 20 per cent, reduce product development times, and help in finding ways to improve quality for next-generation Mercedes Benz cars. The Virtual Reality Centre is driven by a silicon graphics supercomputer, linked to the company's CATIA design software and database. Visual representation is provided on a 'powerwall' (7 m × 2.5 m), a 'curved projection' screen, and in a 'cave' environment. Visit to Mercedes Sindelfingen Factory, Design and R&D Facilities, Stuttgart, 14 April 2003.

83 Source: Adapted from the ideas generated in the European Commission's 'Manufacturing Visions Project' (www.manufacturing-visions.org).

84 In the developed economies, one of the major changes occurring in traditional manufacturing is a result of its comparative expense, and production has moved off-shore to access cheaper labour. Traditional manufacturing has grown in countries like China, to enable production to be close to emerging and potentially large new markets.

85 There are also disadvantages with rapid prototyping technologies. Some machines, for example, only offer parts with maximum sizes of 3-inch cubes. Others are not as restrictive at 32 × 22 × 20 inches, but large parts usually have to be built separately and connected manually. Larger parts can also be expensive.

86 Arup R&D in Jones *RIBA Journal*, 2003.

87 Sources: Jonathan Ward: http://home.att.net/~castleisland/, and Elisabeth Goode, Laureen Belleville, and David Belforte: http://ils.pennnet.com/Articles/Article_Display.cfm?Section=Articles&Subsection=Display&ARTICLE_ID=207992&KEYWORD=rapid%20prototyping

88 Renault's Advanced Manufacturing Centre includes four SLA 7000 systems, an OptoForm direct composite manufacturing system, and a ThermoJet printer. Future additions to the Centre will include 3D Systems' SLS systems.

89 This section on Palm is taken from Bart Eisenberg: http://www.dcontinuum.com/content/news.php?id=149

90 Cynthia L. Istook: http://www.tx.ncsu.edu/jtatm/index.htm

91 http://europa.eu.int/comm/enterprise/textile/documents/conf_apparel_harari.pdf

92 http://www.fashion-online.org/flash.html

93 http://www.avatar-me.com/company/realav.pdf

94 http://www.bodymetrics.com/ProblemDotComFrameset.htm

95 http://www.bodymetrics.com/NewsDotComFrameset.htm

96 Claudia Eckert 'Communication and Representation': www-edc.eng.cam.ac.uk/projects/comrep/index.html

97 ABAQUS/Standard provides a comprehensive, general-purpose FEA tool that includes a variety of time- and frequency-domain analysis procedures. These procedures are divided into two classes: 'general analyses', in which the response may be linear or non-linear; and 'linear perturbation analyses', in which linear response is computed about a general, possibly non-linear, base state. A single simulation can include multiple analysis types (www.hks.com).

98 Finite element analysis (FEA) consists of a computer model of a material or design that is loaded and analysed for specific results. It is used in new product design, and existing product refinement. A company is able to verify that a proposed design will be able to perform to the client's specifications prior to manufacturing or construction. Modifying an existing product or structure is utilized to qualify the product or structure for a new service condition. In case of structural failure, FEA may be used to help determine the design modifications to meet the new condition (www.dexmotmonaghan.com).

Endnotes

99 Interview with Michael McIlrath, Integrated Circuits Laboratory, Electrical Engineering Department, MIT, 4 April 1996.

100 The simulation system is a modified version of DELMIA's Interactive 3D Graphic Simulation Tool for Designing, Evaluating, and Programming Robotic Work (IGRIP). DELMIA is a third-party applications domain of SGI.

101 www.dem.csiro.au/em/majorresearchinitiatives/glassearth

102 Interview, Dr Mehmet Kizil, Lecturer in Mining Engineering, University of Queensland, 30 April 2003.

103 Jones, W. (2003) Rapid Prototyping Techniques, *RIBA Journal*, 12 December, 55–8.

104 Defined as the ability to do things well.

105 Defined as providing the potential to be used for a particular purpose, in this case to change competencies.

106 A 2002 McKinsey analysis of Web services, for example, argues that their likely result is: 'increased fragmentation of value chains and industries as well as more narrowly focused companies', Ismail et al. (2002).

107 Other firms in this industry, such as Sun Microsystems have decided to continue their focus on products and have limited the growth of their service business.

108 As pointed out by Best and Garnsey (1999), Penrose's central organizing concept of 'bases' is also similar to that of 'organizational capability' used by Chandler (1966).

109 Although our simple distinction between competencies and capabilities fails to capture much of the richness of these analyses, it is sufficient for our purposes to highlight the importance of IvT to strategic management.

110 Information for this section was derived from Sabbagh (1996) and the PBS Video documentary series '21st Century Jet: The Building of the 777' (PBS 1996).

111 Another issue managers might need to address is how IvT could enable more creative design outside of the confines of particular modular structures. Fast and cheap experimentation may permit greater innovation within modules.

112 For a description of the kind of workforce to which we refer, see Florida (2002).

113 The dispersal of teams across different locations should not be seen as the 'end of geography' or the 'death of distance'. Geography still matters for innovation. Crucial contributors to innovative activities, such as R&D expenditure and demanding, knowledgeable customers, remain concentrated in a small number of countries and regions around the world. Despite the extraordinary expansion of science and engineering capability discussed in Chapter 4, it is highly unlikely that this number of regions, which contribute significantly to world science and technology, will grow substantially over the next twenty years.

114 It does seem that we are in an endless cycle of communication and interaction, where it is believed to be imperative to be online all the time. Australian armed forces in Iraq in 2004 complained that their email from home is packaged for daily delivery: they demanded instant communications. One is reminded of the cartoon of the exhausted man sitting up in bed working on his PC, telling his concerned wife: 'I'm afraid if I go off-line, I'll die'. IvT and ICT can lead to a corrosion of personal space and time and its intermingling with professional space and time. It can also lead to other senses of social dislocation (cf. Sennett 1998).

115 See the special edition of *Research Policy*, 'Codification of Knowledge: Empirical Evidence and Policy Recommendations', 30 (9), 2001, and *Industrial and Corporate Change*, 9 (2), 2000.

116 We agree with Cook and Brown (1999) that tacit and explicit knowledge are distinct concepts and that it is not necessarily possible to use one form as an aid to acquiring the other.

117 Innovation theory refers to concepts such as 'learning by doing' and 'learning by using'. IvT enables these to take place in virtual environments as well as new forms of 'learning by playing'.

118 There may, of course, be cognitive problems associated with remembering that information is stored, and technological problems associated with incompatible generations of technological media.

119 Marx's Grundisse, p. 507 (McLellan 1980).

120 It also overcomes the problems of definition that emerge when R&D is defined as investment up to the production of the first working prototype. Technologies such as IvT show that prototyping can be virtual, goes through many iterative stages, and is intimately linked to investments in 'doing' that are not included in measurements of investment, despite their strong influence on the creation of designs and prototypes.

121 The development of IvT itself presents many technical challenges, particularly in integrating different software programs. In some applications, it is possible that problems in software development could slow the rate of adoption of IvT.

122 The preference of people to work closely only with those they trust is, however, unlikely to change in the immediate future.

123 Dodgson et al. (2002) developed an 'intensification index' to measure relative performance over time.

References

Abernathy, W. and Utterback, J. (1978). 'Patterns of Industrial Innovation', *Technology Review*, 80(7): 40–7.

Allen, T. (1977). *Managing the Flow of Technology: Technology Transfer and the Dissemination of Technological Information Within the R and D Organisation*. Cambridge, MA: MIT Press.

Antonelli, C. and Geuna, A. (2000). 'Information and Communication Technologies and the Production, Distribution and Use of Knowledge', *International Journal of Technology Management*, 20(1–2): 72–105.

Anumba, C. J., Bouchlaghem, N. M., Whyte, J. K., and Duke, A. (2000). 'Perspectives on a Shared Construction Project Model', *International Journal of Cooperative Information Systems*, 9(3): 283–313.

Archibugi, D. and Michie, J. (1998). *Trade Growth and Technical Change*. Cambridge: Cambridge University Press.

Argyris, C. and Schon, D. (1978). *Organizational Learning: Theory, Method and Practice*. London: Addison-Wesley.

Arthur, B. (2002). 'Is the Information Revolution Dead?', *Business 2.0*, www.business2.com.

Babbage, C. (1971). *The Economy of Machinery and Manufactures*. London: Pickering.

Baldwin, C. and Clark, K. (2000). *Design Rules: The Power of Modularity*. Cambridge, MA: MIT Press.

Ball, P. (1997). *Made to Measure: New Materials for the 21st Century*. Princeton, NJ: Princeton University Press.

Banks, J., Ericksson, G., Burrage, K, Yellowlees, P, Ivermee, S., and Tichon, J. (2003). 'Constructing the Hallucinations of Psychosis in Virtual Reality', *Journal of Network and Computer Applications*, 27: 1–11.

Barlow, J. and Ozaki, R. (1999). Are you being served? Japanese lessons on customer-focused housebuilding. Report of a DTI Expert Mission. London: DTI.

Barney, J. (1986). 'Strategic Factor Markets: Expectations, Luck, and Business Strategy', *Management Science*, 32: 1231–41.

Barras, R. (1986). 'Towards a Theory of Innovation in Services', *Research Policy*, 15: 161–73.

Bartlett, C. and Ghoshal, S. (1989). *Managing Across Borders: The Transnational Solution*. Boston, MA: Harvard Business School Press.

—— and Ghoshal, S. (2000). *Transnational Management: Text, Cases, and Readings in Cross-Border Management*. Singapore: McGraw-Hill.

References

Baumol, W. J. (2002). *The Free-Market Innovation Machine*. Princeton and Oxford: Princeton University Press.

Berg, M. (1997). *Rationalising Medical Work: Decision-Support Techniques and Medical Practices*. Cambridge, MA: MIT Press.

Bernstein, P. (1996). *Against the Gods: the Remarkable Story of Risk*. New York: Wiley.

Bessant, J. (1991). *Managing Advanced Manufacturing Technology: The Challenge of the Fifth Wave*. Oxford: Blackwell.

—— Francis, D., Francis, D., Meredith, S., Kaplinsky, R., and Brown, S. (2001). 'Developing Manufacturing Agility in SMEs', *International Journal of Technology Management*, 22(1–3): 28–54.

Best, M. and Garnsey, E. (1999). 'Edith Penrose 1914–1996', *Economic Journal*, 109(453): 187–201.

Best, M. H. (2001). *The New Competitive Advantages: The renewal of American industry*. Oxford: Oxford University Press.

Bettencourt, L. A., Ostrom, A. L., Brown, S. W. and Roundtree, R. I. (2002). 'Client Co-Production in Knowledge-Intensive Business Services', *California Management Review*, 44(4): 100–28.

Bijker, W., Hughes, T. and Peach, T. (eds) (1987). *The Social Construction of Technological Systems: new directions in the sociology and history of technology*. Cambridge, MA: MIT Press.

Bilda, Z. and Demirkan, H. (2003). 'An Insight on Designers' Sketching Activities in Traditional Versus Digital Media', *Design Studies*, 24: 27–50.

Blauner, R. (1964). *Alienation and Freedom*. Chicago: University of Chicago Press.

Bleaney, M. and Wakelin, K. (2002). 'Efficiency, Innovation and Exports', *Oxford Bulletin of Economics and Statistics*, 64: 3–15.

Boden, M. (1990). *The Creative Mind: Myths and Mechanisms*. London: Weidenfeld/ Abacus.

Bok, D. (2003). *Universities in the Marketplace*. Princeton, NJ: Princeton University Press.

Braverman, H. (1974). *Labor and Monopoly Capital: The Degradation of Work in the Twentieth Century*. New York: Monthly Review Press.

Bright, J. R. (1958). *Automation and Management*. Boston, MA: Harvard Business School Press.

Brill, M. (2001). *Disproving Widespread Myths About Workplace Design*. Jasper, IN: Kimball International Inc.

Brooke, L. (1994). 'Coping with Complexity', *Automotive Industries*, 174(11): 38–42.

Brown, J. S. and Duguid, P. (2000). *The Social Life of Information*. Boston, MA: Harvard Business School Press.

Brusoni, S., Prencipe, A., and Pavitt, K. (2001). 'Knowledge Specialization, Organizational Coupling and the Boundaries of the Firm: Why Do Firms Know More Than They Make', *Administrative Science Quarterly*, 46: 597–621.

Burland, J. B. (2004). *The Leaning Tower of Pisa Revisited*. Fifth International Conference on Case Histories in Geotechnicial Engineering, New York.

Burns, T. and Stalker, G. (1961). *The Management of Innovation*. London: Tavistock.

Bush, V. (1946). *Science: The Endless Frontier.* Washington: National Science Foundation, Reprint 1960.

Calvert, J. and Patel, P. (2002). *University–Industry Research Collaborations in the UK.* Brighton, SPRU University of Sussex.

Carey, J. (1995). *The Faber Book of Science.* London: Faber & Faber.

Carlsson, B. (1994). 'Technological Systems and Economic Performance', in M. Dodgson and R. Rothwell (eds) *The Handbook of Industrial Innovation.* Aldershot: Edward Elgar, pp. 13–24.

Carr, N. (2003). 'IT Doesn't Matter', *Harvard Business Review,* 81(5): 41–50.

Castells, M. (1996). *The Rise of the Network Society.* Oxford: Blackwell.

Caves, R. (2000). *Creative Industries: Contracts between Art and Commerce.* Cambridge, MA: Harvard University Press.

Cefis, E. and Marsili, O. (2004). *Survivor: The Role of Innovation in Firms' Survival.* T. C. Koopmans Research Institute, USE, Utrecht University.

Chandler, A. (1966). *Strategy and Structure.* Cambridge, MA: MIT Press.

Chandler, A. D. (1990). *Scale and Scope.* Cambridge, MA: Harvard University Press.

Chesbrough, H. W. (2003). *Open Innovation: The New Imperative for Creating and Profiting from Technology.* Boston, MA: Harvard Business School Press.

Child, J. and Faulkner, D. (1998). *Strategies of Co-operation: Managing Alliances,* Networks, and Joint Ventures. Oxford: Oxford University Press.

Christensen, C. M. (1997). *The Innovator's Dilemma: When New Technologies Cause Great Firms to Fail.* Boston, MA: Harvard Business School Press.

Clark, K. B. and Wheelwright, S. C. (1993). *Managing New Product and Process Development: Text and Cases.* New York: Free Press.

Cohen, L. R. and Noll, R. C. (1991). *Efficient Management of R&D Programs: The Technology Pork Barrel.* Washington, DC: The Brookings Institution, pp. 37–52.

Cohen, W. and Levinthal, D. (1990). 'Absorptive Capacity: A New Perspective on Learning and Innovation', *Administrative Science Quarterly,* 35(2): 128–52.

—— and Malerba, F. (2001). 'Is the Tendency to Variation a Chief Cause of Progress?', *Journal of Industrial and Corporate Change,* 10: 587–608.

—— Nelson, R. R., and Walsh, J. (2002). 'Links and Impacts: The Influence of Public Research on Industrial R&D', *Management Science,* 48(1): 1–23.

Constant, E. W. (1980). *The Origins of the Turbojet Revolution.* Baltimore and London: Johns Hopkins University Press.

Constant, E. W. (2000). 'Recursive practice and the evolution of technological knowledge', in J. Ziman, *Techological Innovation as an Evolutionary Process,* pp. 219–33.

Cook, S. D. N. and Brown, J. S. (1999). 'Bridging Epistemologies: The Generative Dance between Organizational Knowledge and Organizational Knowing', *Organization Science,* 10(4): 381–400.

Cooke, P. and Morgan, K. (2000). *The Associational Economy: Firms, Regions, and Innovation.* Oxford: Oxford University Press.

Coombs, R. (1994). 'Technology and Business Strategy', in M. Dodgson and R. Rothwell (eds) *The Handbook of Industrial Innovation.* Cheltenham: Elgar, pp. 384–92.

References

Cooper, R. G. (1998). *Product Leadership: Creating and Launching Superior New Products*. Cambridge, MA: Perseus Books.

Crump, T. (2001). *A brief History of Science: As Seen Through the Development of Scientific Instruments*. London: Constable.

Cusumano, M. A. and Yoffie, D. B. (1998). *Competing on Internet Time: Lessons from Netscape and Its Battle with Microsoft*. New York: Free Press.

Czarnitzki, D. and Kraft, K. (2004). 'Innovation Indicators and Corporate Credit Ratings: Evidence from German Firms', *Economics Letters*, 82: 377–84.

Dahl, D., Chattopadhyay, A., and Gorn, G. (2001). 'The Importance of Visualization in Concept Design', *Design Studies*, 22: 5–26.

Davies, A., Brady, T., Tang, P., Rush, H., Hobday, M., and Gann, D. M. (2003). *Delivering Integrated Solutions*. Brighton, SPRU, University of Sussex.

Davis, S. and Meyer, C. (1998). *Blur: The Speed of Change in the Connected Economy*. New York: Warner Books.

DCMS (2001). *Creative Industries Mapping Document*. London: DCMS.

Debackere, K. (1999). *Technologies to develop technology: The impact of new technologies on the organisation of innovation projects*. Antwerp/Apeldoorn: Maklu-Uitgevers nv.

—— and B. Van Looy (2003). 'Managing Integrated Design Capabilities in New Product Design and Development', in B. Dankbaar, *Innovation Management in the Knowledge Economy*. London: Imperial College Press.

DeFillippi, R. J. and Arthur, M. J. (1998). 'Paradox in Project-Based Enterprise: The Case of Film Making', *California Management Review*, 40(2): 125–39.

Den Hertog, F. and Huizenga, E. (2000). *The Knowledge Enterprise. Implementing Intelligent Business Strategies*. London: Imperial College Press.

Design Council (2003). *Facts and Figures on Design in Britain 2002–2003*. London: Design Council.

Dodgson, M. (1984). 'New Technology, Employment and Small Engineering Firms', *International Small Business Journal*, 3(2): 118–19.

—— (1985). *Advanced Manufacturing Technology in the Small Firm—Variation in Use and Lessons for the Flexible Organisation of Work*. London: Technical Change Centre.

—— (1989). *Technology Strategy and the Firm: Management and Public Policy*. Harlow: Longman.

—— (1991). *The Management of Technological Learning: Lessons from a Biotechnology Company*. Berlin: De Gruyter.

—— (1993a). 'Organizational Learning: A Review of Some Literatures', *Organization Studies*, 14(3): 375–94.

—— (1993b). *Technological Collaboration in Industry: Strategy Policy and Internationalization in Innovation*. London: Routledge.

—— (1993c). 'Learning, Trust and Technological Collaboration', *Human Relations*, 46(1): 77–95.

—— (2000). *Management of Technological Innovation*. Oxford: Oxford University Press.

—— and Hinze, S. (2000). 'Indicators Used to Measure the Innovation Process: Defects and Possible Remedies', *Research Evaluation*, 8(2): 101–14.

—— Gann, D. M., and Salter, A. (2002). 'Intensification of Innovation', *International Journal of Innovation Management*, 6(1): 53–84.

—— and Bessant, J. (1996). *Effective Innovation Policy: A New Approach*. London: International Thomson Business Press.

—— Gann, D. and Salter, A. (2005). 'The Intensification of Innovation and the Management of Knowledge', in K. Green, M. Miozzo and P. Dewick, *Technology, Knowledge and the Firm: Implications for Strategy and Industrial Change*. Cheltenham: Edward Elgar.

Dore, R. (2000). *Stock Market Capitalism: Welfare Capitalism—Japan and Germany versus the Anglo-Saxons*. Oxford: Oxford University Press.

—— and Sako, M. (1998). *How the Japanese Learn to Work*. London: Routledge.

Dosi, G. (1988). 'Sources, Procedures and Microeconomic Effects of Innovation', *Journal of Economic Literature*, 26: 1120–71.

Dougherty, D. (2004). 'Organizing practices in services: capturing practice-based knowledge for innovation', *Stategic Organization*, 2(1): 35–64.

DTI (2002). *e-Science: Building a Global Grid*. London: Department of Trade and Industry.

—— (2003). Third Community Innovation Survey. London: Department of Trade and Industry.

Duffy, F. (1997). *The New Office*. London: Conran Octopus Ltd.

Dyer, D., Dalzell, F., and Olegario, R. (2004). *Rising Tide: Lessons from 165 Years of Brand Building at P&G*. Cambridge, MA: Harvard Business School Press.

Edgerton, D. (1999). 'From Innovation to Use: Ten (Eclectic) Theses on the History of Technology', *History and Technology*, 16: 1–26.

—— (2004). '"The Linear Model" Did not Exist: Reflections on the History and Historiography of Science and Research in Industry in the Twentieth Century', in K. Grandin (ed.) *Science and Industry in the Twentieth Century*. New York: Watson.

Edquist, C. (ed.) (1997). *Systems of Innovation*. London: Pinter.

Eisenhardt, K. M. and Martin, J. A. (2000). 'Dynamic Capabilities: What Are They?', *Strategic Management Journal*, 21: 1105–21.

—— Whitney, D. E., Smith, R. P., and Gebala, D. (1990). *Organizing the Tasks in Complex Design Projects*. ASME Conference on Design Theory and Methodology, Chicago.

Elder, J. (2003). 'The management of knowledge in Germany', in F. Gault and D. Foray, *Measuring Knowledge Management in the Business Sector: The First Steps*. Paris: OECD, pp. 89–119.

Eppinger, S. D. (2001). 'Innovation at the Speed of Information', *Harvard Business Review*, 79(1): 149–58.

EPSRC (2003). Spotlight—Border-Crossing Science.

Fagerberg, J. (1987). 'A Technology-Gap Approach to Why Growth Rates Differ', *Research Policy*, 16: 87–99.

Ferguson, E. (1992). *Engineering and the Mind's Eye*. Cambridge, MA: MIT Press.

Feynman, R. (1999). 'There's Plenty of Room at the Bottom', in A. J. G. Hey (ed.) *Feynman and Computation*. Cambridge, MA: Perseus Books, pp. 63–76.

References

Florida, R. (2002). *The Rise of the Creative Class: And How It's Transforming Work, Leisure, Community and Everyday Life*. New York: Basic Books.

Foreman, J. (2004). 'Game-Based Learning: How to Delight and Instruct in the 21st Century', *Educause Review*, 39(5): 50–66.

Freeman, C. (1974). *The Economics of Industrial Innovation*. London: Pinter.

—— (1987). 'Information Technology and Change in Techno-Economic Paradigm', in C. Freeman and L. Soete (eds.) *Technical Change and Full Employment*. Oxford: Basil Blackwell.

—— (1991). 'Networks of Innovators: A Synthesis of Research Issues', *Research Policy*, 20: 499–514.

—— (1994). 'Innovation and Growth', in M. Dodgson and R. Rothwell (eds) *The Handbook of Industrial Innovation*. Aldershot: Edward Elgar, pp. 78–93.

—— and Louca, F. (2001). *As Time Goes By: From the Industrial Revolutions to the Information Revolution*. Oxford: Oxford University Press.

—— and Perez, C. (1988). 'Structural Crises of Adjustment: Business Cycles and Investment Behaviour', in G. Dosi, C. Freeman, R. Nelson, G. Silverberg, and L. Soete (eds) *Technical Change and Economic Theory*, London: Frances Pinter.

—— and Soete, L. (1997). *The Economics of Industrial Innovation*, 3rd edn. London: Frances Pinter.

Friedmann, G. (1961). *The Anatomy of Work: The Implications of Specialization*. London: Heinemann Educational Books.

Galison, P. (2003). *Einstein's Clocks, Poincare's Maps: Empires of Time*. London: Sceptre (Hodder & Stoughton).

Gallouj, F. and Weinstein, O. (1997). 'Innovation in services', *Research Policy*, 26(4–5): 537–56.

Gann, D. M. (1996). 'Construction as a Manufacturing Process? Similarities and Differences between Industrialized Housing and Car Production in Japan', *Construction Management and Economics*, 14: 437–50.

—— (2000). *Building Innovation—Complex Constructs in a Changing World*. London: Thomas Telford Publications.

—— and Salter, A. (1998). 'Learning and Innovation Management in Project-Based, Service-Enhanced Firms', *International Journal of Innovation Management*, 2(4): 431–54.

—— —— (1999). *Interdisciplinary Skills for Built Environment Professionals*. London: The Ove Arup Foundation, p. 47.

—— —— (2000). 'Innovation in Project-Based, Service-Enhanced Firms: The Construction of Complex Products and Systems', *Research Policy*, 29: 955–72.

—— —— and Whyte, J. K. (2003). 'Design Quality Indicator as a Tool for Thinking', *Building Research and Information*, 31: 318–33.

Gardiner, P. and Rothwell, R. (1985). 'Tough Customers: Good Design', *Design Studies*, 6(1): 7–17.

Gault, F. and Foray, D. (2003). *Measuring Knowledge Management in the Business Sector: First Steps*. Paris: OECD.

References

Gawar, A. and Cusumano, M. A. (2002). *Platform Leadership: How Intel, Microsoft, and Cisco Drive Industry Innovation*. Cambridge, MA: Harvard Business School Press.

Geroski, P. A., Machin, S., and van Reenen, J. (1993). 'The Profitability of Innovating Firms', *Rand Journal of Economics*, 24(2): 198–211.

Gerstner, L. (2002). *Who Said Elephants Can't Dance?: How I Turned Around IBM*. New York: Harper.

Gerybadze, A. and Reger, G. (1999). 'Globalization of R&D: Recent Changes in the Management of Innovation in Transnational Corporations', *Research Policy*, 28(2–3): 251–74.

Gibbons, M., Limoges, C., Nowotny, H., Schwartzmann, S., Scott, P., and Trow, M. (1994). *The New Production of Knowledge: The Dynamics of Science and Research in Contemporary Society*. London: Sage.

Gillies, J. and Cilliau, R. (2000). *How the Web Was Born*. Oxford: Oxford University Press.

Grant, R. (1996). 'Towards a Knowledge-Based Theory of the Firm', *Strategic Management Journal*, 17(Winter Special Issue): 109–22.

Grant, W. and MacNamara, A. (1995). 'When Policy Communities Intersect: The Case of Agriculture and Banking', *Political Studies*, 43: 509–15.

Graves, A. (1994). 'Innovation in a Globalizing Industry: The Case of Automobiles', in M. Dodgson and R. Rothwell (eds) *The Handbook of Industrial Innovation*. Cheltenham: Elgar, pp. 213–31.

Greenfield, S. (2003). *Tomorrow's People: How 21st-Century Technology Is Changing the Way We Think and Feel*, Allen Lane.

Groak, S. (1998). 'Representation in building', *RSA Journal*, CXLVI(5487): 50–9.

—— and Krimgold, F. (1989). 'The "Practitioner-Researcher" in the Building Industry', *Building Research and Practice*, 17(1): 52–9.

Grove, A. (1996). *Only the Paranoid Survive*. New York: Doubleday.

Hafner, K. and Lyon, M. (1996). *Where Wizards Stay up Late: The Origins of the Internet*. New York: Touchstone–Simon & Schuster.

Hall, B. H. (2000). 'Innovation and Market Value' in R. Barrell, G. Mason, and M. O'Mahoney (eds) *Productivity, Innovation, and Economic Performance*. Cambridge: Cambridge University Press, pp. 177–89.

Hamilton, J. (2003). *Faraday: The Life*. London: HarperCollins.

Hargadon, A. (2003) *How Breakthroughs Happen. The Surprising Truth about How Companies Innovate*. Cambridge, MA: Harvard Business School Press.

Hays, C. (2004). 'What Wal-Mart Knows About Customers' Habits', *New York Times*, 14 November.

Henderson, K. (1999). *On Line and on Paper: Visual Representations, Visual Culture and Computer Graphics in Design Engineering*. Cambridge, MA: MIT Press.

Henderson, R. and Clark, K. (1990). 'Architectural Innovation', *Administrative Science Quarterly*, 35: 9–30.

—— Jaffe, A., and Trajtenberg, M. (1998). 'Universities as a Source of Commercial Technology: A Detailed Analysis of University Patenting, 1965–1988', *The Review of Economics and Statistics*, LXXX(1): 119–27.

References

Hey, T. and Trefethen, A. (2003a). 'The Data Deluge: An e-Science Perspective', in F. Berman, G. Fox, and T. Hey (eds) *Grid Computing: Making the Global Infrastructure a Reality.* Chichester: Wiley.

—— and Trefethen, A. (2003b). 'e-Science and its Implications', *Philosophical Transactions of the Royal Society,* 361: 1809–25.

Hicks, D. (1995). 'Published Papers, Tacit Competencies and Corporate Management of the Public/Private Character of Knowledge', *Industrial and Corporate Change,* 4(2): 401–24.

—— and Katz, J. S. (1997). *The British Industrial Research System.* SPRU Working Paper, University of Sussex, Brighton.

—— Breitzman, T., Olivastro, D., and Hamilton, K. (2001). 'The Changing Composition of Innovative Activity in the US: A Portrait Based on Patent Analysis', *Research Policy,* 30(4): 681–703.

Hillier, B. (1996). *Space is the Machine.* Cambridge: Cambridge University Press.

Hobday, M. (1998). 'Product Complexity, Innovation and Industrial Organisation', *Research Policy,* 26: 689–710.

Hollingsworth, J. R. and Hollingsworth, E. J. (2000). 'Major Discoveries and Biomedical Research Organizations: Perspectives on Interdisciplinarity, Nurturing Leadership, and Integrated Structures and Culture', in P. Weingart and N. Stehr, *Practising Interdisciplinarity.* Toronto: University of Toronto Press, pp. 215–44.

Hollingsworth, J., Hollingsworth, E., and Hage, J. (2005). *Fostering Scientific Excellence: Organizations, Institutions, and Major Discoveries in Biomedical Science.* Cambridge: Cambridge University Press.

Hough, R. (1996). *Intuition in Engineering Design: Arups on Engineering.* D. Dunster, Berlin: Ernst & Sohn, pp. 18–27.

Hutchins, E. (1996). *Cognition in the Wild.* Cambridge, MA: MIT Press.

Iansiti, M. (1993). 'Real-World R&D: Jumping the Product Generation Gap', *Harvard Business Review,* May–June: 138–46.

Ismail, A., Patil, S., and Saigal, S. (2002). 'When Computers Learn to Talk: A Web Service Primer', *McKinsey Quarterly,* (Special Edition): 70–7.

Jeffrey, S. (2003). 'Virtual Reef: A Visualisation Framework for Marine Simulation Models', *Lecture Notes in Computer Science,* 2659: 679–87.

Johnson, C. and Hansen, C. (2004). *Visualization Handbook.* New York: Academic Press.

Jones, R. A. L. (2004). *Soft Machines: Nanotechnology and life.* Oxford: Oxford University Press.

Jones, W. (2003). 'Here's one I made earlier', *RIBA Journal,* 55–8.

Kaplinsky, R. (1984). *Automation: The Technology and Society.* Harlow: Longman.

Kerr, C., Dunlop, J., Harbison, F., and Myers, C. (1973). *Industrialism and Industrial Man.* London: Penguin.

Keynes, J. (1936). *General Theory of Employment, Interest and Money.* New York: Harcourt Brace.

Kindelberger, C. P. (2001). *Manias, Panics and Crashes: A History of Financial Crises.* Chichester: John Wiley & Sons Inc.

References

King, A. and Tucci, C. (2002). 'Incumbent Entry into New Market Niches: The Role of Experience and Managerial Choices in the Creation of Dynamic Capabilities', *Management Science*, 48(2): 171–86.

King, R., Whelan, K., Jones, F., Reiser, P., Bryant, C., Muggleton, S., Kell, D., and Oliver, S. (2004). 'Functional Genomic Hypothesis Generation and Experimentation by a Robot Scientist', *Nature*, 427: 247–51.

Kline, S. and Rosenberg, N. (1986). 'An Overview of Innovation', in R. Landau and N. Rosenberg (eds) *The Positive Sum Strategy*. Washington: National Academy Press.

Knight, F. (1921). *Risk, Uncertainty and Profit*. Boston, MA: Houghton Mifflin.

Kodama, F. (1995). *Emerging Patterns of Innovation*. Cambridge, MA: Harvard Business School Press.

Kogut, B. (1996). 'What Firms Do? Coordination, Identity and Learning', *Organization Science*, 7(5): 502–18.

Kortum, S. and Lerner, J. (1999). 'What is Behind the Recent Surge in Patenting?', *Research Policy*, 28: 1–22.

Kuemmerle, W. (1997). 'Building Effective R&D Capabilities Abroad', *Harvard Business Review* (March–April): 61–70.

Lambert, R. (2003). Lambert Review of Business-University Collaboration. London: HM Treasury.

Langley, P. (2000). 'The Computational Support of Scientific Discovery', *International Journal of Human-Computer Studies*, 53: 393–410.

Langrish, J., Gibbons, M., Evans, W. G., and Jevons, F. R. (1972). *Wealth from Knowledge: A Study of Innovation in Industry*. Basingstoke: Macmillan.

Laursen, K. and Salter, A. (2004). 'Searching High and Low: What Types of Firms Use Universities as a Source of Innovation', *Research Policy*, 33(8): 1201–15.

Lefèvre, W. (2004). *Picturing Machines 1400–1700*. Cambridge, MA, MIT Press.

Leonard-Barton, D. (1995). *Wellsprings of Knowledge*. Boston, MA: Harvard Business School Press.

Lester, R. K. (1998). *The Productive Edge*. New York: W.W. Norton.

—— and Piore, M. J. (2004). *Innovation, the Missing Dimension*. Cambridge, MA: Harvard University Press.

Lundvall, B. A. (ed.) (1992). *National Systems of Innovation*. London: Pinter.

Mabe, M. and Amin, M. (2001). 'Growth Dynamics of Scholarly and Scientific Journals', *Scientometrics*, 51(1): 147–62.

Macdonald, S. and Williams, C. (1994). 'The Survival of the Gatekeeper', *Research Policy*, 23: 123–32.

Maddox, B. (2002). Rosalind Franklin: The Dark Lady of DNA. London: HarperCollins.

Madhok, A. and Osegowitsch, T. (2000). 'The International Biotechnology Industry: A Dynamic Capabilities Perspective', *Journal of International Business Studies*, 31(2): 325–35.

Malerba, F. (2004). *Sectoral Systems of Innovation: Concepts, Issues and Analyses of Six Major Sectors in Europe*. Cambridge: Cambridge University Press.

References

Mansfield, E. (1998). 'Academic Research and Industrial Innovation: An Update of Empirical Findings', *Research Policy*, 26: 773–76.

March, J. (1991). 'Exploration and Exploitation in Organizational Learning', *Organization Science*, 2(1): 71–87.

Mason-Jones, R. and Towill, D. R. (1999). 'Total Cycle Time Compression and the Agile Supply Chain', *International Journal of Production Economics*, 62: 61–73.

May, R. M. (1997). 'The Scientific Wealth of Nations', *Science*, 275: 793–6.

McCullough, M. (1996). *Abstracting Craft: The practical digital hand*. Cambridge, MA: The MIT Press.

McGown, A., Green, G., and Rodgers, P. (1998). 'Visible Ideas: Information Patterns of Conceptual Sketch Activity', *Design Studies*, 19: 431–53.

McKenna, P. and Maister, D. (2002). *First Amongst Equals*. New York: Free Press.

McLellan, D. (ed.) (1980). *Marx's Grundrisse*. London: Macmillan Press.

Metcalfe, J. (1998). *Evolutionary Economics and Creative Destruction*. London: Routledge.

Metcalfe, S. (1997). 'Technology Systems and Technology Policy in an Evolutionary Framework', in D. Archibugi and J. Michie (eds) *Technology, Globalisation and Economic Performance*. Cambridge: Cambridge University Press, pp. 268–96.

Meyer-Krahmer, F. and Reger, G. (1999). 'New Perspectives on the Innovation of Strategies of Multinational Enterprises: Lessons for Technology Policy in Europe', *Research Policy*, 28(7): 751–76.

—— and Schmoch, U. (1998). 'Science-Based Technologies: University–Industry Interactions in Four Fields', *Research Policy*, 27: 835–51.

Miles, I. (2003). 'Services Innovation: coming of age in the knowledge-based economy', in B. Dankbaar, *Innovation Management in the Knowledge Economy*. London: Imperial College Press.

Miller, F. (2001). 'Simulation—can we compute the future?', *Fraunhofer Magazine*, 1: 6–11.

Mintzberg, H. and McHugh, A. (1985). 'Strategy Formulation in an Adhocracy', *Administrative Science Quarterly*, 30: 160–97.

Mowery, D. C., Nelson, R. R., Sampat, B. N., and Ziedonis, A. A. (2001). 'The Growth of Patenting and Licensing by U.S. Universities: An Assessment of the Effects of the Bayh-Dole Act of 1980', *Research Policy*, 30(1): 99–119.

Mowery, D. and Rosenberg, N. (1979). 'The Influence of Market Demand upon Innovation: a critical review of some recent empirical studies', *Research Policy*, 8(2): 102–50.

Myers, S. and Marquis, D. (1969). *Successful Industrial Innovation*. Washington: National Science Foundation.

Myerson, J. (1995). *Makepeace: A Spirit of Adventure in Craft and Design*. London: Conran Octopus.

Nasser, J. (2000). 'Jac Nasser on Transformational Change, e-business and Environmental Responsibility', *The Academy of Management Executive*, 14(3): 46–51.

Narin, F., Hamilton, K. S. and Olivastro, D. (1997). 'The increasing linkage between US technology and public science', *Research Policy*, 26: 317–30.

Nelson, R. (ed.) (1993). *National Innovation Systems: A Comparative Analysis*. New York: Oxford University Press.

—— and Winter, S. (1982). An Evolutionary Theory of Economic Change. Cambridge, MA: Belknap Press.

Nentwich, M. (2003). *Cyberscience: Research in the Age of the Internet*. Vienna: Austrian Academy of Sciences Press.

Nightingale, P. (1998). 'A Cognitive Model of Innovation', *Research Policy*, 27: 689–709.

Noble, D. (1977). *America by Design*. New York: Knopf.

Noble, D. F. (1986). *Forces of Production: A Social History of Industrial Automation*. New York: Oxford University Press.

Nonaka, I. and Takeuchi, H. (1995). *The Knowledge-Creating Company: How Japanese Companies Creat the Dynamics of Innovation*. Oxford: Oxford University Press.

—— and Teece, D. (eds) (2001). *Managing Industrial Knowledge Creation, Transfer and Utilization*. London: Sage.

NSB (1998). *Science and Engineering Indicators 1998*. Washington: National Science Foundation (NSF), USA.

—— (2002). *Science and Engineering Indicators 2002*. Washington: National Science Foundation (NSF), USA.

—— (2004). *Science and Technology Indicators 2004*. Washington: National Science Foundation (NSF), USA.

OECD (1992). *STI Review: Science/Technology/Industry No 9*. Paris: OECD.

—— (2004). *Main Science and Technology Indicators*. Paris: OECD.

Oxman, R. (2002). 'The Thinking Eye: Visual Recognition in Design Emergence', *Design Studies*, 23: 138–64.

Patel, P. and Pavitt, K. (2000). 'National systems of innovation under strain: the internationalisation of corporate R&D', in R. Barrell, G. Mason and M. O'Mahoney, *Productivity, Innovation and Economic Performance*. Cambridge: Cambridge University Press, pp. 217–35.

Pavitt, K. (1998). 'The Social Shaping of the National Science Base', *Research Policy*, 27: 793–805.

—— (2002). Systems Integrators as 'Post-industrial' Firms? DRUID Summer Conference on Industrial Dynamics of the New and Old Economy—Who Embraces Whom?

—— (2003). 'Specialization and Systems Integration: Where Manufacture and Services Still Meet', in A. Prencipe, A. Davies and M. Hobday, *The Business of Systems Integration*. Oxford: Oxford University Press, pp. 78–91.

PBS (1996). '21st Century Jet: The Building of the 777.' Alexandria, VA: Public Broadcasting Service.

Penrose, E. (1959). *The Theory of the Growth of the Firm*. New York: Oxford University Press.

Perez, C. (2003). *Technological Revolution and Financial Capital: The Dynamics of Bubbles and Golden Ages*. Cheltenham: Edward Elgar.

Perlow, L. A. (1999). 'The Time Famine: Toward a Sociology of Work Time', *Administrative Science Quarterly*, 44(1): 57–81.

References

Perlow, L. A., Okhuysen, G., and Repenning, N. (2002). 'The Speed Trap: Exploring the Relationship Between Decision Making and Temporal Context', *Academy of Management Journal*, 45(5): 931–55.

Petroski, H. (1985). *To Engineer is Human—the Role of Failure in Successful Design*. New York: St Martin's Press.

Pham, D. and Dimov, S. (2003). 'Rapid Prototyping—A Time Compression Tool', *Ingenia*, Oct.–Nov.: 43–8.

Pisano, G. (1997). *The Development Factory: Unlocking the Potential of Process Innovation*. Boston, MA: Harvard Business School Press.

Porter, M. E. (1990). *The Competitive Advantage of Nations*. Hong Kong: Macmillan.

Powell, W. W., Koput, K. W., and Smith-Doerr, L. (1996). 'Interorganizational Collaboration and the Locus of Innovation: Networks of Learning in Biotechnology', *Admistrative Science Quarterly*, 41(1): 116–45.

Prahalad, C. and Hamel, G. (1990). 'The Core Competence of the Corporation', *Harvard Business Review* (May–June): 79–91.

Prencipe, A. (1997). 'Technological Competencies and Product's Evolutionary Dynamics: A Case Study from the Aero-Engine Industry', *Research Policy*, 25: 1261–76.

—— Davies, A., and Hobday, M. (eds) (2003). *The Business of Systems Integration*. Oxford: Oxford University Press.

Price, D. de S. (1963). *Little Science, Big Science*. New York and London: Columbia University Press.

—— (1986). *Little Science, Big Science*. New York: Columbia University Press.

Razac, O. (2002). *Barbed Wire: A Political History*. London: Profile Books.

Rindova, V. and Kotha, S. (2001). 'Continuous "Morphing": Competing Through Dynamic Capabilities, Form, and Function', *Academy of Management Journal*, 44(6): 1263–80.

Roberts, E. B. (1991). *Entrepreneurs in High Technology: Lessons from MIT and Beyond*. Oxford: Oxford University Press.

Rogers, E. M. (1995). *Diffusion of Innovations*. New York: Free Press.

Rosenberg, N. (1963a). 'Capital Goods, Technology and Economic Growth', *Oxford Economic Papers*, 15(3): 217–27.

—— (1963b). 'Technological Change in the Machine Tool Industry, 1840–1910', *Journal of Economic History*, 23: 414–43.

—— (1982). *Inside the Black Box: Technology and Economics*. Cambridge: Cambridge University Press.

Rothwell, R. (1992). 'Successful Industrial Innovation: Critical Factors for the 1990s', *R&D Management*, 22(3): 221–39.

—— Freeman, C., Jervis, P., Robertson, A., and Townsend, J.. (1974). 'SAPPHO Updated-Project SAPPHO Phase 2', *Research Policy*, 3(3): 258–91.

—— and Gardiner, P. (1988). 'Re-innovation and Robust Designs: Producer and User Benefits', *Journal of Marketing Management*, 3(3): 372–87.

—— and Zegveld, W. (1985). *Reindustrialization and Technology*. Harlow: Longman.

—— and Robertson, A. (1973). 'The Role of Communications in Technological Innovation', *Research Policy*, 2(3): 204–25.

Sabbagh, K. (1996). *Twenty-First-Century Jet: the Making and Marketing of the Boeing 777*. New York: Scribner.

Sakakibara, M. (1997). 'Heterogeneity of Firm Capabilities and Cooperative Research and Development: an empirical examination of motives', *Strategic Management Journal*, 18: 143–64.

—— (2001). 'The Diversity of R&D Consortia and Firm Behaviour: Evidence from Japan', *Journal of Industrial Economics*, 49: 181–96.

Sakkab, N. (2002). 'Connect and Develop Complements Research & Develop at P&G', *Research–Technology Management*, 45(2): 38–45.

Salter, A., D'Este, P., Martin, B., Guena, A., Scott, A., Pavitt, K., Patel, P., and Nightingale, P. (2000). *Talent, not Technology: Publicly Funded Research and Innovation in the UK*. Bristol: CVCP, SPRU, HEFCE.

—— and Gann, D. M. (2001). 'Interdisciplinary education for design professionals', in R. J. S. Spence, S. Macmillan, and P. Kirby (eds) *Interdisciplinary Design in Practice*. London: Thomas Telford.

—— —— (2003). 'Sources of Ideas for Innovation in Engineering Design', *Research Policy*, 32(8): 1309–24.

—— and Martin, B. (2001). 'The Economic Benefits of Publicly Funded Basic Research: A Critical Review', *Research Policy*, 30(5): 509–32.

Salter, A., D'Este, P., Martin, B., Geuno, A., Scott, A., Pavitt, K., Patel, P. and Nightingale, P. (2001). *Talent, not Technology: Publicly funded research and innovation in the UK*. London: CVCP HEFCE.

Scherer, F. M. (1999). *New Perspectives on Economic Growth and Technological Innovation*. Washington, DC: Brookings Institution Press.

Schilling, M. (2005). *Strategic Management of Technological Innovation*. New York: McGraw-Hill/Irwin.

—— and Hill, C. (1998). 'Managing the New Product Development Process: Strategic Imperatives', *Academy of Management Journal*, 12(3): 67–82.

Schnaars, S. P. (1994). *Managing Imitation Strategies*. New York/Ontario: Free Press.

Schrage (2000). *Serious Play—How the World's Best Companies Simulate to Innovate*. Boston, MA: Harvard Business School Press.

Schumpeter, J. A. (1942). Capitalism, Socialism and Democracy. London: Unwin.

Schwartz, E. I. (2004). *Juice—the Creative Fuel that Drives World-Class Inventors*. Cambridge, MA: Harvard University Press.

Seely Brown, J. (2003). 'Innovating Innovation', Foreword to H. Chesbrough, *Open Innovation*. Cambridge, MA: Harvard Business School Press.

—— and Duguid, P. (2000). *The Social Life of Information*. Boston, MA: Harvard Business School Press.

Sellers, P. (2004). 'P&G: Teaching an Old Dog New Tricks', *Fortune*.

Senge, P. (1990). 'The Leader's New Work: Building Learning Organizations', *Sloan Management Review*, 32(1): 7–23.

Sennett, R. (1998). *The Corrosion of Character: the personal consequences of work in the new capitalism*. New York: W.W. Norton & Co.

References

Simon, H. A. (1996). *The Sciences of the Artificial*. Cambridge, MA: The MIT Press.
Smart Technology (2001), 164.

Smith, A. (1812). *An Inquiry into the Nature and Causes of the Wealth of Nations*. London: Ward, Lock & Tyler.

Smith, D. and Katz, S. (2000). *Collaborative Approaches to Research*. London: HEFCE.

Steinmueller, E. (2000). 'Will New Information and Communication Technologies Improve the "Codification" of Knowledge?', *Industrial and Corporate Change*, 9(2): 361–76.

Stockdale, B. (2002). *UK Innovation Survey.* London: Department of Trade and Industry, pp. 1–11.

Sutton, R. and Hargadon, A. (1996). 'Brainstorming Groups in Context: Effectiveness in a Product Design Firm', *Administrative Science Quarterly*, 41: 685–718.

Swasy, A. (1994). *Soap Opera: The Inside Story of P&G*. New York: Touchstone.

Takeuchi, H. and Nonaka, I. (1986). 'The New New-Product Development Game', *Harvard Business Review*, 64(1): 137–46.

Teece, D. J. (1987). *The Competitive Challenge: Strategies for Industrial Innovation and Renewal*. Cambridge, MA: Ballinger.

Teece, D. (2002). 'Dynamic Capabilities' in W. Lazonick (ed) *The IEBM Handbook of Economics*. London: Thomson.

—— and Pisano, G. (1994). 'The Dynamic Capabilities of Firms: An Introduction', *Industrial and Corporate Change*, 3(3): 537–56.

Tether, B. and Hipp, C. (2002). 'Knowledge Intensive, Technical and Other Services: Patterns of Competitiveness and Innovation Compared', *Technology Analysis & Strategic Management*, 14(2): 163–82.

Thomke, S. (2003). *Experimentation Matters*. Cambridge, MA: Harvard Business School Press.

Thompson, E. P. (1967). 'Time, Work-Discipline, and Industrial Capitalism', *Past and Present*, 38: 56–97.

Tidd, J., Bessant, J., and Pavitt, K. (1997). *Managing Innovation*. Chichester: Wiley.

Toivanen, O. and Stoneman, P. (2002). 'Innovation in the Market Value of UK Firms, 1989–1995', *Oxford Bulletin of Economics and Statistics*, 64: 39–61.

Toker, U. (forthcoming 2005). 'Workspaces for Knowledge Generation: Facilitating Innovation in University Research Centers', *Journal of Architectural and Planning Research*.

Touraine, A. (1962). 'A Historical Theory in the Evolution of Industrial Skills', in C. Walker (ed.) *Modern Technology and the Organisation*. London: McGraw-Hill.

Tovey, M., Porter, S., and Newman, R. (2003). 'Sketching, Concept Development and Automotive Design', *Design Studies*, 24: 135–53.

Towill, D. R. (2003). 'Construction and the Time Compression Paradigm', *Construction Management and Economics*, 21: 581–91.

Townes, C. H. (1999). *How the Laser Happened*. Oxford: Oxford University Press.

Tufte, E. R. (1983). The Visual Display of Quantitative Information. Cheshire, CT: Graphic Press.

Tufte, E. R. (1997). *Visual explanations: Images and quantities, evidence and narrative*. Cheshire, CT: Graphics Press.

Tuomi, I. (2002). *Networks of Innovation: Change and Meaning in the Age of the Internet*. New York: Oxford University Press.

Tushman, M. and Anderson, P. (1986). 'Technological Discontinuities and Organizational Environment', *Administrative Science Quarterly*, 31: 439–56.

—— and O'Reilly, C. (1997). *Winning through Innovation: A Practical Guide to Leading Organizational Change and Renewal*. Boston, MA: Harvard Business School Press.

Utterback, J. M. (1994). *Mastering the Dynamics of Innovation*. Boston, MA: Harvard Business School Press.

van de Ven, A. H., Polley, D. E., Garud, D. E. and Venkataraman, S. (1999). *The Innovation Journey*. New York: Oxford University Press.

Vandermark, S. (2003). 'An Exploration of Innovation in the Australian Minerals Industry: an innovation systems approach', *National Graduate School of Management*. Canberra: Australian National University.

Vandermerwe, S. and Taishoff, M. (2000). *Amazon.com: Marketing a New Electronic Go-Between Service Provider*. ECCH.

Vincenti, W. (1990). *What Engineers Know and How They Know It*. Baltimore, MD: Johns Hopkins University Press.

von Hippel, E. (1988). *The Sources of Innovation*. Oxford: Oxford University Press.

—— (2002). 'Shifting Innovation to Users via Toolkits', *Management Science*, 48(7): 821–33.

—— and Katz, R. (2002). 'Shifting Innovation to Users via Toolkits', *Management Science*, 48(7): 821–33.

Wainwright, F. (2003). 'Life Safety in Extreme Events', *Ingenia* (October–November): 10–14.

Warnke, P., Springer, I., Wiltfang, J., and Acil, Y. (2004). 'Growth and Transplantation of a Custome Vascularized Bone Graft on a Man', *The Lancet*, 364(9436): 766–70.

Watson, J. (1968). *The Double Helix: A Personal Account of the Discovery of the Structure of DNA*. New York: The New American Library.

Watson, J. (2004). *DNA: The secret of life*. London: Arrow Books.

Wegryn, G. and Siprelle, A. (undated). Combined Use of Optimization and Simulation Technologies to Design an Optimal Logistics Network.

Wheelwright, S. C. and Clark, K. B. (1995). *Leading Product Development: The Senior Manager's Guide to Creating and Shaping the Enterprise*. New York: Free Press.

Whyte, J. and. Gann, D. M. (2003). 'Design Quality Indicators: work in progress', *Building Research and Information*, Special Issue, Vol. 31, No. 5, Sept–Oct.

Whyte, J. K. (2002). *Virtual Reality in the Built Environment*. Oxford: Architectural Press.

—— (2003). 'Industrial Applications of Virtual Reality in Architecture and Construction', *Electronic Journal of Information Technology in Construction*, Special Issue on Virtual Reality Technology in Architecture and Construction, 8: 47–9.

Williams, R. (2002). *Retooling: A Historian Confronts Technological Change*. Cambridge, MA: The MIT Press.

237

References

Womack, J. and Jones, D. (1997). *Lean Thinking: Banish Waste and Create Wealth in Your Corporation*. New York: Free Press.

Womack, J. P. and Jones, D. T. (1996). *Lean Thinking*. London: Simon & Schuster.

—————— and Roos, D. (1990). *The Machine that Changed the World*. New York: Maxwell Macmillan International.

Woodward, J. (1965). *Industry and Organisation: Theory and Practice*. Oxford: Oxford University Press.

Zahra, S. A. and George, G. (2002). 'Absorptive Capacity: A Review, Reconceptualisation, and Extension', *Academy of Management Review*, 27(2): 185–203.

Zuboff, S. (1988). *In the Age of the Smart Machine: The Future of Work and Power*. New York: Basic Books.

Website references

www.archrecord.construction.com/innovation/1_techbriefs/0310Gehry.asp

www.arup.com

www.avatar-me.com/company/realav.pdf

www.bodymetrics.com/NewsDotComFrameset.htm

www.bodymetrics.com/ProblemDotComFrameset.htm

www.business2.com.

www.chromadex.com

www.dcontinuum.com/content/news.php?id=149

www.dem.csiro.au/em/majorresearchinitiatives/glassearth

www.dermotmonaghan.com

www.e4engineering.com

www-edc.eng.cam.ac.uk/materialsselection

www.edc.eng.cam.ac.uk/projects/comrep/index.html

www.europa.eu.int/comm/enterprise/textile/documents/conf_apparel_harari.pdf

www.fashion-era.com

www.fashion-online.org/flash.html

www.gehrytechnologies.com/

www.gsk.com/press_archive/press2003/press_10212003a

www.hks.com

www.home.att.net/~castleisland

ils.pennnet.com/Articles/Article_Display.cfm?Section=Articles&
    Subsection=Display&ARTICLE_ID207992&KEYWORD=rapid%20prototyping

www.innocentive.com

www.manufacturing-visions.org

www.ninesigma.com

www.pg.com/main.jhtml

www.pg.com/science/mngmnt_commit.jhtml

www.polaroid.com

www.rcuk.ac.uk/science
science.gsk.com/news/features/030613-tres.htm
www.sgi.com/pdfs/3413.pdf.
www.skin-forum.org.uk
www.tx.ncsu.edu/jtatm/index.htm
www.walmart.com
www.yet2.com
www.yourencore.com

Glossary

Byte: a unit of information. There are 8 bits in a byte. 1 megabyte $=$ 1 million bytes. 1 gigabyte $=$ 1 billion bytes (1024 megabytes). 1 terabyte $=$ 1 trillion bytes (1024 gigabytes). 1 petabyte $=$ 1024 terabytes (about 10^{15} bytes).

Characterization: construction of a symbol or distinctive mark.

Conceptualization: formation of an idea or notion.

Combination: joining together, uniting for a common purpose.

Do: activities associated with the realizing and operationalizing of new ideas, including producing, exploiting, compiling, executing, assembling, implementing, customizing, diffusing, and completing.

E-science: a new infrastructure facilitating distributed global collaboration in research and development, with access to very large data collections, very large scale computing resources and high performance visualization.

Extrapolation: inferring more widely from a limited range of known fact.

Innovation: successful application of new ideas to products, processes, and services.

Innovation process: managerial decisions, organizational structures, and combinations of resources and skills that together produce innovative outcomes.

Innovation technology: technology applied to the innovation process. It includes Grid-based computing, modelling and simulation tools, artificial intelligence, visualization technologies including virtual reality, data mining, and rapid prototyping.

Integration: completing (an imperfect) thing by the addition of parts.

Interpolation: estimating (intermediate values) from surrounding known values.

Interpretation: explaining *and* elucidating meaning.

Glossary

Intensification of innovation: improved economies of effort and definiteness of aim in innovation.

Mixed reality: a combination of real and virtual media.

Model: a simplified or idealized description of an observed behaviour, system, or process put forward as a basis for further investigation. This often involves the establishment of the key parameters and relationships in a system, construct, or physical phenomenon. Models usually show how something works.

Pattern recognition: ability to use experience and analytical skills to interpret data and find patterns relating to specific phenomena.

Play: activities associated with the selection of new ideas to ensure they are practical, economical, targeted, and marketable, including verifying, simulating, extrapolating, interpolating, preparing, testing, prototyping, validating, transforming, integrating, exploring, and prioritizing.

Prototype: first or primary type of anything; the original (thing or person) of which another is a copy, imitation, representation, or derivative, or to which it conforms or is required to conform; a pattern, model, standard, exemplar, archetype. The first full-size working version of a new vehicle, machine, etc., or a preliminary one made in small numbers so that its performance and methods of mass production can be evaluated.

Schema: pattern imposed on complex reality or experience to assist in explaining it, mediate perceptions, or guide responses.

Think: activities associated with the creation of new ideas and options, including creating, conceiving, imagining, observing, combining, delivering, interpreting, searching, defining, imitating, reflecting, intuition, and experimenting.

Representation: exemplifying, embodying, symbolizing.

Simulation: imitating a behaviour, situation or process, by means of a suitable analogy. This often involves the manipulation of parameters articulated in a model to explore 'what if' questions to ascertain what might happen should parameters be changed.

Transformation: act of making a thorough or dramatic change in form or appearance.

Ubiquitous computing: use of distributed computer networks, sometimes with many tiny microprocessors for sensing, recording, signalling, and controlling activities in a particular environment.

Verification: process of establishing the truth or validity of something.

Virtual reality: simulation of a real or imagined environment that can be experienced visually in the three dimensions of width, height, and depth, and that may additionally provide an interactive experience visually in full real-time motion with sound and possibly with tactile and other forms of feedback. (whatis.techtarget.com)

Visualization: make visible to the eye.

Index

Index

Index

Index

Index

Index